HERE'S WHAT THE EXPERTS ARE SAYING ABOUT *INSTANT INTERVIEWS* . . .

"Every page of this exciting book explodes with the energy of new ideas! You haven't read these techniques before—on the Net or anywhere else. Highly recommended!"
—Joyce Lain Kennedy, America's No. 1 Syndicated Careers Columnist

"With *Instant Interviews* you don't 'look for a job.' You actually interview as you create the best job for yourself. The impact of this remarkable book on your life will be positive, dramatic, and permanent!"
—Deborah Hall-Kayler, President, National Association of Executive Recruiters

"Easily the best book on finding a job ever written! It makes conventional ways of looking for a job obsolete. This will be the breakthrough book of our generation."
—Alan R. Schonberg, Founder, Management Recruiters International

"*Instant Interviews* is must-reading and must-*doing* for these revolutionary times. If you need to work and want the best job, there's no other way."
—Valeria D. Prevish, Business Columnist, *Cincinnati Enquirer*

"Your 'dream job' will remain a distant dream unless you interview for it. *Instant Interviews* gives you the edge you need to get interviewed for the best jobs *now*."
—Gary M. Spinner, President, Mid-Atlantic Association of Personnel Consultants

"*Instant Interviews* will jolt you out of where you are and propel you to the job of your dreams. Whether you want to create that job or get promoted into it, get this book!"
—Jeff R. Goldman, Executive Vice President, Forbes Worldwide

"Don't do another thing to look for a job until you've read and applied *Instant Interviews*! Follow its action plan and you will generate interviews continuously. You'll be using the techniques for as long as you're working—with optimum success."
—Patricia A. Turner, Publisher, *Employment Marketplace* magazine

Instant Interviews

Other Books by Jeffrey G. Allen, J.D., C.P.C.

INSTANT INTERVIEWS

101 Ways to Get the Best Job of Your Life

JEFFREY G. ALLEN, J.D., C.P.C.

Bestselling author of
The Complete Q&A Job Interview Book

WILEY

John Wiley & Sons, Inc.

Published by John Wiley & Sons, Inc., Hoboken, New Jersey.
Published simultaneously in Canada.

For general information on our other products and services or for technical support, please contact our Customer Care Department within the United States at (800) 762-2974, outside the United States at (317) 572-3993 or fax (317) 572-4002.

Wiley also publishes its books in a variety of electronic formats. Some content that appears in print may not be available in electronic books. For more information about Wiley products, visit our web site at www.wiley.com.

Library of Congress Cataloging-in-Publication Data:

Allen, Jeffrey G., 1943-
    Instant interviews : 101 ways to get the best job of your life / by Jeffrey G. Allen.
        p.   cm.
    Includes index.
    ISBN 978-0-470-43847-3 (pbk.)
        1. Employment interviewing.   2. Resumes (Employment)   3. Job hunting.   I. Title.
    HF5549.5.I6A442 2009
    650.14'4—dc22

                                                                2008045569

Printed in the United States of America

10 9 8 7 6 5 4 3 2 1

To my wife, Bev, our daughter Angel, our daughter-in-law
Kathy, and our grandchildren, Jonathan, Gabby, Kevin,
Amanda, Brandon, and Justin.
You're in every syllable I'll ever write. Yet no words can
express my love for you.

Dedicated to all those
would-bes who
could be and
should be and

Who now
can be and
will be and
—watch out—
are!

May these pages live through your lives.

Contents

About the Author . . .

Jeffrey G. Allen. J.D., C.P.C. is the world's leading placement lawyer and author of more bestselling books in the career field than anyone else. His popular interviewing books include *How to Turn an Interview into a Job, The Complete Q&A Job Interview Book, The Interactive Interviewing Technique, The Resume Makeover, The Perfect Follow-Up Method to Get the Job, The Perfect Job Reference, Finding the Right Job at Midlife, The Career Trap* and the three-volume series, *Jeff Allen's Best.*

Jeff turned a decade of recruiting and human resource management into the legal specialty of placement law. He has served as special advisor to the American Employment Association, general counsel to the California Association of Personnel Consultants, legal advisor to the California Institute of Employment Counseling, director of the National Placement Law Center, and is a founder of Search Research Institute.

Jeff is a certified placement counselor, certified employment specialist, certified personnel consultant, and certified search specialist. He has been featured on television and radio, in magazines and newspapers, and is a popular speaker. *The Fordyce Letter* (the recruiting monthly) recently celebrated the 25th anniversary of Jeff's essential "Placements and the Law" column.

Introducing Instant Interviews!

Twenty-five years ago, I jumped up in the jobjungle, swung from the nearest tree, and Tarzanned.

I've spent my entire career in the job placement field, and it all comes down to this:

1. The interview is almost all that counts
2. The interview is a highly predictable, controllable event, with only the places and the faces changing

Those were the first words in my first book, *How to Turn an Interview into a Job*. They rumbled in the jungle like a herd of charging bull elephants. The books flew off the shelves as they still do today.

In following the pages that followed those words, jobseekers became lifetime *jobgetters*. These days they generate job offers whenever they interview. Bigger and better job offers.

Their success was limited only by the global climate change over a quarter century. The underbrush grew above the height of the hunter. The traditional terrain—classifieds, job fairs, then the Internet—become nothing more than a mirage.

These *passive* ways of looking for a job or finding a job did nothing to *generate an interview*. Any successful recruiter will tell you they're virtually useless for a jobseeker today. Only active jobgetting skills work for the professionals—and only those skills will work for you.

That's why I wrote *Instant Interviews*. The law of the jungle didn't change: Survival of the fittest. The law of hiring didn't change either: No interview, no job.

Right now, you're probably all dressed up in your jeweled jungle jacket with no place to go. Ready for a searchin' safari. Mangled machete in one hand, rusty resume in the other. Thrashing around through the hidden job market looking for the career path. Mumblin', stumblin', and fumb-lin'. Passively missing everything below your binoculars. Living that old saying, "You can't see the forest for the trees." Getting *tired* long before you get *hired*.

The best-kept secret among the natives is that the *candidates* are hid-ing, not the *jobs!* Every day, I watch the braver ones from my treehouse-office, wandering around in the marshes blindfolded.

So, before we begin using techniques, let's get rid of those subcon-scious spears.

Scan the *Instant Interview* titles (Dos) in the Contents (you will any-way). Then, take a piece of paper and a pen. Scribble down a list of the first 10 reasons that pop into your mind why you can't, won't, shouldn't, or would get arrested for doing them. Nothing fancy, and do it *fast*. We want to catch those first (hence the word *instant*) excuses.

When you're done, walk over to the first mirror you see. Then *look at yourself tearing up the list*. Throw it away and don't even keep a copy. Tell nobody. Your secret's safe with me.

It's a jungle out there. A jobjungle.

So, straighten your imaginary pith helmet. Shoulders back, eyes for-ward (not the other way around). Smile on your face. Mangled machete in one hand, rusty resume in the other. (If the machete's rusty and the resume's mangled, just switch hands.)

The only spear to fear is fear itself.

That concludes your warmup exercise. Now, it's "Forward *march!*"

I'm with you every step of the way.

Foreword . . . and Forward March!

Before we get down to business, I want to give you a gift that will change your life.

It's a little exercise that's as easy to do as it is *not* to do. But the difference between those who enjoy success and those who endure failure is found in substituting little exercises for big excuses.

There's a natural tendency for you to simply *scan* the 101 Instant Interview techniques and think one of the 10 things that follow:

1. "It'll never work."
2. "If it worked, everyone would do it."
3. "I tried it and it didn't work."
4. "It's not something I can do."
5. "I'll embarrass myself if I try that."
6. "I'm too (*old, young, fat, skinny, pretty, ugly, important, unimportant, masculine, feminine, smart, dumb, professional, self-conscious, nervous, whatever*) for that."
7. "It's just too (*simple, hard, complicated, silly, crazy, whatever*) for me."
8. "Everyone's doing it, so I don't stand a chance."
9. "I'll try it later."
10. "I'll just do it my way."

These cause jobseekers to become destroyed, not employed. They're the 10 most common causes of *instant interview inertia*. Someone calls our office for help, and my assistant announces, "There's an *eight* on the line." I already know he didn't do the exercises or he'd be calling me from his cell phone asking whether to accept the offer he just received.

There are an infinite number of excuses. They all work. You won't, though. If your subconscious is creative enough, it can spear you to the ground before you ever reach the jobjungle. Behavioral psychologists call this overthinking. We call it underdoing. Unemployment underdoing.

So many people wait for the Sunday sunrise and listen for the thud. They're up—physically and emotionally—kings of the jungle—trading that machete for a newspaper and fantasizing about gainful employment. Planning for the next job fair.

Then, Monday morning, it starts. They s-l-o-w-l-y descend into the quicksand. Gasping and grasping until the next Sunday thud. The Sunday syndrome starts again.

Human resourcers place the ads in papers for reasons having nothing to do with hiring. Reasons like showing their companies are prominent, showing they're into affirmative action, showing they're about the community, or showing their business is growing. Maybe even showing top management they're doing something other than taking outside recruiters on tours of the facilities. That's why you don't know anyone who recently got a job through a classified ad or a job fair.

But why wait 'til Sunday when armchair jobseeking on the Internet can click you into oblivion 24/7? Every tease conceived by the human race is right in that electronic box. Why think outside it? That's why you don't know anyone who recently got a job through an Internet posting either.

Any recruiter in the rainforest will tell you that the Internet is nothing more than a large *lead source*. More often than not, a *misleading* lead source. All those hidden hunters would be better off watching Animal Planet since the interview action's underfoot.

The *active job market* is where the *action* is. Where the fearless few generate endless interview invitations like crazy. Always out there in the marketplace, ready to leap at the lead. Then to pounce on the potential.

They think: "Good, *better*, BEST. Perhaps I'll take this one—nah—how about *that?* Well, let's see. Let's write it down. This one pays twice as much, but I need to travel. That one gives me a car with unlimited mileage, but there's no long-distance travel required. I really like the management of that other one, though. H-m-m-m-m. Decisions, decisions."

So, here we are, a quarter-century later. Working on this concept of persuading one person to pay another to watch that person do something they won't or can't do for themselves. (Note that I said *persuading,* not *motivating.* When you *persuade,* you *steer.* When you *motivate,* you *watch.* One is *active,* the other is *passive.*)

Employers treat a job as though it were some tangible thing. They enhance it by calling it an *opening,* a *position,* or even an *opportunity.*

They write it down, give it a makeover, add adoring adjectives, print it, list it, post it, mail it, announce it, advertise it, box it, and dress it up as an "executive search assignment" for recruiters. Yet it's not some tangible thing. The best evidence of this is that the person who gets hired rarely resembles the person described in the wish list.

If you really understand that rainforest reality, this should hit you like a bolt of lightning:

Interview Insight

Successful people create their own jobs. They simply make their own openings, jump in to them with both feet (usually without a clue as to where they'll land), and change what they do as they go along. They eventually become the job and become indispensable in the process.

It just makes you want to pull down that "Help Wanted" sign, tear it in half, put back the "Help" half, and take the "Wanted" half home to tape on your mirror.

I'm going to guide you through your very own customized jungle treasure hunt. But you've got to let me take you by the hand. Learn the lay of the land. Page by page. Don't just scan the titles. *Study* the *techniques*. That's what separates the seekers from the getters. I'll teach you all the jungle jive you need to know along with the moves. Timing. Closing tips.

The more you practice, the faster you'll get more and better interviews. You're just learning to ride a bike through the thicket. Once you've learned it, no one can ever take it away from you.

If you want a different result (let's just say tons of interviews), you've got to do something different.

How does permanent job security, lifetime unemployment insurance, a high standard of living, even higher self-esteem, and unlimited potential sound? Too good to be true? Fun?

Time for your coming-out party. A few bars of "Jungle Boogie" and you're hiding no more.

Say, "BOO!"

Here *we go!*

Instant Interviews

Do 1: Appearing Magically—Like a Genie!

There are six reasons we'll cover appearing magically before any other technique.

Doing it instantly:

1. Gets you into an interview
2. Exercises you (with your endorphins flowing—active rather than passive)
3. Trains you to answer the (always asked) interview questions naturally
4. Enables you to own the dialogue
5. Boosts your self-confidence dramatically
6. Makes the other 100 Dos more effective

Right now, my wish is your command. (That will change rather abruptly once you start pumpin' interviews, so I'd better work fast!)

We'll get to your warm market (family, friends, and acquaintances) later. But let's cover that instantly infinite cold market now, or you'll never get there.

Unsuccessful jobseekers burn through their warm market, then stop stone cold. They stay in that warm, fuzzy comfort zone, wasting valuable time, surrounded by those who commiserate rather than connect with them. They spend their time psychoanalyzing why nobody wants to hire them rather than talking to the ones who do.

FEAR is the culprit. The letters stand for *False Evidence Appearing Real*. Now you're going to learn to spell it right: F-U-E-L. That means Finding Unlimited Employment Leads.

We'll turn your fear into fuel.

You'll need:

- At least a thousand business cards with your name (full name and middle initial), address, phone number, fax number, and e-mail address. Keep them simple and readable, black on white. The price drops like a depth charge for quantities, and you'll be using them a *lot*.
- Twelve large binder clips.
- Two small boxes to file business cards. Label one box "Appointments" and the other "Revisits."
- A voice mail setup for all landlines and cell phones that answers:

  Hi! This is (First name, Last name). I'm not available at this time. Please leave your name, number, and a brief message at the tone. I'll return your call as soon as possible. Thank you.

There are six steps to the genie technique:

1. Identifying Yourself
2. Introducing Yourself (The most important step)
3. Gathering Information
4. Showing Your Appreciation
5. Motivating Yourself, and . . .
6. Repeating the Process

I'll also show you how to use the "Magic Four Hello" and "Magic Four Goodbye."

Before we start, pick a time to appear.

Early mornings are better because:

- By getting out of the house fast, you'll be less likely to get distracted by everyone and everything around you.
- You'll be more likely to find managers who personally open their businesses in the morning to get the workday started for the employees they supervise.
- In the early morning, public places are less busy. People are freer to talk.
- You'll be more alert.
- Prospects will be more receptive to new ideas (morning coffee is still working), and . . .
- It's cooler in the summer. (You'll be walking outside.)

Now let's take the process chronologically and go through the six steps:

Identifying Yourself

Here's how to take the crucial first step:

1. Decide on an *offeror*. An offeror is your target prospect.
   Think about two things:
   a. Who responds well to you?
   b. What type of person will you be most comfortable approaching? Some jobseekers approach people who look like them. Others approach the ones who look like those most attracted to them. ("Me Tarzan, you Jane"—or vice versa.)
2. Suit like a recruit, wearing:
   a. Business casual clothes (quality sportswear). The slacks or skirt must have front (side) and back (rear) pockets. Four total, or you'll play havoc with our filing system.
   b. Quality walking shoes
   c. Sixteen of your business cards in your left front pocket. (You've got serious business to do.)
   d. A quality ballpoint pen in your left front pocket
   e. Breath mints in your right back pocket
   f. A watch
   g. No cell phone. Resist the temptation—it's the worst possible distraction.

(Put your keys in your left front pocket, too, and your wallet in your right front pocket. And, yes—you can leave your magic lamp at home.)

3. Go somewhere you know you'll find your offeror. Office buildings, industrial parks, and shopping centers are best. Anywhere there are employees, since managers want to set a good example by greeting and being courteous. (Security guards are no problem. Just act like you know what you're doing and are in a hurry.) Don't approach any offeror unless he's alone. Getting an interview from a group will not work. No manager will be receptive if her subordinates are watching.

4. Always go alone. You'll get no interview if anyone is with you.

5. Be there when business starts (usually 8 a.m.), Monday through Friday (with the exception of Wednesday mornings, for reasons I'll explain shortly). If you're looking for anything in a retail store or other business that's open on weekends, go out then, too—unless of course you're preparing to start your new job Monday. Weekend interview scouting is so much fun. Smiles, happy people, balloons, bright colors, sales, free food samples. Every store is just waiting for you to arrive.

Introducing Yourself (the Most Important Step)

Take no more than five seconds to scope out the place, and walk over to the person who appears to be in charge.

About half the time, before you connect with the offeror, you'll speak to a *gatekeeper*. That would be a receptionist, secretary, assistant, or any other front-liner. Amateur jobseekers make a big deal out of this, but it's silly-simple.

Just walk up to the gatekeeper confidently, look him in the eye, smile, and say, "I'd like to see the manager." (Of course, if you see a name posted anywhere, say "Mr." or "Ms. Whoever.")

If you're asked your name, say it proudly.

The reply from the gatekeeper will be something like:

"What's it about?"

Whew! Someone who speaks English. We're in now! Fire back with:

"It's a personal matter."

Watch his face. Perfect! Coupling the word *personal* with the word *matter* makes any gatekeeping grunt worry about his job. *Personal* means, "It's your boss's confidential, private business." *Matter* hints that you could be an investigator or a lawyer. Someone who depends on someone else for a living will let that someone else know immediately if there's a personal matter concerning that someone else. Otherwise, that someone may need *Instant Interviews*.

If the offeror isn't around or is busy, just reach into your left front pocket, feel for one business card, smile as you withdraw the card from your pocket, and ask for a call "immediately" (a *major* word) as you hand the card to the gatekeeper. Be nice and say your "voice mail will be on" (a *big* phrase) if you're not "in the office" (an even *bigger* phrase). Be businesslike, friendly, but own the conversation—you and that spiffy business card.

Take any business cards or brochures that you can stuff in your right front or back pockets. (You don't want to mix them up with yours!)

You'll get that return call. Why? It's called the "fear of the unknown," and the offeror won't spell FEAR backward. We'll cover how to handle the call in Do 40.

But for now, let's assume you're about to connect with the offeror. We s-l-i-d-e right into . . .

The Magic Four Hello

The *Magic Four Hello* has four quick steps:

1. Direct eye contact. (If he's too ugly, look at the bridge of his nose.)
2. A smile. (Image consultants give smile classes! Practice in front of a mirror.)
3. The words, "Hi, I'm (*First name, Last name*). It's a pleasure meeting you."
4. A firm but gentle handshake. (No dead flounder dangling at the end of your wrist. No live shark either. Practice shaking one hand with the other. Alone. People probably already think you're crazy.)

Why is it magic? How does it work? Why are we having this conversation? Are we figuring out magic tricks or getting interviews? Just think "Poof!" and behold:

- You look him in the eye, he looks you in the eye.
- You smile, he smiles.
- You greet with your name, he greets with his name.
- You shake his hand, he shakes your hand.

Can it really be so primordial? Are we still having this conversation? Can you see why it's *instant interview* time? The whole process is so predictable and controllable!

Then you ask a question—something that is job-related and will get the prospect talking about his work. The actual words are not important. It's that you're acting interested, positive, and upbeat. You do this in a complimentary, admiring way.

After using this technique successfully for decades, I'm convinced you can do it walking backward and talking in sign language if you do it right.

You can't ask the wrong question to the right person, and you can't ask the right question to the wrong person. Knowing that should have you asking away, as relaxed as a wet noodle.

It's all in the delivery! It's not what you *say*—it's what you *convey*.

But since you still crave a phrase that pays, here are some examples:

How were you able to design your lobby so well?

How were you able to increase your market share so dramatically?

Where will you be setting up future factories?

What's your secret to finding and training the best people?

What do you like best about managing such a successful business?

After the first few hundred times, you'll be yawning because everyone will be interviewing you. After a while, you'll want to see if you can blow it, just for fun. As long as you've done it for at least two weeks solid, go for it! Here are a few off-the-wall openers I've used to get the identical, successful results:

Did you marry into the Bloomingdale family?

Are you a "lifer" at Consolidated?

When are you going to give the competition a break?

Even nonsense like that will open up the offeror if you use the Magic Four Hello. I think it's the smile, but who's trying to figure out the trick when it's so obviously magic?

This is what behavioral psychologists call *pacing*. I was going to tell you how to get the huge amount of scientific research backing it up, but if I do, you might be tempted to check it out. Ergo, that would get you tired rather than hired. (Well, there is one place you can look. Just promise you won't do it until you start pumping out interviews. It's Chapter 4 of *How to Turn an Interview into a Job*.)

Gathering Information

One way or another, you've opened the door. The way to enter into the instant interview is with a sentence like:

"I've been watching the success of Dynametrics and would like to join your team."

Analyzing the Successful Approach

Note why this approach is so powerful:

Watching shows that you've been attentive, but not compulsive. This is supposed to be casual, or you'd have just sent in a resume with a cover letter like everyone else. (We spell *résumé* without the fancy accents. You should too, for reasons I give in Do 5.)

Success means different things to different people. But any manager will have successes to brag about and can only appreciate that you've observed them.

Like to join is not the same as *asking* to join. Keep in mind that, until the genie appeared, there was probably no thought of anyone's joining. Newbie salespeople will ask for the sale here—and lose it because the prospect isn't ready for the close.

Your is a major mover. Have you ever noticed how odd it sounds when the manager of a global company says something like, "I'll have my operations manager get on it right away!"—as if it's really *his* company? As though the people really work for *him*? He's probably an *at-will* employee who could be gone tomorrow if "his" company wanted it. But he feels that he owns the place. So flatter him. You agree that it *is* his.

Team is one of those sports words that has been adopted by employers everywhere. Along with *team members, teammates, associates, partners,* and even *owners.* And we'll use *team,* too, pretending it's more than a group of randomly selected what-have-you-done-for-me-today employees.

Note also that this is not a question. You're not asking for a job. Who wants someone who wanders in unannounced interrupting the workday when there are no openings? No—you're declaring that you want to be there because the person's so great—no room to turn you down there.

The next thing to do is listen. It's very difficult. But if you have two ears and one mouth, remember why. The response is usually, "We don't have any openings right now."

That's expected because we set it up that way. It gives us the opportunity to give our usual reply: "I wasn't looking for just any job. I want to be a part of an organization that will reward me commensurately with my results."

Are you getting rhythm yet? *Want, part, reward* for *results*, and a multisyllabic *commensurately* to boot! Here's someone who:

- Knows what he wants.
- Understands he's only a part of a bigger thing, not someone who's likely to go around turning the desks upside down.
- Wants to get paid for results, not effort. (Where has he been all of my life?) And . . .
- Uses big words like *commensurately*. (You might even hear some offeror say, "Oh, you read *Instant Interviews*, too? You're hired!")

The natural Pavlovian response is to say, "Well, we have no openings right now. What kind of work do you do?" What this *really* means is: "I need to have a reason to pay you. How can you help me?"

Here's the time for us to pause, take a deep breath, and discuss the myth of experience. With the exception of a job being a tangible thing (as discussed in the introduction), *experience* is the second most jumbled-jungle word in the forest.

You might ask, "How can you get experience if you don't have experience?" What a wrongheaded question! Yet society has programmed us to ask it almost before we learn to spell *j-o-b*. In fact, it's not even a question at all. It's an excuse.

You have exactly the same amount of experience as anyone else your age! It's the generic life experience that makes you shake your head at the younger generation (no matter how old you are). You did goofy things when you were their age, right? What happened? You developed common sense, a work ethic, values. You learned to handle yourself, discipline yourself, think for yourself.

Let's use me as an example. (I'd use you, but you're the genie in this relationship. That's my wish and I'm stickin' to it.) I've written more books on interviewing than anyone in the history of publishing. In fact, my editor once threatened to report me to the Library of Congress! I've also probably read every book on interviewing ever written and heard every expert on the subject. I even enrolled in Bible study class one time because the ad said they'd be discussing the *Book of Job*.

But this isn't about my experience or yours, is it? Here's how I can explain it best: One time I was on a book tour doing an all-night radio talk show somewhere west of New York City. It was my last appearance of a v-e-r-r-r-y long day, and I was late to board a plane for the next city's wakeup show. Someone called in and asked, "What do the J.D. and C.P.C. stand for after your name?" (They stand for *Juris Doctor* and *Certified Placement Counselor*.) As I was taking off my headset, this just popped out: "The J.D. stands for *Just Do it!* and the C.P.C. stands for *Courage, Persistence, and Confidence!*"

I'd be surprised if I use more than an hour or so of everything I learned in law school in my specialized law practice. Ask any brain surgeon or nuclear physicist, and they'll tell you that it's all about knowing what to do, not learning about what it is.

Studying, passing the exams, getting the degrees, qualifying for the license, going for the certifications—they're all just speed bumps, roadblocks, and detours on the road to success. It's all an obstacle course that anyone can master if they concentrate enough and have the opportunity. Ultimately, those obstacles are just a way of keeping the supply of highly paid pros down, the demand up, and impressing the buyers. These folks can be excellent at what they do. But the experience they use isn't from hurdling the obstacles. It's from living. And you're experienced at that!

So much for the experience excuse—too much, in fact. Much too much time is wasted on *excusing* rather than *enthusing*.

So the only question now is, "How can you state experience you have that will get you hired?" *Now* you're talkin'—er —askin'.

The answer is, "Generically, genie!"

You must be ready to recite a memorized script like this:

Worksheet

I can assist you in many ways. My college training was in _____, and I graduated in _____. That taught me the discipline of studying and focusing on a specific goal. After I graduated, I worked as a/an _____ at _____ where I excelled in working with others and increasing the bottom line year after year. When the company relocated to _____, I was designated as a "key employee" and asked to go there. I was then recruited away, however, by _____ to become a/an _____ and it was an opportunity I just couldn't pass up. So I can help you here at _____ by _____.

(That last sentence is the only place where you ad lib with a little focus on what you think the offeror thinks she needs—thereby granting her *one* wish.)

Congratulations! You were just *instantly interviewed!* You just knocked that one cold.

Now ask for a business card. If she has none, take your pen out of your left front pocket (this is why a disposable pen with an advertisement is a nonstarter). Find a small piece of paper the size of a business card, or just tear one to that size. (The back of any business card except yours is perfect.)

Ask the offeror to write down her full name (including middle initial), exact title, office address, phone and fax numbers, and e-mail address. Get the business web site address too, so you can see what you just talked yourself in to. Don't be too pushy, but show that you want details. If she writes it down, you're practically sharing an office already. If you write it down, that's fine, too. So, ask her to do it and be gracious about assisting. Put the business card or paper in your left back pocket. And don't forget to put the pen back in your left front pocket.

If the offeror gives you an application form, leave it there until you complete your rounds for the day. Just say you'll pick it up later. If she asks for a resume, great. You can customize yours to fit exactly what she thinks she needs. You can then mail it back. No, you don't hand-carry it back, even though doing so might be cheaper. It doesn't get any better than what you did at this stage—it only gets worse. So stay away until you're invited back.

Don't volunteer to use e-mail for the return of forms, and try to avoid filling them out online. They're likely to be deleted inadvertently (or *vertently*) by some worried rival employee. If the offeror requires e-mail, just say, "If you don't mind, I'd like to submit a hard copy, too." They don't object, and your paperwork will be read readily.

Now get out of there! But I don't mean turn around and head for the door.

Here's how it's done . . .

The Magic Four Goodbye

Four quick steps here too:

1. direct eye contact
2. a smile
3. firm but gentle handshake
4. The words, "This looks like a great match! Thanks very much for taking the time."

This entire process should take no more than 15 minutes. You're a magic genie, not a begging jobseeker. Genies don't talk much. They disappear much! That's why you wear a watch (in addition to it making you look more professional). And please remember this:

If you stay, say, and play, they won't pay.

When you're out of there, take the business card (or piece of paper) out of your left back pocket and your pen out of your left front pocket. Write the date (XX/XX/XX) in the upper-left corner and a grade on the upper-right corner (A, B, C, or D). This only takes a moment. Don't overanalyze it—just flash on how you rate the probability of getting an offer and how you would like working there. Then put the pen and card back in to the pockets where they belong.

So you should be able to knock out two of these capers every hour. Start at 8 A.M., and you will have pumped out eight face-to-faces by noon—with eight business cards left for after lunch.

But who eats when this is so much fun?

People don't get fun jobs. Repetitive jobs are the only ones people get. People either *make* fun jobs or they never make it at all. Look around you. Do you want to end up like them?

Making jobs is all about timing. Have you ever noticed what happens when you first get the idea to buy something? Wallpaper, furniture, a car? Something creates that impulse buy, and— *click!* Your brain's locked in. You measure everything else against how well it satisfies your sudden desire. That's why visualizing a goal is such an incredibly powerful way to actualize it.

You're not having an interview, you're having an *inner view!* Every person since the dawn of civilization wants someone else to do his chores. This is just a manifestation of the quest for happiness inside every human heart.

It starts at birth and ends at death. People spend their entire lives, from the time they wake up to the time they go to sleep, trying to fulfill that wish. It guides what they buy, what they eat, where they go, when they go, who they call, who they befriend, who they marry, who they hire. Then they dream about it through the night. Genies appear to deliver happiness when the time is right—when there's desire. Translation: *anytime.*

You're the reason for that saying, "I don't know what it was about him, but we just *clicked!*"

Showing Your Appreciation

I once wrote a popular book called *The Perfect Follow-Up Method to Get the Job*—an entire book devoted to the subject. But using this technique, there are only two things to do and there's only one way to do them.

They are:

1. Send an e-mail when you arrive home to every offeror you met.

It should state:

Hi, *(First name)*,

I just wanted to let you know what a pleasure it was meeting you today. I really appreciated having the opportunity to discuss what you are doing at _____.

I look forward to speaking with you again soon.

Thanks.

Best regards,

(Your first name)

(All of your contact information)

If you're sending a resume or completing an application, indicate when you'll be sending it.

That's it! No long-winded sales pitch, no life history. Just a simple expression of appreciation.

2. Mail a thank-you note dated the following day (prepared when you sent the e-mail the night before) to every offeror you met.

It should state:

Dear (First name),

I just wanted to let you know that _____ appears to have exactly the opportunity I've been seeking.

Thanks again for your time.

(Your first name)

Redundant? Repetitious? How else does one effectively advertise? When you enclose another business card (which you must), you're penetrating even deeper into her subconscious.

Motivating Yourself

Now, you take scissors and trim the papers you have down to business-card size, and you insert all the cards (including the trimmed papers) in a large binder clip. That is your binder clip for the week, so you will use it for all left rear pocket cards you get from Monday through Friday. The next week, you will use another binder clip, and so forth.

Wednesday morning is your time to smile and dial in the office. Every Wednesday at 8 A.M. sharp, you should be making your first call to the offeror on the first card in the binder clip from around two weeks before. Waiting this long gives the offeror time to reflect on your meeting, read your e-mail and thank-you note, see your business cards repeatedly, and perhaps review any forms or resume that you submitted.

The purpose of the call is achieve one thing and one thing only: to make an appointment to meet again. That's when you'll get the offer (unless the offeror is desperate)—not now over the phone.

What's that? You're nervous about making the call? Gotta gulp another cup of joe? Hold on a second! Can't we just wait awhile? 'Til she's had a chance to settle down?

Not a chance! Genies poof out of bottles; offerors don't poof out of phones. Didn't we discuss what F-E-A-R stands for? If you're nervous, you're relying on *False Evidence Appearing Real*. You don't understand your *victim*—the offeror. You're already *hopelessly hired* in her head. You know it; she doesn't. It's still in the subconscious where the neurons remain until fired. They must be awakened—even annoyed—into firing about hiring.

If your little heart is thumpin' like a drum machine when you look at that card, that's the call to make first. Don't tell me your symptoms. I'll tell you they're hunger pangs. This is a numbers game. Just Do it! Smile and dial that number *now!*

If you spend more than five minutes on the phone, you're interviewing, not arranging. That will unhire you because those neurons in her brain are still in the dormant state of imagination. Wish fulfillment occurs when the genie appears. That's the whole basis for free trials of almost everything that you can't return some other way.

A successful jobgetter listens well, probes, asks questions, uses the same words as the offeror, and avoids shooting from the lip. The call is the means to the end—an appointment.

Here's how it might go:

Receptionist: Good morning, Bonomo Company.
You: Hi, is Mildred Eptibottom in?
Receptionist: I'm not sure. Who's calling?
You: (first name, last name.) *(Don't say, "It's the genie ready to grant her wish.")*
Receptionist: May I tell her what it's regarding? *(Don't say, "It's the genie, and I think I left my bottle in her office a few weeks ago.")*
You: It's a personal matter. We discussed it a few weeks ago, and I have some more information for her. *(Notice it's always "nothing but the truth.")*
Receptionist: One moment please, I'll ring . . .
Assistant: Ms. Eptibottom's office. May I help you?
You: Whom am I speaking to?
Assistant: This is Irving, her assistant.
You: Hi, Irving! This is (first name, last name). We met when I was in your office a few weeks ago. It was nice meeting you! *(Translation: "I'm not after your job, so don't be so jumpy!")*
Assistant: Oh yes, I remember. Mildred received your thoughtful note!
You: Well, I really appreciated the time. She sounds great, and I just wanted to take a moment to mention something to her.
Assistant: I think she's in a meeting. May I take a message? (Irving's playing "shield the boss" as every assistant does. It's your move.)
You: I'd like to discuss it personally with her, if you don't mind.
Assistant: Well, let me see if she's available.
You: Thanks. (You're in!)
Offeror: Mildred Eptibottom.
You: Hi, Mildred! This is (first name, last name).
Offeror: Hi, Genie! *(Sorry, I couldn't resist.)* I received your resume and appreciated your note.
You: I wanted to again thank you for making the time to meet with me a few weeks ago.
Offeror: It was my pleasure.
You: I've done some research on what we discussed and would like to share it with you briefly. I've figured out how to greatly improve your cost control system.
Offeror: We really need to do that. What would you suggest?
You: It's not something I can explain really well over the phone. When can we meet?

Offeror: Well, we're not in a position to hire anyone else this year.

You: Oh, I understand that completely. I'm just fascinated by the opportunity at Bonomo to cut your costs dramatically with just a few ideas.

Offeror: That sounds great. I guess it never hurts to talk.

You: I'm a great believer in solving problems one at a time. If I can show you how to save money and make more, the budget constraints will take care of themselves. Let's see what happens. Bonomo has such a quality product. I just like the challenge of helping you become even more successful! I'll be near your office on business next Thursday, June 4.

Offeror: I should be in the office. What time would you like to meet?

You: How about 8 A.M.?

Offeror: That sounds perfect. We can have a cup of coffee together and talk.

You: Great! I'm looking forward to assisting.

Offeror: Thanks for calling. See you then.

You: Thanks.

Bingo! You're in and never even mentioned the word *interview.*

The call won't be exactly like that. But it will be surprisingly similar if you set it up the same way.

Try to weave the following interview words into your conversation. They make offerors want to hear what you have to say. They will want to hire you. Photocopy a stack of these pages and write out a short sentence with as many of the words you think will help you with each offeror.

Worksheet

Name of Business: _____

Name of Offeror: _____ . _____

Title of Offeror: _____

Date of Appointment: __/__/__ Time of Appointment: ____ AM/PM

Bring: _____

Comments: _____

Work as many of these interview words as you can into your conversation with the offeror:

ability _____

accelerate _____

accurate _____

active _____

affect _____

aggressive _____

analyze _____

attitude _____

capable _____

careful _____

commensurate _____

common sense _____

conceive _____

conduct _____

confidence _____

conscientious _____

controllable _____

courage _____

develop _____

diplomatic _____

direct _____

discipline _____

dramatically _____

drive _____

dynamic _____

effectively _____

efficiency _____

eliminate _____

energetic _____

enthusiastic _____

establish _____

evaluate _____

excel _____

excellence _____

expand focus _____

forward _____

generate _____

great _____

good _____

guide _____

implement _____

improve _____

incisive _____

initiate _____

innovate _____

lead _____

listen _____

monitor _____

motivate _____

opportunity _____

participate _____

perform _____

persistence _____

(continued)

(continued)

persuade _____

potential _____

precise _____

pride _____

produce _____

professional _____

proficiency _____

provide _____

recommend _____

reliable _____

responsible _____

results _____

reward _____

simplify _____

skill _____

solve _____

streamline _____

strengthen _____

successful _____

systematic _____

tactful _____

team _____

thorough _____

train _____

trim _____

urgency _____

vital _____

win _____

Those sentences you write are the words of the winners in life. Let them work for you just by writing them in sentences before each appointment. It's exactly the same way you learned to speak in sentences when you wrote in your first-grade workbook. It becomes automatic, and you'll be surprised at how the words pop out naturally in all of your conversations!

This little exercise will continually increase your self-esteem and the respect you receive from others. It will start with your first instant interview and end with your imminent internment.

Next, simply write the date of the call on the back of the card, along with one of these four things:

1. XX/XX/XX Appt. XX/XX/XX at ____ AM/PM (Means *appointment date and time.*)
2. XX/XX/XX N/A LMVM (Means *not available, left a voice mail message with name and number.*)
3. XX/XX/XX N/A LM w/ (first name, last name) (Means *not available, left a message for the named person with your name and number.*)
4. XX/XX/XX N/I CB in ____ wks. (Means *not interested, call back in ____weeks.*)

Now place the card at the back of the stack in either the:

- Appointments box if you arranged to meet the offeror, or the
- Revisits box if you're waiting for a return call.

Any calls when you can't even leave a message remain in the binder clip. You try them again at 8 A.M. Thursday and Friday of that week. If you connect, complete and place the card at the back of the appropriate box, then dash out of the house.

You've got eight encounters to complete before lunch.

Repeating the Process

The next Wednesday at 8 A.M., you go to the binder clip for the second week, and repeat the process. Then you go to the box labeled Revisits and call those offerors again. Finally, you go back to the prior week's binder clip and try to reach any offerors left in it again.

You'll be astonished at how the cumulative effect of following this discipline will get you a massive inventory of instant interviews and job leads. You'll be a C.P.C. too! After a month, you'll either be working or just enjoying the process so much that you're holding out for your dream job.

Many fringe benefits will drop out of the sky just by following the discipline. Here's one example.

Learning from a Success Story

A lawyer I recently assisted was looking for a position in a corporate legal department. He was an average student from a very average school, with an employment record that you'd charitably call average. Since being admitted to practice law several years ago, he'd been writing appellate briefs for other lawyers, making pretrial court appearances for them, and attempting to establish his own general law practice. He had no corporate law experience. His previous work experience actually consisted of only part-time jobs as a server in restaurants while he was in college.

One day, he decided to hit the downtown office buildings. He parked in an outdoor all-day parking lot for a few dollars (the early-bird rate) at 7:30 A.M. and walked into the home office of a bank. A large sign on an easel read, "All candidates for employment must apply at the Human Resources Department on the Third Floor."

A month ago, he'd have fallen into the third-floor funnel when the elevator doors opened, lain there in a coma, and allowed his twitching remains to be poured into the HR department where they would be processed, stored in accordance with all applicable federal and state laws, and in four to six weeks, a rejection letter suitable for framing would have been mailed to his last-known address.

But he'd been appearing like a genie for almost a month, so he was experienced in wiggling his way through the world of work. With all the self-confidence of a super sleuth, he walked over to the directory in front of the security guard and saw that the legal department was on the 22nd floor.

He glanced down at the name of the bank's vice president, general counsel on the directory, and signed in on the entry log book to see him. In response to the guard's question "Do you have an appointment?" he honestly answered, "Yes." (It was with another offeror the following day.)

The guard attempted calling up to the 22nd floor to verify the appointment, but doing so is a very time-consuming and virtually useless act in most large office buildings. It requires some receptionist somewhere (who isn't at the water cooler) having prior knowledge of who some muckety-muck meeting-master has invited for a visit. The guard was predictably far more concerned that the lawyer's signature on the log matched the one on his driver's license. (He can feel he's doing his job.)

Our friend then was given a visitor's pass and courteously directed to the bank of elevators for the 22nd floor. Since he was in genie mode, he was dressed casually and didn't have a resume. The receptionist asked who he was there to see, and he used the general counsel's name. When asked if he had an appointment, he simply again stated, "Yes."

After watching several people scurry past him for a few minutes, he finally said, "I'm sorry, but I have another appointment. I'd like to speak to any staff attorney who's available." A junior associate came out immediately, and he laid the Magic Four Hello on her. She then invited him back into the inner sanctum, gave him an instant interview (around five minutes) along with an application form. He gave her his business card, asked her for hers, thanked her, and said he would mail back the application with his resume.

As he was waiting for the elevator, he dated and graded the visit on the front of the business card, and deposited it safely in his left back pocket. (The grade was a B since the attorney told him there were "no openings for this quarter" and to check with the bank's HR department for other opportunities.)

He followed the e-mail, thank-you note, mail application, and resume routine to that staff attorney. Then two weeks later—*Bam!*—he pulled that card from the binder clip and lobbed that call right into the general counsel's office. A gruff voice answered and said, "I'm sitting here with this stack of applications when I'm trying to run an understaffed department! What was your name again? Okay, here's your app. How does $125K for the first year sound? Fine. That's one less thing I have to do today. You're hired. I'm sending your paperwork down to HR so they can check your references and set up a personnel file. Report for work there Monday morning."

Our friend was completely blown away because he thought the GC was going to only set up an appointment! When he called me afterward, I assured him that his secret was safe with me and that it was probably just because the GC hadn't read *Instant Interviews*. My friend was satisfied with this reply but then called the GC's office to inquire about where to park when he reported for work Monday morning. He knew—but thought he'd *hallucinated* about getting the job!

Being hooked on being himself, that afternoon he was back on the beat instant interviewing in some other office building.

That fellow has the best job of his life at the bank. He smiles a lot now. Not because he loves his job, but because he loves himself. He knows that he can always pull off something as good or better, anytime anywhere. He learned more about himself (and certainly had more fun) in one month of using the genie technique than he learned in two years of banking experience gained by bouncing checks.

Will you be hopelessly hired every time? Of course not! At least not until you've done it for a while. The working world isn't a perfect world. That's why *you* can get hired over and over, and someone with *better credentials* can't.

And every single visit—no matter how it turns out—will make you better at the 100 more instant-interview self-marketing techniques that follow.

Do 2: Making and Taking the Instant Interview Magic Potion

Want to interview stronger and longer?

Pow!

Here's the Instant Interview Magic Potion. A delicious drink that will power you through a whole morning of instant interviewing.

The potion stabilizes your metabolism and curbs your appetite. That allows you to concentrate on what you do best—instant interviewing. (Follow the making-and-taking instructions carefully to maximize potency and effectiveness.)

Your Basic Disclaimer

It's not really magic. It will only *seem* that way!

I have no way of knowing whether you're allergic to water, let alone the other ingredients.

Consult with your doctor before imbibing, ingesting, inhaling, or otherwise taking the potion.

The Potion's Magic

If you fortify your body and mind in the morning, you'll be energetic, alert, and able to go the distance. The magic is that you'll be doing it and no offerors will.

This will make you appear even more confident, upbeat, and energetic than your coffee-and-donut breakfast, greasy-fast-food lunch audience. They'll want you around even more.

It's common knowledge that a processed carbohydrate meal causes your blood sugar level to rise rapidly, temporarily increasing your energy. But it also drops rapidly, causing sluggishness and irritability. You don't need a spike in your blood sugar. You need sustained energy, mental acuity, and no hunger. That requires high-octane, nutritionally balanced fuel.

Your body is too precious and unique to run with anything but the best you can. We started with a delicious high-protein, low-fat, low-carb smoothie. Adding the coffee gives just enough caffeine to boost your brain activity without making you jumpy.

The potion is not only instant. It gives you sustenance, so you won't run down at sundown. You need to be there for your loved ones when the day is done.

The Potion's Ingredients

Protein Powder (Whey or Soy)

Start with vanilla, but you can use other flavors as well. I rotate between vanilla, chocolate, and strawberry (using up one container at a time).

Protein powder gives you staying power and bulk for appetite control. Whey is a byproduct of milk. So, if you're lactose intolerant, you may want to use the soy powder.

Oatmeal (Uncooked)

The high-fiber and rib-sticking qualities of dry oat flakes can't be matched by any processed cereal or bread. Aside from the many other benefits of oats, the soluble fiber absorbs the potion and acts like a natural timed-release vitamin.

You can use regular or instant. Cook it the night before if anyone in a white coat's following you and taking notes on a clipboard.

I know it sounds a bit weird, but what magic potion doesn't?

If doing things like it says on the box could get you interviews, jobseekers would be jobbing rather than seeking. Working rather than eating.

Raisins

Another natural energy booster. Fibrous, filling, and tastes great.

Almond Butter

Almond butter contains loads of minerals like magnesium, phosphorus, and zinc, as well as healthy fiber. It has no trans fats, is low in saturated fat, and is rich in monounsaturated fat. It gives you yet *more* staying power and appetite control.

Instant Coffee

Coffee contains caffeine, which makes you quicker on the uptake because the neurons in your brain are firing more quickly. So you think faster. You're happier too, because coffee is a mood enhancer.

Drinking instant coffee in the potion buffers the acid. Moreover, it reduces the spiking of caffeine since it's metabolized evenly and slowly. A natural, sustained release occurs.

Banana (Frozen)

No other fruit has more digestible carbs than bananas. All three natural sugars—sucrose, fructose, and glucose. Fiber too. The boost of natural energy will have you ready to rock. And rock you will.

Sugar-free, Fat-free, Instant Pudding Mix

Start with vanilla here, too. Then enjoy the variety of flavors available. I just discovered Blackberry Fusion. Delicious.

The pudding adds flavor, protein, and bulk.

Packet of Sugar Substitute

This is for a little extra sweetness. Don't add—or add more—according to taste.

Water

Because your body needs it. And the ingredients won't blend well without it.

Crushed Ice

Ice cubes are fine, too (as long as the lid's on the blender).
And, to give the final wizard's touch, you'll add. . .

Secret Ingredient X

Ever get a recipe from a great cook who deliberately left something out? Something that would take the dish from great to spectacular?

Nutmeg. It's is a classic spice for attracting *happiness* and *money*. Translation: Instant interviews!

And it's a delightful flavor.

Just don't use too much. A pinch is enough.

Secret Ingredient Y

Baking soda. It's practical (and wizardly clever). A half-teaspoon of baking soda cuts the acid in the coffee. It also reduces urgency, offsetting the diuretic effect of coffee. Add a little, and you'll be less likely to cross your legs and walk like a mummy—very instantly. Or go running around looking for a restroom while accepting the offer of your life.

Baking soda fizzes when mixed with water. Use a little, get delightful effervescence. Use a lot, and your cauldron will erupt! The potion will be sour too.

Making and Taking the Potion

Start the night before by freezing a few bananas. Peel and cut them in half. Put the halves in a plastic bag in the freezer. You'll also need to make ice cubes if you don't already have them frozen.

In the morning, mix the elixir in a cauldron—er—blender.

Here's how:

1. Pour in two teaspoons of instant coffee with one cup of water. (Yes, one cup of black coffee is fine.)
2. Add one-half of a frozen banana.

3. Blend the coffee and the banana, then turn off the blender. Let the mush sit for a few minutes while you collect and add the other ingredients.

4. Add three tablespoons of protein powder. (The scoop inside the container is usually the size of a tablespoon.)

5. Add a cup of dry oatmeal.

6. Add approximately two dozen raisins.

7. Add a tablespoon of almond butter.

8. Add one packet of sugar substitute. (None or more according to taste.)

9. Add one half-cup serving of the sugar-free, fat-free, instant pudding mix. (Four half-cup servings are in the regular 9 oz. box.)

10. Add two cups of crushed ice. (Don't overfill the blender. Leave at least an inch between the top of the liquid and the lid.)

11. Push "Blend."

12. Pause a moment here. You're about to add the magic.

13. Add a pinch of nutmeg.

14. Add a half-teaspoon of baking soda.

15. Say the incantation, "Sixteen interviews today!" as you . . .

16. Blend again.

Assuming you're able to digest this smoothie, you'll probably never leave home again without drinking it. There's just no better way I've ever seen to move you through your moves with optimum results. It just naturally increases your number of successful I.I.'s!

You'll power consistently on all eight cylinders without taking the time and money to eat out.

Let the potion work its magic on *you!*

Do 3: Maintaining Magic Potion Potency Throughout the Day

It's essential to keep the Instant Interview Magic Potion fueling you throughout the day.

Taking the potion when you get up (or after your workout at the job-gym, Do 45) will easily power you through the morning of instants. But it'll eventually need a booster to keep its magic working.

We want you to be as sharp as a tack, energetic, and enthusiastic until you've done all 16 appearances (then taking the bows at home).

You never know which door opens to your dream job, and you've got to be 100 percent engaged.

Here's what I suggest:

The Boosters

Keep containers of protein powder, dry oatmeal, raisins, almonds, and instant coffee mixed with a small amount of baking soda (to reduce the acid and your urgency) in your car. Take a fresh banana, too. These are high-octane additives in the potion.

Also keep a bottle of water, a 6 oz. plastic cup, and a plastic spoon.

Keep a bottle of your favorite mouthwash in the car as well.

Other Snacks

You can add any other snacks, as long as they're unprocessed, natural, and lean.

Packages of peanut-butter sandwich crackers, high-protein bars—things like that. Just be sure they're items that won't spoil or become gooey if the weather is hot.

Lunch Ideas

Plan what you'll eat for lunch the night before. The food doesn't have to be elaborate, and you don't have to spend hours shopping.

Stock your refrigerator with whole-wheat bread, lean sliced chicken or turkey, low-fat cheese slices, lettuce, sliced pickles (if you like them), and low-fat spreads. That way you can make a high-nutrition sandwich in minutes the night before, slip it in a sandwich bag, put it back in the refrigerator, and you're ready to rock after taking the potion (or packing it to take after your workout at the jobgym).

Foods to Avoid

Onion (ergo no relish or salsa), garlic, and cheese. They smell. And so will you if you consume them.

If you're unable to get back to your car for lunch, opt for a light meal. Whole-wheat sandwiches, salads, and nothing that has a diuretic effect. (You don't want to interview instantly in restrooms since the seating arrangement is problematic.)

Rinse out with the mouthwash before you leave your car-office.

Try this and you'll be zoomin' through those buildings like a buzzsaw all day!

Do 4: Breaking Out of the Box—Job E-X-P-A-N-S-I-O-N

If you're happy and you know it, clap your hands!

Let's keep you working there and get you a promotion. More responsibility, more pay, bigger title.

This Do's for you.

For half a century, the federal and state governments have been issuing underemployment statistics.

Why are we paying for this? Is there any employee who can't have more responsibilities? Who can't be worth more? Isn't the number underemployed 100 percent?

Our statistic is 100 percent, too—100 percent success in expanding any job. Why? Because a j-o-b is a b-o-x. Just a container. An arbitrary limitation that our commonsense, politically correct system expands. You're a jack-in-the-box! We all are.

Viktor Frankl, the brilliant author who wrote *Man's Search for Meaning*, observed over half a century ago, "We don't know we've been in prison until we break out."

With the publication of *Instant Interviews*, underemployment will be dramatically reduced. All it takes is adapting our system. The result is an advanced instant interviewing technique.

It works 100 percent of the time because—it works!

The greatest benefit of job e-x-p-a-n-s-i-o-n is the maintenance of absolute job security throughout. It's using what you've got to get what you want. Not empire building, but value-adding—acquiring more responsibility that's worth more.

Every job (and every wage) can be expanded. Easily up to 40 percent if you do it right. We do this by isolating expandable areas called *job components*. Each is worth 10 percent. The more components, the more e-x-p-a-n-s-i-o-n.

Think of your job as a profit center. What do you contribute to the bottom line? How can you increase that contribution?

We'll call you "Jack." Let's say you're in middle management with the title of cost estimator. You take engineering mockups of mechanical switches and determine what they will cost to produce. The company manufactures the switches directly, primarily because it wants to maintain quality control for tight tolerances in the materials. That also eliminates any delivery problems.

How can you make your job more profitable? One way may be to out-source the manufacturing instead of doing it in-house. There are subcontractors who can do this, but top management has resisted the idea.

As usually happens when there are more than two employees, there's a political consideration in this job e-x-p-a-n-s-i-o-n. The vice president of manufacturing is an empire builder and jealously guards against any outside work being done.

S-o-o-o, what you do first is get your facts straight. Call the outside subs and meet with them to discuss outsourcing the manufacturing work to them. This is within your present job description—it's just not politically correct.

Then have that source give you a detailed, realistic proposal to do the work. One that will anticipate every objection. Specifically, the cost, the tolerances, quality control, and the delivery. It must be absolutely bulletproof.

You get corroboration by using another source as well.

The result—as you knew would happen—was that the cost to produce would be less (due to much lower operation expenses), and quality control could still be monitored in-house. Completion would be faster, so delivery would be, too.

You go to your direct supervisor. You explain the merits of the idea to him. It will also free up the manufacturing group to take on new business. All it would take is a little marketing that you would do.

There are four job e-x-p-a-n-s-i-o-ns here:

You would be willing to handle the contract negotiation with the subcontractor (Job Component 1), the quality monitoring (Job Component 2), delivery timeliness (Job Component 3), and the marketing of the manufacturing capability (Job Component 4).

You've used the third-party validation of job e-x-p-a-n-s-i-o-n by the proposals. You've explained why it will make your job more profitable to the company. You've shown professionalism. (No attacks on the status quo or the status quoers. No hidden agenda.) More important, you've shown initiative.

Your supervisor likes the idea and supports you. He reports to the corporate controller, a numbers guy. The controller reports to the president. So does the vice president of manufacturing—a gruff ex-military officer who resists change.

So you ask your supervisor if he would set up a meeting for you with the controller. (That's your I.I.) He's happy to do it, because he sees that this will give him more power and money. He offers to attend, but you tell him you've got a good relationship with the controller (actually, you don't know him that well, but this is an instant interview; you already rehearsed with your supervisor and don't need any interference).

You ask your supervisor to arrange the meeting with the controller in your little (until expanded) office. This is a smart request, since otherwise we've got you entering the inner sanctum of someone with greater power. We have nothing against the controller or his office, but you're being aggressive enough with the idea itself. In your office, you're in the driver's seat.

You greet the controller with, "Hi, Craig! Have a seat." Otherwise, give him the Magic Four Hello (Do 1). Then, you simply give him the two proposals and let them work. You do not sell. The facts do.

The interview with the controller focuses on the bottom line only. He's a numbers guy, right?

The hooks for him are clearly:

- You will negotiate the deal (Job Component 1—no additional cost)
- The switches are cheaper to manufacture (more profit)
- You will monitor the quality (Job Component 2—no additional cost)
- You will be responsible for timely delivery (Job Component 3—no additional cost)
- You will get new manufacturing business (Job Component 4—more profit)

The controller asks you whether the cost estimator job description includes these things. You say it doesn't, so it will have to be expanded. He says that doing so might throw off the salary-rate ranges.

You suggest a new title of "Development Analyst" and will write the job description for approval tonight. ("No need to take company time.") He likes that because he's a numbers guy. Everything must equal everything else.

Can you see how we adapted the basic instant interviewing technique to job e-x-p-a-n-s-i-o-n?

The controller asks you which vendor you like best. (That's the clue that he's made up his mind. Does the I.I. ever fail?) You suggest the vendor you originally picked.

I purposely chose an actual case using four job components because it demonstrates how to expand them simultaneously. They key is to isolate the components. Then you do your homework, factor in the politics, and instantly interview with the right point person.

Now, four years later, the company is generating twice the sales from the job e-x-p-a-n-s-i-o-n. The employee has been promoted and is working in an expanded version of his boss's job. He's earning about three times his pay before the job e-x-p-a-n-s-i-o-n and has received additional benefits.

Bigger bowl, bigger fish. Bigger box, better life.

Employed? Then, you're underemployed. Then, not now.

It's a fact, Jack!

Do 5: E-Mailing, Faxing, and Mailing Your *Rest-You-May*

Were you expecting a resume Do here? Okay, but the *instant* way!

(Remember to spell it *resume*—without the accented letters. It'll make your instant interview submissions a lot easier.)

I'm not a big history buff, because looking in the junglejeep rearview mirror while in the fast path causes crackups. But here's one bit of history every instant interviewer must know.

Okay. Stop at the clearing with that old "Offerors Only" sign. It looks just fine. Park right here. Gee, look at that litter. Resumes strewn all over. What a mess.

Now, let's talk for a moment.

In days of yore, candidate background information used to be called a *curriculum vitae*. (The derivation is actually from the Latin term *fahget-aboutit*.) During the Industrial Revolution, a grad student in Advanced Uselessness wrote his Ph.D. dissertation on the concept of shortening the term to CV. However, frustrated jobseekers attached some rather antisocial words to those letters.

Then, as people starting removing their clothes and our society became more open, someone called it what it was: a *rest-you-may*. The idea was to address the basic reason anyone who goes through the hassle and expense of hiring. So, they can *rest*. The rest-you-may gave them information to decide whether to interview.

It actually worked well for a while. When businesses received the rest-you-mays, they thought they looked like restaurant menus. So, they started calling up the jobseekers and ordering pizza and beer. When the jobseekers showed up, some serious partying ensued.

Then as employer tastes changed to soufflé and Bordeaux, the rest-you-may didn't work as well. So, someone shortened the term *rest-you-may* to *resume* because it sounded French. Resume writing became a service industry. Millions of books were sold (thank you), and the Internet was flooded with tips. Some were savvy, others were silly. But jobseekers didn't know the difference. They started churning out copies of the samples. Employers were overcome. Resumes, by whatever name, lost their impact as the now-you-can-relax direct-mail pieces they were in the first place.

So, we're going to allow history to do what it does best—repeat. Let's go back to the basic, magnetic rest-you-may.

Your resume will work because it's not background information. Nor is it a clone of someone else's paint-by-the-numbers masterpiece.

No—your resume is a front-end, gotta-have-him, *impulse buy* that gets interviews. Instantly.

The resume, like every other device we're going to examine, is only that—a device to get you an interview. So, the value of your resume depends on whether it gets you interviews—instantly.

You shouldn't use a resume service. The discipline of fighting your way through every syllable is better at making you a great self-marketer than almost anything else you can do. You draw down the information to state your wonderfulness powerfully and concisely. Then you form the same word patterns in your speech.

Smart, yes?

Getting Offeror Attention

The offerors of the working world don't ask you to send a resume because they want to interview you. They request that piece of paper for one of four reasons:

1. They want to get you off the phone
2. They're not sure you're right for the job

3. They want to delay making a decision
4. They're unauthorized hiring authorities with no power to hire you

Our focus is not to make your resume suitable for framing, but simply to get you an instant interview.

No reason to rest. Not when you're this close to your goal.

Resume Dos for Interviews

Use your resume to step you straight into the offeror's office.

These ways:

1. Keep the resume short. No more than two pages. Readership drops 80 percent with every additional page.
2. Make the font size at least 10 point. Better yet—12.
3. Use black ink on white or ivory stock. Gray text or paper is often difficult to photocopy. Any other color combinations are o-u-t.
4. Leave a one-inch border. That makes it easier for the offeror to write comments.
5. Bullet—but only for a few important points.
6. Double-check. Did you leave out your contact information? Is a number wrong? Did you check all of the spelling?
7. Follow up. Regardless of the employer's instructions for sending resumes (e-mail, fax, or pasted in to an online form), *always* follow up by mailing a hard copy. Why? Just in case. And to stand out, because your average jobseeker won't bother.

Resume Don'ts for Working Won'ts

1. Don't use the word *resume* with the accented letter *e*. The only exception is if you're applying for an old-age home position as a patient. HR (stands for "happy rejector") types have been screening those out for decades.

I don't know why anyone would even *use* the title *Resume* on a resume. Would they shuffle into an interview with Post-it notes on their eyeglasses that say *Glasses?*

2. Don't update anything in your own handwriting. It draws attention and looks like you didn't take the time to correct an error.

3. Don't include contact information for references. Why let offerors wiggle out of an interview by calling them? Say instead: *Personal and professional references are available upon request.*

4. Don't state salary at all, even by implication. Not desired, not current, and not past. The probability of your missing the amount an offeror has in mind is 100 percent. Save this for our negotiation prestidigitation.

5. Don't give an objective. If you're answering an ad or know the job being offered—and don't want any other—it's okay to repeat whatever the offeror says.

6. Don't use a cover letter. A letter to an unidentified offeror can RSVP "Will not attend" before you even receive the invitation. The only time to use a cover letter is when you know exactly what the offeror wants. Since the *offeror* doesn't, this is an accurate footshot. Footshots have you infirmed, not interviewed.

7. Don't include a photo. Doing so shows you completely reject a half-century of equal employment opportunity laws. You'd be happier if your envelope was misaddressed, since you wouldn't receive a rejection letter.

8. Don't state vital statistics (sex, height, weight, marital status, and so forth).

Racing from Resume to Interview

The best way to instant an interview is with the most seemingly focused but generically written resume you can develop. Leave enough out so they *must* talk to you. Make them want you to fill in the blanks through an *interview!*

There's a Spanish word that says it all. It rhymes (almost) with *resume.* It's *andale (ahn da lay).* It means *to move* or *to work.*

Andale!

You move. You work!

Do 6: Getting Your Resume Scanned

Getting your resume scanned favorably really increases the number of interviews!

ATSs *(Applicant Tracking Systems)* are now being used by almost every major employer. With them, companies can draw on a huge database of candidates without paying advertising or placement fees. The candidates have already applied, and in some cases have even been interviewed. So they tend to be more qualified and interested than ones who are sourced on the Internet.

Keyword Indexing of Candidate Files

If your resume comes in as hard copy, they scan it. The computer may try to read the words (it's called *optical character recognition*). If it does, it sees keywords (Do 15). Even if it doesn't read, it takes an electronic picture of the pages. Then it asks the offeror to input some keywords.

If you submit your resume online, the first thing the software does is comb it for keywords.

So, no matter how the resume comes in, keywords control its destiny. The computer stores the keywords in its electronic document *index*. Whenever an offeror wants a resume, she enters a keyword into the search software.

If you have the right keywords in your resume, there you are!

Planning for Scanning

That little scanner is looking for highlights. Things like attributes, accomplishments, names of colleges attended, languages spoken, job titles, locations, and sometimes names of other companies (competitors or ones that have good training).

This is one time it's acceptable to go over two pages.

Scanning Secrets

1. Format properly. This is no time to get fancy. The computer will need the cleanest original you can produce, printed by laser or a high quality inkjet. Use recognizable terms such as *Accomplishments, Honors, Awards, Education,* and *Experience.* All the terms that make a resume look like a professional profile of you.

2. *Select the right paper.* Use white only. (Unlike with a hard copy of your resume, ivory is not recommended. Scanners don't pick up the characters as readily when there's less contrast.) Make sure it's quality paper with a hard finish, too. (Lower-grade paper is rougher and makes the type fuzzy.) Print on only one side of the page.

3. *Have your name prominently at the top of each page.* Full first name, middle initial, last name, and any professional designations.

4. *Use standard fonts.* Times New Roman and Courier are the best choices. Don't go over 14-point size.

5. *Make headings stand out.* Use bold or caps.

6. *List each phone number on its own line.*

7. *Be as specific as possible about your skills.* Include work habits such as "team player" and "can meet deadlines." Then add to them for maximum matches.

Scanning Silliness

Unstants do exactly the wrong things in setting up a scannable resume.
Here are some examples:

- They jazz the resume up with graphics, boxes, or lines.
- They use italics, bullets, or underlining.
- They use newsletter or other nontraditional resume layouts.

Scanning is here to stay and getting bigger all the time. Now you know how to get your resume scanned *in* for an *instant!*

Do 7: Writing the ASCII Resume

ASCII stands for *Amazing Success Comes to Instant Interviewers!*

Average jobseekers think it means the American Standard Code for Information Interchange. That's why they don't use it and don't get interviews.

Using the ASCII format gives you a common language for all of the word processing programs. It's the basic, unformatted text that works with any of them.

This means the offeror won't get conversion losses or destruction of your e-mailed resume upon opening it.

Answering about ASCII

If you've been jobseeking online, you're probably run across ASCII. Many of the job web sites and employers ask you to submit your cover letter and resume in this format. It's easy to do, and you'll have it down after you've done it once or twice.

Questions? Here are the FAQs and your answers:

Converting or Creating Plain Text

How do I create the file?
It's not how you create it; it's how you save it. As a plain text file (.txt extension). Do not use rich text format (.rtf), which includes formatting. For example, if you have the resume file open in Word, select *File > Save As* from the menu. Then select *.txt* from the *Save As* options before you click the *Save* button. You can also paste or type a new version into a plain-text program such as Notepad or Wordpad, and then save it as a .txt file. (Check the pasted version first. You may have to retype some of it to get rid of extra characters.)

How long should my lines be?
They can't exceed 80 characters. ASCII text doesn't wrap to the next line. You have to make your own breaks (like with getting interviews). Always use Left Alignment (technically known as *flush left*), not centered.

What about fonts?
It doesn't matter. The display will default to the user or offeror's basic font.

How can I line up text?
You can't do this with any predictability. If you must, use spaces. That's the way to center as well. Keep tapping the space bar. The displayed results will depend on how the offeror's computer is set up.

Will I destroy the features my resume software creates?
Absolutely—as with the spacing, only more so. You can't even use bullets. (I don't recommend bulleted lists anyway. But if you must use one, you can use hyphens.)

All Facts and No Frills

ASCII text eliminates all the subjectivity of resume graphics. This places your resume on a level playing field with all of the jillions of others the offeror receives.

Follow the guidelines in Do 5 and Do 6, and your resume will be coming across the offeror's screening screen in bright colors. If you could see what most ASCII resumes look like, you'd realize this in an instant. That's exactly what an offeror does.

After you submit this ASCII resume, keep a copy. Use it the next time an employer requests it. You can also paste it into any resume text field in any online form. (If you try pasting from your Word version, you'll see why I did this Do for you.)

ASCII and you shall receive—*instantly!*

Do 8: Getting You Covered with the Better Letter

Resume cover letters are a great interviewgetter!
You just have to know the right times to use them.

Peeking Under the Covers

I'll get to the content of the better letter in a minute. But let's peek under the covers of almost all cover letters first.

When it comes to resumes, *resumania* reigns. Average Jobjoes research, study, draft, redraft, rewrite, cut, paste, scan, copy, diddle in dictionaries, thumb thesauruses, and otherwise quite literally drive themselves crazy with these nonsensical pieces of paper. Go to any high school or college library, any reference section of any public library, any copy center, any computer bank, any career center—almost anywhere they hide. It's as though the effort bears some relationship to the results.

Those people could actually be interviewing! With the publication of *Instant Interviews* that insanity can finally be clinically diagnosed and instantly treated. Good for you!

If you were here, I'd show you my battle scars. I tried to help folks when I wrote *The Resume Makeover*. It was the first—and is still the only—book ever written that offered a free diagnostic of the reader's resume.

My idea was that they'd read the book, follow the directions, then send us the resume for a written critique and return. We were so excited about that one. For the first time, we'd actually produce a resume book that would get someone a job other than the author. The book was an instant bestseller.

If I could show you the van Goghs that came in, you'd van-go crazy too. And that was after supposedly following the baby-step examples in the book! (The idea helped a lot of people get hired, but only after we personally coached them on how to write and then use the resume.)

Now, I'm teaching you the valuable lessons we learned. Among them is that unless you have a properly drafted resume (Do 5), covering it with a letter will not work.

Our cat Sylvan used to do that with a newspaper. He was very intelligent, so I don't know who he thought he was kidding. We still saw the lump and detected an unsavory aroma.

So, the story with cover letters is: Do them right and they'll help a good resume. Do them right and they'll cover a bad resume like that newspaper. Do them wrong and save your postage.

Writing the Better Letter

The first thing to ask yourself is "What am I trying to accomplish with a cover letter?" If it's focus, you must know who and what you're aiming at. That means the specific offeror and the specific gig.

This is not usually known, and you don't want to guess.

Unless it's a referral or a really specific, serious, absolutely structured job that you know has exactly the requirements and duties you're going to mention.

Go for the referred offeror, and generic the gig.

Think of the better letter as an ad for your resume. You don't want it piled and filed. You want it read and spread!

What do all ads have?

Reasons to buy.

Think of someone at a newsstand yelling "Extra! Extra! Read all about the genie!" (Do 1).

The offeror should be enticed to read more about this wonderful person—you. So avoid resume language, and personalize your approach.

Here are the four elements of the better letter:

Your Contact Information

You can't get interviewed if the offeror doesn't know how to find you. Make it easy by including all your contact information—even though it's on the resume. That means full name (including middle initial), address (using "Unit" for any apartment as you would for an owned one), phone and fax numbers, and e-mail address (definitely—free on the Internet).

Make it easy for the offeror to contact you and she's much more likely to do so. Duh. Yet only around half of the cover letters out there have contact information. Then when they become separated from the resume, Sylvan could have used them.

Your Hook

Your sentence must communicate your purpose. Avoid the usual canned intro and personalize the hook. Once you've personalized a hook, you'll never have to write a canned cover letter again. Oh, sure, you'll have similar contents and closing, but the hook will make the offeror feel you're writing just to her. Why have just an okay hook when you can have a hooray one?

This is an okay hook when responding to an ad:

Enclosed is my resume, which I hope you'll consider for the executive assistant position posted in the *Offerors' News*.

Notice how much more pull there is in the hooray hook:

Your executive assistant ad in the *Offerors' News* caught my eye because it's exactly like the position I've been seeking.

This second hook gives you a natural lead-in. The rest should read like a letter, not a mini resume. Express interest in working for the company (no position listed).

An okay way would be:

I am writing to you because after five years of experience as a warehouse foreman at a food processing plant, I am now seeking greater challenges and responsibilities.

Now, the hooray way:

I've followed the growth of Sandstone Sanding during my five years as a warehouse foreman. I'm impressed by what I've seen and welcome the opportunity to speak with you regarding how my experience will contribute to its expansion.

Your Whatever

You've hooked the offeror. He wants more specifics. That's what you offer in the body of the cover letter. If you're responding to a classified ad, repeat the requirements back as qualifications. Usually no more than two or three items. This is always a one-page letter.

Keep the letter flowing as you describe your years of experience, your skills, and successes. Using bullets or subheads sounds like you're just copying your resume.

Don't include your salary expectations, even if the ad requested them. You'll be instanting forthwith and can work your salary spell then.

Your Next Move

You've written a great letter. Now, a firm handshake. Say you'll contact the offeror the following week. If it's a blind ad, give your phone number and e-mail address again. You want to discuss your ideas and the company's needs.

You want a one-on-one meeting. You always want a meeting. You're Mr. or Ms. Meeting. You meet and greet. You greet and meet. You take a seat when you meet. You repeat when you meet. Offers are sweet when you meet.

See what I'm saying? Accept this. Turn yourself into an interviewin', offer-gettin' meeting maniac! Different symptoms from resumania. They include juggling many offers simultaneously.

Personalize that better letter, and you're—well—*covered!*

Do 9: Broadcasting a Letter with High Bandwidth

High bandwidth. Fast, powerful, and transmitting a crystal-clear signal. That's our broadcast letter.

Unlike a cover letter that sometimes accompanies a resume, the broadcast letter *is* the resume. Only you're free of the rigid format and wordiness. That allows you to be creative.

Here's the system:

Google the Type of Business and Geographic Area

While mass-mailed resumes are typically sent to HR departments, *broadcast* letters should be sent to managers directly. Let's assume you're looking for a job in cookware sales. You google "cookware distributors Seattle." Then write down the address and phone number.

Obtain the Name and Title of the Contact

Call businesses and find out the name of the manager of a specific department. In our example, you just say to whoever answers the phone, "I'm sending a letter to your sales manager. What's his name and exact title?" Try to get the full first name and middle initial.

Be sure to get the title right, too. Is it sales manager, manager of sales, or director of sales?

These things may take a few more minutes, but it's essential to showing that you've done your homework.

Few broadcast letters have this important touch. Yours will and will be *read!*

Use a Preprinted Letterhead or Create Your Own

Broadcast letters don't have to be on a preprinted letterhead. Just print a letterhead on your computer that has no abbreviations (except your middle initial) like this:

Jonas D. Jobseeker
1072 Campbell Street, Unit 7

Craftville, Illinois 30718
555-555-5555
555-555-5555 Fax
jdjobseeker@gotmail.com

Always call an apartment a *Unit*, so it appears you own your home. You can use abbreviations on the matching envelope's return name and address.

Use 10-Point Type with Black Ink on White Paper

Ivory stock is also acceptable. The weight should be at least 24-lb.

Broadcast letters are serious business correspondence—not flyers—so avoid colored ink or stock.

Format the Letter Properly

From top to bottom, it has the following components:

An Address Section
Steven B. Harwood, Manager of Sales
Cookware Distributors, Inc.
521 South Verdugo Road
Northfield, Illinois 30719
A Standard Salutation
Dear Mr. Harwood:
A Message that says, "Instantly Invite Me to Interview."
I am seeking a sales position with Cookware Distributors, Inc.

Over the past nine years, I have held progressively responsible positions in consumer product sales.

During that time, through my management of our sales force, the company has consistently broken all sales records. Moreover, I have increased the sales of newly developed products while devising creative techniques for marketing them.

Advance Notice of Follow-Up
> *I will call you within the next week to arrange an appointment for us to meet.*

A Complimentary Closing

Nothing beats . . .
> *Very truly yours,*

A Signature Line

Your full name as it appears on the letterhead. Sign it yourself (no computer signature) in black ink.

This looks simple, so why do inactive interviewers constantly botch up broadcast letters? Because they read cover letter and resume books. These load up the broadcast letter with facts that at best don't matter—and at worst don't get read.

The broadcast letter is one page, easy to read, and gets right down to the bottom line. What's the message? *You must interview me!* Exclamation point. Period.

Whether it's increasing sales, using technical ability, or implementing a new accounting system, always give the *benefit* you conferred.

What else would you want an offeror to think about for a week?

Call the Recipient a Week after You Mail the Letter

Use the letter as your opener with words like:

> This is Steve Harwood. I wrote you last week about meeting to discuss my contribution to Cookware Distributors. I'll be in Northfield next Wednesday and can meet at 10 A.M. or 2 P.M. Which is better for you?

Note the reference to the letter and the choice of times.

The letter is your place card. The alternative choice doubles the probability of an acceptance (less restricts, more confuses).

Send out 100 of these and you'll generate around 20 interviews. A big boost to your interview inventory!

Follow Up on the Follow-Up

Assume that even though you followed up on the letter, you haven't had a return call. No sign of an offeror anywhere. That's no reflection on you or the letter.

Your letter may simply not be received at the right time. You may hear back some time in the future when the company needs you even more than it does now. You aren't going to wait around worrying about it. Oodles of offerors await!

Keep track of when you sent the letter, then follow up with a phone call in a week. Do this every week for a month. Then just file it for a month or so and try again.

But with a high-bandwidth broadcast letter as I've suggested, it's likely you won't be doing a lot of tickler filing.

Because you'll instantly be getting *interview invitations!*

Do 10: Faxmailing for Nofailing

While you're out on the jobjungle trail personally interviewing, your cover letter and resume will be beating *two* paths to offeror doors!

We call the instant procedure *faxmailing*. Since we started it, hundreds of jobseekers received interview invitations who wouldn't have even been *considered* otherwise.

If you've ever been inside a business that has more than one person (and some that have only one), you know what happens. Resumes get piled, filed, written on, spilled on, forwarded to, turned over, separated from, crumpled up, torn up, and thrown out. And those are the ones that *arrive!*

While I was working at one supposedly well-run company, I bought a three-foot-high traffic signal from a toy store and placed it beside my desk. Some manager would run in breathlessly and say, "Hurry and place this ad in the Sunday *Times* before the deadline!" Then after the deadline passed, he'd saunter back and say, "Cancel the ad. We're placing the req on hold." I'd bend down and turn the signal from green to red. A loud bell would ring.

Faxmailing instantly *doubles* your chances of having the cover letter and resume result in an interview. If the package is received by the *same* offeror, you've had the benefit of powerful direct-mail repetition. If it's received by a *different* offeror, you're being considered again by someone with totally separate criteria.

If an ad says "mail resume," call and find out the full name, title, and fax number of the offeror. If it says "fax resume," call and find out the offeror's full name, exact address, title, and fax number.

Obvious. Yet nobody else will faxmail but I.I.'s.

Designing the Fax Cover Sheet

Always use a cover sheet for your transmittal. You're a pro and you're sending personal information.

It should be on the same letterhead as your cover letter and resume. This will restate your contact info and your image. Be consistent, and the similarity will reduce the chances of the sheet becoming separated from the rest of the transmittal. Include the number of pages so the offeror can verify receipt of all four (including the cover letter and no more than a two-page resume).

The body should say only:

Please deliver immediately.
Thank you.

At the bottom, the following words should appear in smaller print:

This transmission is intended for the use of the individual to whom it is addressed and may contain information that is confidential, privileged, and exempt from disclosure under applicable law. If you receive this transmission in error, please return it to the sender via the United States Postal Service. Thank you.

Assembling the Mail Package

Don't include a copy of your cover sheet with the mailed package. The idea is to have someone else read the contents.

Even though it's easily folded and stuffed into a Number 10 business-sized envelope, it's far more likely to be read if placed without folding in a 9 × 12-inch full-sized one. A real subtlety, but even the better letter (Do 8) and best resume (Do 5) are DOA if they're not read. People pay bills with regular envelopes. Oversized ones get opened. Don't you open the ones you receive?

Use white envelopes. With a black marker, draw a stripe around the edges. It won't be noticeable until it's in a stack. The offeror will open it first because it'll stand out.

Faxmail and then call to follow up (Do 40).

No reply from a local offeror? Plan an instanting day around its facility!

Do 11: Dollaring for Instant Interest

Do you want an offeror to know you're a valuable asset? Send her a dollar bill!

Who does that? Clark Conventional? I don't think so. Clark Conventional spends half that on a stamp and twice that on a worry pill.

Here's how it's done.

Go to the Bank and Get 20 Crisp Dollar Bills

These will cost $20, so be prepared. The good news is that they cost no more than the funky ones in your wallet.

So, give George a facelift. Bad enough he's green and shrinking.

First impressions, you know.

Pick 20 Local Places Where You'd Like to Work

Let's say these are a music store, a recording studio, and a record label.

Working at these places would make you very happy because you love music. No boss, co-workers, or work could change that.

Only you're a brain surgeon. Even worse, you've got the shakes. So not fixing brains any more is a no-brainer. You can control it with pills, but not that well.

You go to a career counselor and take a battery of tests. You discover *job incompatibility* between brain surgery and working in a music store.

Job incompatibility is a careerfolk bigphrase that means, "You ain't done it, so you can't do it."

It's one example of how the fancy phrase becomes a new disease. Once you've got it, you need a cure. Only there's none because you're unqualified. Go find something else. How about watch repair?

This is why the whole job thing is so gross. You were in one box, and all that you can do is get into a smaller one.

My first question is, "What's this with you and music?" Of course, it turns out you sold records in high school, hung around a recording studio in college, and visited a studio when artists were recording.

You've got a photographic memory for artists and songs (naturally— it's what you love), know all about recording studios (because you've visited every one in town just for enjoyment), and have a friend who works for that record label (that fits—friends have similar interests).

Now, you . . .

Write the Letter

Here's what a job-to-die-for letter looks like:

Digital Beat Recording Studio
230 Hiphop Highway
Singatune, NY 21873

ATTN: Carey Beat, President

Dear Carey,

I visited Digital Beat last year, and my goal is to assist you in making it the most successful studio in Singatune.

The dollar enclosed is my first contribution. I'd like to follow it with doing more than you ask for whatever you think would grow the business. From what I've seen locally, we should be able to double the business within 18 months.

I've become thoroughly familiar with the latest digital conversion techniques, have a lifelong love of music, can help you book artists fast, and see a big potential for Digital Beat acting as their agent.

I'm also a technically proficient professional with 24 years of experience in the surgical field. However, it's not my passion. Booking and recording artists is. I'll call you next week and look forward to speaking with you.

Thanks for your anticipated interest!

Very truly yours,

Noah U. Cutter

Encl.: $1 bill

Note that we used contractions like "I'd, "I've," and "I'm." This is not a formal letter—we're enclosing a gimmick! Besides, we're writing to a recording studio owner-operator, not the dean of a university.

Next you . . .

Google Recording Studios

Click on the addresses of web sites so you'll know the names of new equipment, their uses, prices, and as many buzzwords (and buzzphrases) as you can find. Write down the information. Practice the words. When people in any business talk to each other, buzzwords are the shorthand they use to let each other know they're hip.

When you use buzzwords properly, an offeror is very impressed. It sounds like you know volumes. But all you're saying is a word. This makes them the most effective device possible to get an interview. That's why we used the words *digital* and *conversion* in Noah's letter.

Call the Offeror

Carey probably answers his phone when he's there. Try not to leave a voice mail. Just call back. When you reach him, here's an idea of how to handle the call:

You: Hi, Carey. This is Noah Cutter!

Carey: (Laughing) I spent your dollar! (See—they always remember. Worth the stamp, too.)

You: Well, let's get busy making a lot more. I'm really excited about the new synthesizer Harrold Electronics just introduced!

Carey: You sure seem confident we can increase our business!

You: It's not even confidence. It's right there. The acts, the bookings, the studio upgrades to increase the rates—everything!

Carey: When can we meet?

You: Tomorrow morning, if that works for you.

Carey: You're on.

You: I'll be at the studio at 10 sharp.

Carey: Looking forward to it.

You: Me, too!

Interview Insight

While we're on the subject of money—do you pick up coins when you're walking? Even pennies? I do too.

When I pick up a coin from the street, I think about when that coin meant the difference between eating and starving. Then I drop

(continued)

(continued)
it back down for someone to pick up who needs it. It's a little dumb exercise that does wonders for my sense of perspective.

But if it's a *heads-up* penny, I figure that's a sign and I keep it.

That does wonders for my sense of something greater than I can possibly know.

Use the 20 dollars for 20 sets of the 4 steps I gave you. You should instantly get 20 to-die-for interviews!

And a to-live-for livelihood!

Do 12: Maximizing Instant Availability Announcements

The IAA (Instant Availability Announcement) is another super way to get you interviews while you're out interviewing.

These announcements have traditionally been in newspaper classified pages under "Help Available" or "Work Wanted" sections for a variety of services. Sometimes, they're in magazines too.

But they're surprisingly effective for getting management and professional positions as well. You can post yours on the Internet. Or you can fax it. You might even consider paying for an ad. (There's a little more to know about that, so we'll deal with it in a moment.)

Explaining Yourself

The way to penetrate with an IAA is to specifically state what you *want* and what you have to *offer*.

An example is:

Seeking executive chef position. Five years experience in Westchester County. Willing to relocate for the right position.

It doesn't take much space or many words to announce the two things you want.

Leave out:

Past salary

Current salary requirements

Any salary range

Information that will identify you. (You want to attract, then decide. Just like help-wanted advertisers.)

IAAs tend to draw sophisticated offerors.

Placing a Classified IAA

Since everyone uses the Internet, newspaper help-available sections are much smaller than they used to be. That's what makes them so terrific! The reach isn't worldwide, but the audience is local, and the staying power of print advertising is far better than through screen transmission.

Moreover, you can remain anonymous. This is a great time saver and hassle stopper, as employers know. You just review the responses and answer those that interest you.

Set up a separate mailbox for e-mail responses. There won't be any way to trace the contact information back to you. You can advertise yourself all over the place, and no one will know it's you.

Writing the Classified IAA

It's so easy. You just:

- Study classified ads for jobs similar to the one you want.
- Circle the three primary qualifications those ads request. Are they asking for a degree? Knowledge of word processing programs? Minimum two years experience? Get inside the employer's head. Mark the three you think are most important.
- Work backward using the three primary requirements. They want someone with "good people skills," you have "good people skills." Isn't this fun? You're just giving 'em what they think they want. What they get is you. Instantly. Then they *know* what they want.
- Rely on the classified ad rep for tips. HR people do. Ad-sales reps can save you a ton of money by helping you take advantage of upcoming

features (perhaps a special jobs or career section), timing your ad to reach different demographics (as between midweek and weekend editions), using rateholders (those two-line ads that run to take advantage of multiple insertions), and other tricks of the trade. Reps frequently have control over placement of the ads, too. Go for the front page, back page, inside upper-right insertion, or other optimum space.

Deciding Where to Place the IAA

Which publication to use will depend on an infinite number of variables. They include the type of position you want, whether you want to place the ad locally or nationally, whether you want to place it out of town in advance of a scouting trip (Do 60), or whether you want a niche publication in your field.

Call all the publications that have the demographics you want. Tell the reps that you know there's no limit to the amount you can spend on advertising, but you have a very limited budget. Then, listen well. They know which ads work and which don't. You're not writing it for views, you're writing it for *interviews*.

I've advertised in some of the most beautiful pieces you can imagine, but nobody responded. Then I've run the same ad in some oddball publication and tons of inquiries poured in. The lesson here is that you always start slow and recognize that the size of the ad doesn't matter if the placement or the publication is wrong.

IAAs mean increased interviews with no time taken away from instanting. They're worth maximizing this way!

Do 13: Blasting Instant Availability Announcements

Let's explosively blast your IAA with pure dynamite!

Faxing Fast

First we're going to review how to fax it to the offerors of the working-world. You can easily get their fax numbers by calling target companies and just asking.

Here's what you say:

You: Hi. Could I have your fax number?

Receptionist: We have more than one. Which department are you trying to reach?

You: (*Ask for anything but HR, such as:*)

The head of marketing

The head of community relations

The head of internal affairs

The head of transportation

The head of your IT department

The list goes on, but you get the idea. You're trying to reach an offeror—a "head of"—who has fax access. You probably won't even be asked why. It's a routine request.

Just be sure to ask for the offeror's full name (including middle initial) and title. It's worth waiting for a moment to get this information.

Then be . . .

Internetting Instantly

1. *Go online.* The same sites that advertise jobs also allow postings from jobseekers.

2. *Look up trade magazines, online and otherwise.* Many have full sections of availability announcements.

3. *Contact alumni and club magazines.* They often have large availability sections too—at little or no cost. This is a great resource because people like to work with other members.

4. *Find former supervisors and co-workers.* Then e-mail them the announcement.

5. *Use your computer address book.* E-mail the announcement to your friends and acquaintances.

6. *Let everyone you can know you're available and able.* Tell them exactly what you're looking for.

Networking Socially

Why do people think social networking sites are for socializing?

Most make it easy for you to state your experience. Emphasize it in your profile, minimizing the strictly social information. Avoid music, outlandish statements, or anything you don't want the working world to know forever.

You might also check out some of the niche sites that serve the placement industry. Recruiters list their areas of expertise, and many receive excellent candidates that way. Since they're into networking, they'll cast a wide net if you look placeable (Do 26).

In addition to being able to broadcast your experience, these sites allow you to post your IAA.

Boom!

Do 14: Shifting into Overdrive with the Callback Card

Nothing will get you jumping up and down like returning from a day of instants to voice mails from offerors with interview invites!

Our *callback card* will cause ceiling bumps—and keep you v-e-r-r-r-y busy. Your automatic transmission will be effortlessly shifting your magnificent, mean, meetin' machine into overdrive while you're appearing on your genie rounds.

I didn't include the technique in Do 1 because it's too easy to rely on the callback cards rather than instantly interviewing. There's no better *passive* technique, but it's no substitute for your face.

Keep a box of the cards in your car. Then, stick a dozen or so in your left back pocket every time you leave on your genie rounds. (It's tempting to take more, but you need to sit comfortably.)

Unlike the business card, your callback card can be as spiffy as you like. It's your walking advertisement, costs only a fraction more than ordinary cards, and gets your name and qualifications out there like no direct-mail piece ever could.

First, we'll talk about the design and then the use.

Designing the Card

Use the same printer that did your business cards. This will not only get you a better price (since your quantities will be high), but will help keep the look. As you'll recall from my comments regarding the cover letter/

resume/fax cover sheet system (Do 5, Do 8, and Do 10), restating your image packs powerful punches. The same is true for the business card/callback card set. (You'll be giving out your regular card to the offerors when you interview.)

The callback card should show:

1. Your name and contact information exactly as it appears on your business card. The layout and size will be different, but the info should be the same. If you have a web site, include the URL.

2. The position you are seeking. Not the one you necessarily have. This can appear above your name, below it, or in the center of the card. You decide what gets the most attention. I like the center because an offeror doesn't care about your name. She cares about what you can do.

3. A concise, bulleted list of your accomplishments. This is a mini flyer-resume.

4. Here's an example:

   Catherine C. Callback

   Marketing Manager

   (contact information)

   M.B.A. with proven track record of success.

   7 years experience in media sales.

   2 years experience in sales management.

   Highly qualified and available to increase your business!

5. You can also use the back of the callback card for a short sizzle statement about your attributes. Something like:

   Highly motivated professional who believes that dedication and staying ahead of the competition are the keys to success. The product or service is only as good as the integrity of the people behind it.

   The printing cost is a little higher, and the probability of it being read is lower. But it enhances the card. I recommend it.

Distributing the Card

My favorite place was in front of an elevator in busy office buildings from 8:30 to 9:00 every workday morning. It's like giving candy to the nine-to-five trick-or-treaters.

Let's say you're an insurance adjuster. You just go to the building direc-tory and look for companies, agencies, claims offices, whatever. Then you remember the floors, get into the elevator, pressdebutton, and take the callback cards out of your right back pocket. As the crowd hustles out, you stand at the elevator threshold, give each suit a card and say, "I'd appreciate a call sometime today when you get a chance! Thanks." If you can, get right back in and pressdebutton for the next floor. When you're done, you can work the security office and parking office (Do 61), then go back upstairs to start appearing like a genie.

The classic sales technique is to give out cards to elevator passengers who are staying on as you're *leaving*. This works too, but not quite as well.

You should be able to think of many ways to distribute the callback card as you're out and around. It's intended for callbacks only, but wait until you start passing them out. People will start interviewing you stand-ing up! Just be a pest about it. Walk up to likely offerors and say, "Gee. You look successful! I want to be just like you. How about taking a few minutes of your precious time to talk about yourself?" (Well, not *exactly* like that—but you could do worse!)

The cumulative impact of passing out the callback card is staggering. A week or two and you'll want to tape a label on the voice mail playback button that reads *Callbacks!*

Do 15: Interviewing Instantly over the Internet

Here's how to rev up your own personal job search engine to run 24/7:
Prospect online. Automatically. Even while you sleep!

Outing the Offerors

It's a lot like looking for a date. You'll attract two types of suitors:

Locals

There are tons of great offerors in your community that only show up online. They do this because it's cheap and it looks efficient. They fre-quently offer jobs to consider even if they (say they) pay less than you're asking. (There's no law against considering. I do it considerably.)

Locate them online. I'll tell you how shortly. Pursue them like an Internet stalker. These are hot leads because they live where you live. You know their customers. You know their territory. You don't have to relocate.

When you appear like a genie (Do 1), you'll be offered far more because you're far better than they imagined.

And then their imaginations go wild!

Out-of-Towners

You might know someone who met her dream lover through an online dating service. Then left her old life behind and moved away with him. It happens with dream jobs, too. Actually, more often.

There's literally a working world of opportunity out there.

Relocating is fine with employers—until you bring up reimbursement of moving expenses. Meet, then retreat if necessary. Maybe you'll be willing to invest in the opportunity. Lots of employers don't reject out-of-town candidates. Their attitude is "show up and let's talk." (We'll discuss how to get reimbursed for a scouting trip in Do 60.)

It takes a bit more practice to work the out-of-towners, but not all that much. You'll be glad you learned how to do it.

Spearing Search Engines

There's another way Internet job banks work like online dating services. Their computers search for matches of keywords. The words in the profile and preferences you provide are matched with words describing qualifications and features of jobs. The *exact* words. So, if your profile contains only "engineer" but theirs refers to the job only as "engineering administration," the match might not occur.

It's a preposterous premise, but you're gonna love it for what it presumes. Global businesses have built these information superhighways that run right through the jobjungle. It's an electronic Autobahn. Highly efficient and f-a-s-t.

Only the natives *don't drive!* How funny is *that?* They watch and wave from high above in the trees, from behind bushes, and on the ground inside camouflaged huts.

But it's the instant interviewer's Internet. You own it. You can make it work for you.

That's because you're not focused on *jobs*. All you're interested in is *interviews*. Big difference. Instant, life-changing difference.

Feed the jungle beast what it loves—keywords. *Lots* of *keywords!*

Think of every variant of every term that could describe your dream job.

Register at a job web site and then use an electronic resume.

The right resume—with the right keywords—will have you lookin' for love in all the right places, all the time.

You'll be like a headhunter in heat, sleeping with one eye open. All you want is to attract those offerors, then pounce.

Finding Offerors Online

It's easy. Just go to any search engine and key in: "resume database services." The hottest new web addresses will jump right up—usually in the order of the ones that get the most hits.

I can't give you a list of keywords to instantly magnetize you to that job. Every gig has different keywords. But you can figure them out easily:

1. Search online for jobs that look like the one you want. Job web sites typically enable searching by location, job title, professional field, and so on. You don't have to hit every possible job, just find a few representative ones.

2. On the job description page, pick out keywords and write them down. These words don't necessarily fit other jobs.

3. Use the same words in your resume. (Similar words might work too, if the search engine is smart or if a business included them.) The keywords instantly transform you into a hot, heat-seeking torpedo. (Finding synonyms in a pocket or online thesaurus will geometrically increase your damage.)

4. If you're using Microsoft Word, include the keywords in File Properties of the resume .doc file. (In many versions of Word, the path is: *File > Properties > Summary > Keywords*.)

Again, the whole auto-matching process is so arbitrary that you're just helping it work—to generate interviews automatically. While you sleep!

Inputting Your Resume

The electronic resume is constructed differently from the rest-you-may (Do 5). In fact, it's not a resume at all. It's simply those keywords you input. The computer electronically matches them with the same words some business entered.

So you don't have to be elaborate. Electronic resumes can be even more generic than traditional ones.

It's all so silly because offerors don't know what they want—especially as defined by a few keywords. But the job description was written by someone who thinks he knows—and will talk about it.

Many sites have online forms that permit you to attach and upload a resume file. Use the file format they request (.doc, .pdf, and .rtf are some examples). Others want you to paste the text (Ctrl-C to copy, then Ctrl-V to paste) into the form. Double-check the result because Word documents in particular don't always paste cleanly into web pages. If your document contains special characters, you might have to retype them in the form. Even some punctuation, like quotation marks and apostrophes, may have to be retyped.

Benefits of Going Online

What does online job dating cost? Nothing. In fact, don't use sites that charge a fee. That online call will turn into a date anyway.

Go belly-to-belly with the live bodies. But be just passin' through electronically. Lookin' for love in all the right places. It's so easy.

You'll be lookin' even while you're sleepin'. With your two "I.I.'s" wide open!

Do 16: Courting a Corporate Partner—Online

In the previous chapter, we checked out online job dating. Just you and millions of others. What an intimate little group.

Want to narrow your search?

Let's do it.

Instant Internetting

Online matchmaking is even more fun when you have a specific business or industry in mind.

How many of the apps you've posted online received mass e-mailed or suspicious file attachments? From someone in a third-workingworld country who wants to pay less than minimum wage? Or from someone hyperventilating about investing your money in a pyramid scheme? Or perhaps someone trying to trick you with a get-rich-quick scheme?

These are computerized clues that you're doing something wrong.

Using employer database services is not hazardous to your health. *Relying* on them is!

Continue your face-to-face instant interviews. Just add these sites to automatically work for you 'round the clock.

Picking Corporate Partners

The corporate courting dance is a two-step:

1. Use the search engine. Input the name of a business you respect.
2. Do a search for your type of work. Some corporate sites will appear.

Treat these leads the way you'd treat any other legitimate job opportunity:

1. Research the web site. Find out all you can about the business and its needs.
2. Note the buzzwords (and buzzphrases) so you can buzz like a bumblebee.
3. Do another in-depth online search for the business name to see if you can dig up any news stories, prognoses, and problems (translation: *opportunities*).
4. Restructure your online resume (Do 15).

Facing the Fictional Facts

Are web sites created by employers to find top candidates slanted? Of course they are! Imagine yourself as an offeror in an online situation. You can't see the jobseekers. And truly you don't want to see them either. All you want is the perfect candidate to magically pop up on your computer.

That's what the site builders try to accomplish. But it's like virtually everything—virtual or ritual—in the interviewing process. The more efficient the system, the more it screens you out. We don't do dat.

S-o-o-o, let's discuss . . .

Getting Screened *In*

Here's how to write a reply e-mail that will make them pick you out:

1. Write it as a personal note. But begin by talking about the business, not about yourself:

   Your online posting intrigued me because it's exactly the type of position I'm seeking.

2. Directly state what you've done and what you want. Nothing vague:

   After more than five years as a customer service representative in the automotive industry, I'm excited about moving into a management position.

3. State your qualifications—but only the ones that specifically apply to this job and this business.

4. Ask for a reply.

5. Sound *enthused!* (Be bug-eyed! You're trying to enthuse digitally.)

6. Conclude with:

   I appreciate you considering me and look forward to hearing from you soon.

   Best personal regards,

   Jillian J. Jobseeker

Jill's smart. Note that she doesn't sign it "Best Personal Regards" (or "Yours Truly" instead of "Yours truly") but keeps the capital letters down to the proper minimum. Most people don't pay attention to good writing form in e-mail. You should.

She'll get an instant interview. You will too. All you needed was to find the right sites.

Overflowing with online offerors!

Do 17: Getting Personal to Get Interviewed

It's a great strategy to target a business where you want to interview. Even better to know someone on the inside!

A personal referral to someone who works at the business is a big foot in the door.

Let's start with a letter.

Maximizing the Referral

Use it for all it's worth. Wave it like a flag, march in instantly, and get interviewed. You march in with three steps:

1. Lead with the name of the referral. Average jobseekers don't. They're doing maneuvers out in the offeror's parking lot. Don't bury the name at the bottom of your letter. Use it like the bayonet it is:

   My colleague Rhoda Referral suggested I contact you regarding the copy-writer position.

   Or . . .

   Our mutual acquaintance Rhoda Referral asked me to call you to inquire about joining Motomotive Manufacturing.

2. Follow up with facts about yourself and how you fit—fast. Please don't ever tell anyone in the workingworld that you're on a career path. (Yuk! How soon will you be back on the path again?)

3. After stating your specific goal, state:

   In my two years at Alfred Advertising, I've written copy for Collegiate Cars and other major accounts.

4. Close with Rhoda's name again at the end of the letter.

Something like:

   I'll let Rhoda know I contacted you and will call you next week to arrange a meeting.

That's all you want—an opportunity to meet (interview). Instantly. The rest will take care of itself.

Mentioning the Referral in the Interview

Here are some more ways to use the name shamelessly (better than to shame namelessly) during the instant:

1. Be cordial, but not too familiar. When you accept the offer, this contact will become a co-worker or boss. So keep your professional detachment.

2. Don't reveal your salary expectations. If you're asked just about current salary, just say something like "I would expect to be paid

com-men-sur-ate-ly with my con-tri-bu-tion to Motomotive." Interview etiquette demands that you be savvy. Don't press your fiscal face against that salary screen, attempting to shoot blindfolded at a moving target.

3. Expect the offeror to tell you he's not in charge of hiring for the department you want. This is frequently the case with personal referrals. No matter. You're inside. They don't know what (and really don't know who) they want anyway.

4. Always send a thank-you note to the person who referred you. If you're hired, send flowers. The referrer will refer you again—not for the flowers, but because you value her.

It's not *what* you know, but *who* you know.

True, you know!

Do 18: Surveying to Get Instantly In

Talk to an offeror *right now!* Well—as long as it's during business hours.

Why does taking a phone survey work so very instantly? Because the offeror:

1. Is flattered at being asked
2. Likes the power of participating
3. Is interested in the subject (we'll see to that)
4. Can use the results
5. Doesn't have to take the time reading, completing, and sending back a form

That's why the completion rates on phone surveys are five times higher than those on written ones. Many close to 100 percent.

This is how to do it.

Choose a Riveting Subject

The best survey subjects for instant interviews are salary and opinion.

The reason is self-interest. If the offeror is an owner, she either wants to be competitive or wants to express herself to someone who actually might care.

Salary and opinion surveys are also popular for people like you, since the media likes to report them. This boosts your credibility and exposure (if you decide to formalize them).

Write a Short Survey

This shouldn't take more than a few minutes with our guide:

Salary Survey

_____

_____ (date)

Respondent (Offeror) _____ Title _____

Business Address _____

_____

Phone _____ Fax _____ E-mail _____

Hello Mr./Ms. _____. My name is _____ with

_____ (think of something) _____. You've been

selected to participate in our annual salary/opinion survey. I understand that you're a/an (title of job) and I'd like to ask you a few questions.

It should take less than five minutes. Of course, we'll be pleased to furnish you with the results. Is this a good time for you to talk?

Salary Survey Questions

For a salary survey, ask:

How long have you been in this job?

What are your three primary duties?

How many people do you directly supervise?

What is the exact title of each job?

What is the salary being paid for each job?

Opinion Survey Questions

For an opinion survey, ask:

How long have you been in this job?

What do you like most about your job?

What are your three primary duties?

How many people do you directly supervise?

What are their job duties?

What attributes do you like to see in them?

Are you looking to hire anyone now?

What qualifications are important to you?

What makes you want to hire someone?

What opportunities for advancement exist for someone you hire?

Close with an Appointment

Ask tie-downs like:

That appears to be exactly the opportunity I'm looking for! Why don't I come over and we can meet personally?

I'd like to discuss this further with you since I know someone who fits exactly. It's me! How about our getting together for a few minutes tomorrow morning?

It sounds like I can do a lot of good working for you! Let's get together tomorrow and discuss it. I'll be in your area tomorrow morning between 9 and 11. What time would you like to meet?

Then go over and grant her wish! (Do 1).

Do 19: Reading Between the Classified Ad Lines

It's so easy when you work *backward!*

The newspaper help-wanted classified ads look like an organized listing of job openings. The ads are in neat columns, alphabetically grouped, and often numbered by a code for the position. (Same with an Internet job board.)

Organization begins and ends in the newspaper's word processor. The ads are a totally unpredictable, random, free-for-all.

But at least the advertisers have put their money where their mouths are—they're paying for responses. That means you can work your incredible instanting!

There are four types of ads.

The Ones That Don't Say What They Mean (25 Percent)

Confusing words are usually the sign of a confused mind, a committee decision, or both. This occurs most often because the offeror is rushing to meet an ad deadline. The salesperson in the classified office is equally frantic. So, the result reads like an eye chart.

A quarter of all ads are unintelligible, except for the job title (which may be inaccurate). A call-in response is particularly effective, since the offeror probably *still* doesn't know what he wants.

If you call early enough, it's like picking wallpaper. The first jobseeker he sees is the one he'll choose. He's very impressionable, and your first impression really counts.

So genie him if it's an open ad (Do 1). Otherwise, send a *mirror letter* like what I discuss in the next Do.

The Ones That Don't Mean What They Say (35 Percent)

These ads appear most frequently and are the most difficult to identify. Many of them are intentionally misleading. Others are just looking for someone else. Don't take it personally. It's totally *not* about you.

Intentionally misleading ads are designed to bait and switch you into another position, or identify you as someone seeking employment.

These are the ones that seem to be written for you and are designed to draw the largest response possible. Glamour jobs in media and fashion industries are often featured, as are hot jobs in management, marketing, and human resources.

Although there are some ways to spot these ads, why bother? Take the bait and check them out. It's a numbers game, so mechanically go for every one. Let them attempt to switch you all they want.

Nobody plays the game like us!

The Ones Who Don't Know What They're Saying (25 Percent)

These well-intentioned folks are the ones who take open requisitions and recite them in the ads. It takes a lot more than buzzwords (and buzz-phrases) to really understand the specialized jobs in many businesses.

Fully a quarter of the ads contain misstatements or omit essential duties. Either the offeror didn't do his homework or is just covering himself.

You get the interview by studying the ad and playing it back. You only need to know slightly more than the offeror. You always will.

The Ones Who Say It and Mean It (15 Percent)

There are some straight talkers out there.

Their seriousness means they've already gone through their apps, posted the job on the bulletin boards, offered referral bonuses to employees, researched salaries, placed job orders with recruiters, and have otherwise been thorough.

These employers are worth instanting on. They know who they want and will value someone with your training.

That's about all there is to know. You'll reply no matter what I say.

Read on to do it the *instant* way!

Do 20: Responding to Classified Ads

Now that you know how to read between the ad lines, let's respond for instant interviews!

Tracking the Ads

Read the help-wanteds daily. Also check the employment web sites of all the newspapers in your area. Circle (or bookmark) any that even remotely look good.

Ads can be *open* or *blind*. If open, you know the identity of the employer. If blind, you don't. If there's a phone number, use it. Find out all you can.

Read the ad and pick the three most important requirements. (Theirs, not yours.) These are usually the first ones. The others are just nice to have.

Replying with a Mirror Letter

If you're responding to an ad, don't send your resume without a mirror letter. You just use the better letter format (Do 8) and reflect (mirror) the first three ad specs exactly.

Resumes are too general to align with written specs. It's a much more productive use of your time to be out instanting than to be torturing your resume trying to fit some ad. A mirror letter can be knocked out quickly and you're on your way.

Here's how to reply to the ad:

1. Use your letterhead. You already know how important that is (Do 8).
2. Try to address the person by name. "Dear Ms. Offeror." If you don't have a name, use her job title.
3. Do not say, "Enclosed is my resume." The offeror has eyes.
4. Begin with a hook:

   Your ad in Sunday's Offeror Outlook mentions exactly the kind of position I've been seeking. As a marketing director with ten years in the industrial field, I have experience in developing a national sales program, reaching sales goals, and coordinating product support.

   Note the three experience items just mentioned. They were the first three specs mentioned in the ad.
5. Ask for the interview. The ad may say "Send resume" or even "Walk-in applicants will not be interviewed." There's nothing wrong with stating you'd like to appear. (There's also nothing wrong with appearing! They know what they want when they see you.) So, even if the ad discourages it, say you'd like to meet to discuss your qualifications and their needs.

Now, you never should pass up the classifieds again!

Do 21: Mining the *Yellow Pages*

Those *Yellow Pages* are instant interview gold mines! Any phone is your probe.

As with gold mining, you have to be intuitive and persistent. I was tested on the use of *Yellow Pages* very early when I was touring for *How to Turn an Interview into a Job*. TV talk show hosts would invite me on for the first segment, then challenge me to get some really frumpy audience member a job at the bottom of the hour.

It was really no big deal. I'd just take the person backstage, do an instant interview role-play as though I was the offeror, find a phone and

YP, then start smiling and dialing with the YP. Then by the time the show was ready to sign off, we'd have an interview or two arranged.

This may sound low-tech, but some form of book has been around ever since man has drawn pictures. The phone's been around a while, too. So has the ballpoint pen.

You can surf, click, and e-mail on the tube for a day and not get the results you can get in a few minutes by looking, calling, and writing in the margins of a YP.

Where else can you instantly find such a diverse list of offerors willing to tell you what they do (and how they can use you)?

There are specific mines and ways to mine them.

This is how it works:

Know the Differences in *Yellow Pages*

There are major differences in the type of advertisers and reach of these books. If you don't see the words *Yellow* and *Pages* following one another, you probably don't have the original AT&T version ("The real Yellow Pages").

The others have lower rates, so tend to get advertisers who don't have the money for the official YPs. I've tried using them, and there's just not the same responsiveness. Due to the long lead times of directory publishing, however, the alternatives do snag startup businesses that are very receptive to interviewing.

Sometimes you have to check the covers of the alternative YPs for the areas covered because the listings are so different! (That's a good thing for us.)

So get an official YP, all the alternatives around, and a stack of blank, lined index cards. Open the official YP and . . .

Go to the Heading for the Field You Want

Turn the pages to your field and notice who has the biggest ad. That business can at least pay for the ad. Is it successful or desperate? Who knows? Either one has reasons to wish for you to appear (Do 1)! Either one can turn your life around.

Write down the name, contact information, and anything else the ad reveals about the business on an index card.

There will be other listings for similar businesses too. Each gets a separate card. Once you've got a stack from that listing, google each offeror. Add more info about them to the card.

Look for Similar Businesses

The YPs are very helpful in this way. There's a section that's usually called "See Also." Turn to those listings, then look through the entire book. You'll discover industries that wouldn't have occurred to you. Many might be a perfect match for your talent and background. List them on the index cards and start the online research process.

Go to the *Yellow Pages* Online

Google "Online *Yellow Pages*," and you'll come up with links to sites that let you search types of industries and locations. It's as easy as typing in the industry followed by the city and state.

Of course, you have to know what field you want. That's another reason to start with the YP books.

So mine the YPs and offerors will be yours!

Do 22: Breaking the Code in Business Periodicals

Let's see how to access these primo instant interview invitations!

A bewildering number of business newspapers, magazines, and journals exist throughout the country. The problem is that average jobseekers don't know how to get invites through them. So they shuffle to libraries, look at fine-print outdated directories, play with the public computers, and tell themselves they're actually working on working. No thanks.

Go straight to newsdirectory.com, see what publications fit your fancy, and find its web site.

Most have streaming (breaking) news or post recent features. Read the ads, too.

Write down who's doing what, where, and with whom. Google away with names, titles, places, events, new products, new services.

Then send short e-mails (no more than a few sentences) just mentioning the person or event, congratulating if appropriate, offering assistance, and attaching your Instant Availability Announcement (Do 12).

Reading the news this way will tell you more about what's going on than the classified and display ads will. In fact, as you do this for a while using newspapers, you'll find that the want ads follow the news.

Your time isn't infinite, it's instant. So moonlight move on these very live sources after hours. Let your moves work their magic.

Then check your e-mails after you've worked yours!

Do 23: Teaching a Class

Where else can you get instant prestige, free advertising, and new contacts—like *that?*

Many adult-school classes are taught for only a day or weekend. The longest ones are about eight weeks. Be creative, and you could have a new pool of offerors in no time.

One jobseeker taught an eight-week class. She was good at it, so developed a cadre of people seeking her services and inviting her to speak. Although she started out thinking being an instructor was just a good PR move, she fell in love with it. So she continued doing it for the joy of helping others and to know the fascinating people who enrolled in her classes.

Teaching the right subject in the right place will explode your potential!

It also leads to after-hours income and benefits that can be quite amazing.

My CPA started teaching evening tax courses at a community college, and even if he didn't like it so much, he would have stayed for the pay and tenure benefits. My dad taught ethics at a law school in his (very) later years, and he regretted that he hadn't done it when he was still practicing law. He was a modest person (I was the only one who knew he never lost a case). But I caught him using "Prof." on his magazine subscriptions.

These stories are typical.

There's not much better on a resume or cover letter than mentioning a teaching assignment. It's instant credibility. The class subject doesn't have to be mentioned if it's not relevant.

There are four basic sources of teaching jobs.

University Extension Departments

Call or e-mail the colleges and universities in your area. You'll need to fill out an application. Include a short bio of yourself (Do 52). It's the bio that will pique their interest.

Adult Education Departments

Most school districts have adult education programs. You probably receive course catalogs from them. Go through each catalog. What courses offered are similar to courses you could teach?

It doesn't have to be a business course. What do you do when you do what you don't? How about your hobby? Your favorite sport? Offerors have lives away from the office as well.

Maybe there's a course on French cooking. Businesspeople French-cook. How about a course on travel? It would probably take one trip to the library to clean out the shelf and become familiar with the subject. Businesspeople travel.

I've never met a teacher who wouldn't teach you everything you have to know. Have you? Just ask the school for a faculty list and suggestions of whom to contact. They live to teach.

So if a subject or "Gee—I couldn't be a teacher" are holding you back, let loose.

Classes Offered by Private Businesses

In many cases, very successful private businesses.

You can find local ones in the *Yellow Pages* under the heading "Schools," "Colleges and Universities," or similar headings. The number of them will surprise you.

You can also google *colleges* and the city you want, or narrow your search with something like *business colleges* or *martial arts schools*.

Online Learning

This is a great opportunity if you're concerned about standing in front of a classroom. Try it once, and you'll be amazed at how easy it is. You have a most admiring audience in adults there to learn, meet, and have fun.

Google *online education* or *online learning*. This is a really cool way to teach. Just a short commute to your computer room, and you can do it in your sweats. While you're imbibing your Magic Potion (Do 2).

These businesses are so sophisticated that you can hold your classes on conference calls in a virtual classroom where students can hear and see whatever you put on your computer screen (usually a PowerPoint slideshow). You can also post lectures, respond to student questions, and check assignments after hours.

I encourage you to explore this wonderful, giving-back way of life that will enhance your self-esteem and generate tons of interviews!

Do 24: Giving a Speech

Who me? Instantly?

Yes, you. Instantly enough. If you've just started the I.I. system, follow the relaxation and visualization techniques (Do 42). Google *self-hypnosis public speaking* instantly and get a single, simple CD on its way to you ASAP. Get the best deal. They all work. Don't skip a session. Use the F-O-C-U-S Principle (Do 59). And with it, visualize yourself as you're instructed on the CD.

Your incessant interviews and the mind-body exercises will work like nothing you've ever experienced in your life. Please stay with me on this and believe what I'm telling you. Try it. You'll be so proud of yourself for what you alone accomplished.

You Can Speak

If you can talk, you can give a speech. In fact, you've probably done it many times at parties, your kid's school career day, or at a local city council meeting. It's so easy once you get yourself out of the way. Besides, you're probably an expert at many things. Everyone is at something. Share what you know with a group.

Every group, from local service clubs to national associations, needs speakers for its meetings. They'll give you credentials you never even knew you had. You'll think they printed your photo on the wrong article. Instantly many, many interview leads too.

Listen to the next few speakers you see (few people do). Some are really not spectacular. Do they say "uh," "well," and "ya know"? CEOs do it!

Those who do listen are there to learn. I always measure my success in speaking by the content I've conveyed. If people are staying and taking notes, I've done my job. If they come up to me after I'm through and ask more questions, I've done my job. If they go away from the session able to get more interviews than they thought jobs existed, I've done my job. The less I self-aggrandize, the more aggrandized I get.

You're already becoming an expert on instant interviewing! Call me and we'll get a quantity discount on *Instant Interviews* for you to use as the text. That would make me very happy. Just think what you'd be doing to help—truly help—so many people! It would be the most wonderful call for me to receive.

Choosing Where to Speak

If it's a local group, it really is your choice. They crave anyone who'll talk about something even marginally related to their mission. The toughest assignment any member can get is to be on the speakers' bureau or be the program chair. If the contact doesn't do everything but wheel you into the room, I'd be surprised.

Pick a group with a strong publicity person. Someone who regularly gets speakers listed in the local media and on the group's web site. Contact her and say, "Hi! I'm going to be your August speaker, and I wondered if I could give you a photo and short bio." (Do 52.) Copy articles for your files and add the information to your resume.

Most are very grateful for the assistance.

Outlining with Index Cards

When you outline your speech (Outline! Not a word-by-word document you're going to read), use lined index cards. List more points than you will have time to make.

Here's a magic trick that will make you very famous. On the back of an index card (as backup only), write the first sentence of each paragraph in your speech. Then memorize what you've just written. The rest will flow naturally.

Ten Tips for Speech Success

They are:

Tip 1: Practice with a Recording
Record an informal talk with a memorized beginning and close. It will give you a sense of pacing and let you know how much you need to practice.

Tip 2: Ask for a Podium

It's a great place to stash your note cards. When you're feeling confident, walk around, from one side of your audience to the other. Return to the podium when you need to. It's your home base.

Tip 3: Speak with Confidence

Don't worry about you and how nervous you are. Think about your audience and how you can help them with usable information.

Someone I know was told by a college speech professor that she would never be able to teach because she was too nervous. He gave her a B in the class anyway because her speeches were so well written. She took his advice and didn't pursue a teaching career.

After becoming extremely successful in another field, she was able to shove aside her own fear and concentrate how she could help those in the audience. Today she is a highly rated (and paid) speaker.

Tip 4: Quote from Others

Quotes make you sound smart, and audiences love them. Mine have become known as "Jeff's Gems."

Here are a few you are welcome to use as your own:

"Our business hours are seven A.M. to twelve midnight, seven days a week. I won't apologize for waking you up if you won't apologize for sleeping." (Clients love after-hours calls. I've always done it. If you're a professional, do it. In the "Dictionary of Success" *impossible* means *untried*.)

"Success isn't due to knowledge, it's due to activity."

"If confused employers recruited like ones who knew who to hire, we'd have full employment."

"You can't see the movie from the outside of the theater."

"Stop staying around people who have your problems and start staying around ones who have your solutions."

"Motivation leaves, commitment stays."

"The sun always shines—it all depends on where you're standing."

Thanks to the Internet, quotes are easier than ever to find. Sites even have quotes arranged by subject. Libraries are loaded with quotation books too.

Tip 5: Bring Handouts

This is an essential instant interview device. Include your bio and contact information at the bottom.

People love handouts. Keep them and refer to them. Refer to you too.

Tip 6: Consider a PowerPoint Presentation

If you are at all computer-literate (or know someone who is), a Power-Point slide show will bring your presentation to the next level and give you great visual aids.

Tip 7: Ask Questions if Possible

If the audience is small enough, ask questions as you move through your talk. Listen carefully, and respond concisely.

Tip 8: Don't Apologize for Not Being a Professional Speaker

You're who you are. They're there to learn, you're there to teach.

Emerson's famous quote is, "Do the thing and you'll have the power." He also said, " Concentration is the secret of strength." I like them, but I love, "The only gift is a portion of thyself."

That's what you're giving!

No apologies.

Tip 9: Take Questions Before You Finish

Instead of saying, "Are there any questions?" and letting your talk wander, ask before you finish. Say, "Before I close, I'd like to know if there are any more questions." Answer the questions, then say your memorized close.

Leave them wanting more.

Tip 10: Donate the Speaker Fee

Will the honorarium change your standard of living? If so, take it. Most people do.

Those who don't get interviewed faster and more.

A client of mine was asked to speak for a fledgling nonprofit event. The budget was tight, but they were paying for hotel, transportation, and food. It said in the invitation that they were hoping to pay a three-figure speaker fee. The client told them she would like to donate it back to the nonprofit.

When she arrived at the hotel where the event was taking place she was already a celebrity. She was even mentioned by the kickoff speaker for her "generosity."

Okay, maybe donating isn't possible for you. It was for her (barely), and it was a writeoff. But you'll probably be offered only minor expense reimbursement. Consider donating it back to the organization or possibly ask them to donate it to their favorite charity. Either way, you'll stand out as a generous, giving person.

Yes, you. People will call on you again and again. With instant interviews!

Do 25: Making Your Own Recordings

If you speak at any event, record it. It's a sure way to even more instant interviews!

You probably won't like what you hear. No matter. Some of the most accomplished public speakers have the same reaction. But you're really not the best judge of this.

The best judge of this is the offeror who sees on your resume the title of your talk and the words "This was so popular that it was recorded and distributed to interested parties." This is absolutely true.

Use a digital recorder. If you're asked for a copy, you can easily burn one on a CD and complete a label from a stationery store with your name, the title, and the date. No serious offeror will take the time to listen through it. Anyone who does is either looking for someone to conduct workshops or has so much time that he doesn't need to hire. Besides, the offeror already knows what you sound like.

You may well have a market for your recording. The sponsor of the talk may want to sell it to members who didn't attend. Or other groups may want to benefit from it. These things may lead to many instant interviews and leverage your name and expertise with almost no additional effort or expense.

I was retained as general counsel for the California Association of Personnel Consultants a few years after I started practicing law. It was at the CAPC's annual conference. That day I gave a seminar and recorded it on a little portable tape recorder.

When I returned home, I had some graphics done on an audiocassette-notebook package and ordered copies of the cassette with labels. We assembled the packages by hand for the first few months. Then the sales started taking off, so I paid my accountant's retired mother to assemble them. I next recorded a second seminar in our bathroom (great sound, couldn't hear dogs barking). That became the *EMPLAW Cassette Series*. Then my accountant's mother started doing the fulfillment. Thousands of copies were sold over the next 20 years.

The tapes were more than a great help to those who bought it. They positioned me as an expert in the field and I received many, many calls for assistance just because of the name recognition.

With digital recording being so inexpensive, clear, and easy to reproduce, this is something you can do far more easily.

The seminar recording business is huge because there's a high demand for industry-specific and content-driven audio. Advertising on a web site is a low-cost way to get yourself into a passive income stream of direct mail sales.

No matter what your subject is, people want to hear from someone knowledgeable. Experts are always in demand, and they get instant interviews effortlessly.

Recording any speech, seminar, or workshop in front of a few people (or not) will enable you to market yourself worldwide.

Those digital minirecorders are great. You just record the entire session (up to eight hours nonstop), then just plug it into your computer, open the file in your editing software, snip the clip you want, save it in an MP3 file, and you've got yourself a podcast. Now it's saved for reproduction.

An effective recording is:

- Short
- To the point
- One clear thought

Think about the central message in a sound bite. Come up with one and state it fearlessly. Own it as though you're the first person in the world who thought of it.

Finally, you can upload your audio clips to a hosting service, and just be famous without even knowing it.

Digital distribution is called *self-syndication*. As you start posting your links, you build your own network for advertising and get . . .

Instant interviews!

Do 26: Expediting Executive Recruiting

In this Do, I'll show you how to work with the most important people you'll encounter in the jobjungle—the headhunters.

MPC. Just three letters. But knowing what they mean and being them will unlock a workingworld of opportunities for you!

It's a "Most Placeable Candidate"—an MVP in the jobgame. Every successful recruiter looks for one. That's who you're going to be now.

Understanding Who Recruiters Are and What They Do

Executive recruiters are not technically working for you. Their clients (employers) pay the fee. For good reason.

Recruiters are the sharpest, quickest, most amazing people I've ever known. And after being in and around their business practically every day (and night) for 42 years, I know them really well. If you do too, and become an MPC, your career will skyrocket. They'll be your eyes and ears to good, better, and best for as long as you care to work.

Treat them with respect, demonstrate the self-confidence that you're gaining through instant interviews, and let them know you can go the distance. "Running with an MPC" means using your background as a leader to generate job orders (aka *search assignments*) they can fill with you and perhaps others.

Recruiters spend their days (and nights) searching for people like you. Most candidates—regardless of whether they look good on paper—don't present well in person. And you now know that nothing else matters.

The vast majority of candidates just waste a recruiter's time. If you're doing instant interviews, you won't be doing that. Tell them, and give them my regards. Getting you placed is just a matter of doing the match. "Running with an MPC."

A recruiter is a free agent. Only about 10 percent are retained for anything beyond expense reimbursement. So the recruiter expends his own time, money, and (often highly sophisticated) resources on something that may never happen. Thus, he's very conscious about whether or not you're marketable. I summarize their philosophy as, "Fill it and bill it or kill it."

There's also usually a *guarantee period* when you're placed, so you'll have the benefit of their third-party expertise. This helps to get you oriented, trained, and treated properly during the critical probationary period.

In addition to a thorough knowledge of approved job orders, recruiters have a sixth-sense understanding of what employers want—far more than the employers themselves. This isn't just because they're so sharp. It's also because they objectively look inside companies, speak to anyone they like inside, and network with other practitioners. They know what I've been teaching you—that the JO (job order) bears no relationship to the candidate they place. It's just a start for them.

Let's say a recruiter spots a weak manager. It happens a lot. He might just call the manager's boss or boss's boss. He's got no agenda except to accomplish a placement. If someone's in the way, he's all over it or he's out of there.

Isn't that someone you must know? Everywhere in the world? Place *Instant Interviews* under your pillow, for goodness' sake!

Make a full disclosure to a recruiter too. There's no room for game-playing in the relationship. He'll keep confidences as long as it doesn't prejudice a client. Tell him what you really will accept, what you really earned, and why you're really looking. If you don't, he'll find out anyway, can't help you, and won't bother.

Above all, don't play games about where you've applied or sent your resume. If you try this, you'll incur the wrath of a headhunter—and they never forget. Either you're honorable or you're not. They're fine if you want to place yourself, but they need to know that up front.

I talk to recruiters who've placed candidates from the time they were trainees to when they became CEOs of major corporations. Many hire from the same recruiters who placed them—four or five times! How could they not? They've had a trusted jungle scout watching over them, introducing them, and counseling them on successful career moves they couldn't have found on their own!

Having worked a desk, I can tell you recruiting is at once wall-to-wall people and solitary confinement. The highs are really high and the lows are really low.

So what drives these high-velocity folks? The same thing that drives this ex-recruiter and I hope drives every instant interviewer. The good they strive to do. That headhunter's shield protects a servant's heart.

Locating Executive Recruiters

As jungle scouts, headhunters are heard but not often seen. If you google *executive recruiters, executive search,* or *executive search consultants,* however, and type in the name of the city where you reside or where you want or are willing to *relo,* many names will appear. You can also add any discipline to narrow your search. Well over half the recruiters specialize in a certain field.

Because it's a phone-Internet-intensive business, the location of the recruiter doesn't matter. I even know some remarkably successful recruiters who work from motor homes while touring the country. But most are virtual, solo practitioners working out of their homes.

Three Kinds of Networks

There are three kinds of networks that leverage the geometric power of the Internet with practitioners who know how to do the match so it works:

They are:

1. The large branch office and franchise chains (with offices often owned by local entrepreneurs).
2. The large multiple listing services. Independent recruiters are members.
3. Specialized groups that post in chat rooms and social networks. This is now becoming the most popular way for independents to do "split-fee deals" (usually with one recruiter responsible for the candidate and the other for the client).

Now—What about You?

Get your resume in shape (Do 5). It needs to be focused and concise. It can't waste anyone's time.

Take charge. When you call the recruiter, be articulate and come across as highly motivated. They can sense it. That's all they think about, and it has nothing to do with what you did before. It's all about your ability to self-market. Tell them you're an instant interviewer and what you've found on your own. You have what they want.

Show me someone who's enthusiastic and articulate, and I'll show you someone a recruiter will work around the clock to place. Someone he'll stay with for the rest of her employable days.

Now *that's* an MPC . . .

And that's how instant interviewers are expediting executive recruiters!

Do 27: Writing for Newspaper Special Sections

It's how to get instantly published!

Special sections (aka *special publications*) are those parts of a newspaper in which advertisers pay to tell their stories.

A mobile home dealer writes an article about how to buy an RV. A real estate broker with a full-page ad writes about how to pick a sales agent. An accountant gives tax-filing tips.

It's called an *advertorial*. But it should be called an *additional*.

That's because there's usually not enough text for the editors to complete the publication. So they scramble for new material. Only they have to pay for it, and there's no budget because there are not enough advertisers. That's our cue.

Picking an Advertorial Topic

If you have something you'd like to write about (or they have a suggestion), that's your chance to submit it online and get it printed with your photo and bio.

Unlike the news or features departments, advertorial editors are concerned with sales of advertising space, not the content of what's around it.

If you want instant interview invitations, this is a major play.

Just write a short article (a thousand words or so) on some local topic that interests you. You can start by calling one of the advertisers and ask if they'd like you to talk about the wonders of their business. They're delirious to have you do it, since it's extra exposure for them. They basically own the advertorial department, so they're the de facto editors.

Getting Placed

Next, write your short piece, a short bio, and have someone take your picture. E-mail them to the editor and you'll be published.

You might even get the editor to place the article in a career section or create one for you. This is just a layout process, unlike the sections readers pay to read.

It's so effective that you have to wonder why it's legal! Probably because nobody ever does it but . . .

You will *now!*

Do 28: Guiding a Counselor at a Free Career Center

Career centers are a relatively new concept. They're usually operated by nonprofit corporations that receive grants and other government subsidies to help jobseekers find jobs.

This is really nothing more than a transfer of the responsibilities of the traditional unemployment office. Its responsibility is getting people back to work. Government agencies, charities, senior centers, and other enablers refer jobseekers to the centers. Totally free to the jobseeker.

The centers are usually in high-end office buildings in high-rent districts. They're professional, well staffed, and very efficient. They have: job postings, reference materials, phones, phone directories, employer directories (for finding jobs and e-mailing resumes), resume-writing classes, interviewing classes, job retraining, networking with other walking wounded, and employer show-and-tells.

Did I leave anything out? I don't think so. I didn't say that people get jobs there, did I? Nope. Fine.

People *don't* get jobs there. The employers who interview on site are there for PR. Many are often multilevel *upliners* looking to build their *downlines* (multilevelspeak for, "You pay to have your own business selling our goods or services through *your* downline.") Those aren't interviews. They're sales pitches.

The concept is well intentioned, and the social workers at the center have nice titles. It's all so professional. Carpeting. A water cooler. With paper cups. Always a logbook, a receptionist, an appointment with a career adviser. But no jobs. Yet it's probably the best job-intelligence gatherer you'll ever harness.

Unlike the media that rarely get hiring activity right, career centers are real time. They just don't communicate what they learn very well.

We're going to help yours do just that.

Call Your Unemployment Office

Ask for the name of the closest career center. Then call and make an appointment with the most senior career counselor or career adviser there. This is imperative. We're talkin' people with the interest and the information, but not the intuition to get you instant interviews. So meet with the most experienced person.

Politely Listen to the Advice for a Few Minutes

Then tell him that you'll complete the forms and do whatever is required to keep the taxpayer dollars flowing to the center.

Keep Checking In

In exchange, you'll call him once a week to check in. He'll call you back the same day and give you an update on any new job listings at any level with nongovernment, nonutility, non-MLM (multilevel marketing) entities.

Tell him that you would also like him to notify you in that call about any *trends* that he's picking up in the job market. Tell him that time is money and you have neither. You expect straight, nonbureaucratic, *concise* intel. Finally, tell him if he does this every week for three months, you'll write a letter to his CEO that his mother could have written.

He'll go out of his way to help you. It will be extremely valuable.

The Payoff

Within a few minutes on the phone:

- You'll have your finger on the pulse of *specific jobs* being offered. That tells you about where companies need help. For example, an opening to design medical devices tells you that your background in production control would be useful. So you might appear like a genie (Do 1) or call in to a supervisor in the manufacturing area.

- You'll be monitoring *hiring trends* too. When you know what's hot and what's not, you can target your search to those businesses. You're in production control? Head for the furniture manufacturers because they're placing job orders for a variety of positions.

After three months, write that letter. He'll keep helping you and you keep helping him.

You transformed yourself into a powerful jobjungle tracker!

Do 29: Inciting Potential Offerors to Interview

The key to any instant interviewing is to *incite* someone to initiate an interview on the spot.

You've seen how we vividly give someone a hook (Do 8). That's *inducement*—a reason. That's *passive*.

Inciting is used in the phrase "inciting a riot." It doesn't mean giving someone a reason. It means lighting a fire under him. A burning desire—even a compulsion—that energizes him to act. Inciting can be very constructive, too.

Here are a half-dozen instant inciters.

Know You Can Do Whatever You're Asked

This goes beyond thinking positively. It's *saying* and *conveying* the word *Done!*

The words are "Sure!" "I will!" "No problem!" Save "I'll try" for your kids. (That way you'll never break your word to them.)

Offerors are incited by positive I.I.'s. She must hire you. You can do anything!

Be Responsible for What You Say

How many people would say, "I can't start for another two weeks. I've got projects they want me to complete at my job. They want two weeks' notice anyway."

Ouch! *Can't* wouldn't incite a centipede. Phrasing it that way—like your work is on top of you (instead of the other way around)—is not something a superhero does.

How about, "I want to complete the critical projects at work so my employer will win the contract."

You probably can think of only a few people who accept personal responsibility. They're probably the most successful people you know.

Focus on What's Sticking, not the Person Who's Stuck

The offeror says, "I'm so far behind in my work that I can't even think about hiring anyone right now."

Please don't say, "Gee, I understand. You really need to get your act together."

Oh, you won't say it like that. You might say, "That's too bad. Hope things settle down. I'll give you a call in a few weeks and see if you straightened things out."

To *incite* you say, "Why think about it at all? Why not just *do* it now? I won't accept any money from you for two days. Then we can discuss it, okay?" (Note that you didn't ask him to pay you for what you thought the services were worth. You *assume* they'll be invaluable.)

Don't fight, incite.

Visualize and Verbalize a Cup Half Full

It will runneth over, but not if it's empty. You need some solution to begin.

An example is, "Our cash flow is slow right now, and we need to pay for stock as the holiday season approaches."

You incite, "That can really work to your advantage at tax time. I'll help you *accelerate* (great winner's word) the *velocity* (wow) of your receivables, so payment is made right after your fiscal year ends on December thirty-first! I'll get just enough payment from your customers so you can *offset* (!) my salary as a business deduction."

Boom. Done.

Build Up the Offeror

He says, "I can't hire you. I'm just the director of communications."

You incite, "That's a position with a lot of responsibility. Why don't we talk to the vice president of marketing together? How can we lose?"

We always incites in getting interviews. People are afraid they'll repeat hiring mistakes of the past.

Inject them with your strength and confidence. You have it in abundance because you have nothing to lose. As Sir Isaac Allen once said, "It's impossible to fall when you're on the floor."

Ask to Work

Don't be a "Gee-whizzer" about this. Don't say, "Well, I guess good things come to those who wait. I'll be hoping to hear from you soon." (Ugh!)

Say, "When do I start?" "Make me an offer!" "Let's get busy!"

Incite right.

Now you know how to talk so an offeror listens. This will work to incite if you know how to listen so an offer talks. Around twice as much as you do.

It's why your *inciteful* self has one mouth and two ears!

Do: 30 Answering Inside Job Listings: Gold without the Shaft

If you're working now, the very best move—particularly while you're instant interviewing—is often another job with your current employer. *Internal interviewing.*

There are the obvious reasons like maintaining seniority, keeping vested benefits, receiving the same or better pay, knowing how the company works, and being familiar with its products. These reasons are very compelling, particularly if you don't have a job offer to compare them with.

But less obvious reasons should inspire you to jump at the chance: You know where the company has weak departments, where you can make a positive contribution, where the high profile jobs are, what managers are popular, which ones to avoid, what projects are hot, what the policies *really* mean, how to score high on performance reviews, how to get raises, which areas have the best promotion potential, and umpteen other things that take any new hire a long time to figure out. (Many never do.)

The big thing we need to discuss here is *politics*. Pure, raw, and ever-present.

I learned this lesson early in my first HR job after working that desk as an executive recruiter. I learned it from an amazing man who combined the vigor of youth with the wisdom of age. It has probably saved tens of thousands of workplace warriors when I wrote about it in *Surviving Corporate Downsizing.*

It's the deceptively simple military protocol known as the *chain of command.* It means that you go *through* your next higher-up. Check what I'm saying. Not *over*, not *under*, not *around. Through.*

Shinnying Up the Chain of Command

Let's look at how the chain of command works to finesse interviewing for a contract administrator posting. In this case, you know and like the contract administrator who's getting promoted. You discussed the job, and he's promised to teach you everything he knows. His boss is a gem—well respected and knowledgeable. The job pays 25 percent more than you're making as a buyer. You get to travel, meet professionals, and are responsible for running large projects.

Your boss keeps you around because you know your job well. However, he's got personal issues and is insecure about himself and his role in the company. He was passed up for a promotion recently and tries to keep a low profile.

So, you can't look better than him or your job is in jeopardy. You also can't say anything to anyone about his personal issues (he drinks too much—maybe does drugs too).

In fact, you're the one who has to cover for his mental lapses and times away from the office when he's on a binge. Worst of all, the boss doesn't think he has a problem.

You're this far along in *Instant Interviews*, so no problem with self-confidence and bailing if the right offer comes. The only thing is you've been working full time, and often doing your boss's job too. Your interviewing, therefore, is done on nights and weekends. The offers are now coming at you a few times a week, but this contract admin gig looks like a no-brainer. You like everything about the company. An immediate increase in pay, benefits, and responsibility while losing the baggage.

What can you do?

Option 1: Go Over Your Boss's Head

Simple enough. Just march over to HR and tell them you want to apply. They'll send your personnel file over to the new manager and arrange for an interview.

Discussing the problem with HR is not an option. It's hari-kari. When your boss finds out (because the new manager will instantly call him about your performance), he'll do what comes naturally. He'll say you got those good reviews *but* . . .

This is an insult to your boss, and you'd deserve what you get. You say, "My boss would sabotage the deal if I told him first."

I agree with you.

This is not only Option 1. It is *Reason 1*. More internal interviewers lose their jobs (usually within six months) from taking this option than the next two combined.

Please don't be among them. If you've done it, instant interview as much as you can. You'll get a much better job. I just want you to leave on your own terms.

Option 2: Go Under Your Boss

This would be calling your buddy in the job now and asking him to put in a good word for you with his boss.

You're instant interviewing these days, so probably wouldn't whine. But you'd look awfully strange.

Your boss should be doing that bidding for you.

So Option 2 is a non-jobstarter. Probably a jobstopper.

Option 3: Go Around Your Boss

This involves asking a sympathetic manager to be creative in letting the hiring manager know about you. It's usually some offhanded remark or informal suggestion to the manager to check you out.

Sounds really good until you realize that the sympathetic manager has absolutely no stake in the outcome. You have no control over the dialogue either.

Your intermediate instant interviewing skills should make the answer obvious to this one.

Stay back. Way back.

That leaves us with . . .

Option 4: Go Through Your Boss

Your instant interviewing skills are now about to leapfrog you into executing this option with dispatch.

Confrontation time (if necessary). Take that gulp—don't worry about his mood, his mental state, or his metabolism. You can get instant interviews anytime you want. You just don't happen to want right now.

Get going. Walk in, sit down. Smile, and look him right in the eye.

Oh, he's on the phone? So what? It's during business hours. His door wasn't closed. He didn't wave you away. Plop yourself down and wait.

Ah, good, he's hanging up. I've got clients calling with real issues, so let's get this done:

You: Steve, I see there's an opening in Norm Castell's group for a contract administrator. I'd like to apply.

Steve: Yeah, I saw that. Aren't you happy here? I gave you a pretty good review last time. You seem to be improving.

You: Yes, I'm happy, I suppose. I appreciate all you've done and I've liked working here.

Steve: Okay, then. Let's just forget we had this discussion and get back to work.

You: I just won't do that. (Note the word *won't*. You don't say *can't* when there's a challenge. Losers do that. You're definitely a *can*-didate.)

Steve: What do you mean you "won't"? Are you planning to apply anyway?

You: No. Actually, I was going to ask you to do it for me.

Steve: Me? Just why would I want to lose a good employee and have to find, train, and supervise someone new on the Spencer procurement?

You: There are several reasons. For one thing, I have other opportunities that I'm considering. (Remember what I said about that word *consider* in Do 15.) For another, I'd help you find and train my replacement. I'll be just two floors up. In fact, I'll work extra hours if necessary.

Steve: Well, I guess that would work.

You: I know it would. I'll babysit the Spencer account and transition the new hire. I also will say nice things about you to our management. That's how I can show my appreciation.

Steve: Well, I can't argue with any of that.

You: I knew you wouldn't. You've always treated me fairly. I've drafted a letter for you recommending me for the job. If you like, I'll print it and bring it in. I don't want that requisition filled before I have a shot at the job.

Steve: Okay. What do you want me to tell Norm?

You: Whatever you can truthfully say about my ability. I'll prepare some comments for you to use, okay?

Steve: You're sure making it easy for me.

You: That's the least I can do.

Steve: So you really think I've been a good boss?

You: You're not a *boss*. You're a *leader*. I'll make sure that's understood wherever I go.

Steve: I'm in shock, but I'll get over it.

You: Sounds like *we* already have!

There's something subtle we did here that turned the outcome around. You gave Steve several *hooks*. Transitioning, training, the letter, the suggested comments. A way to do what you wanted.

I do that in court, and it wins cases consistently. If you don't give the judge a *reason* to rule in your favor, don't expect her to do it.

Whenever you're in a negotiation—whether it's personal or professional—do that.

I don't know about your boss, but we were stone sober in this chapter.

The reason is because I appreciate you beyond adjectives. Just look at the magnificent job you've done here. Look at what your dedication to being the best has done.

Look at yourself. Why, you're 10 feet tall!

Congratulations. Nothin' can stop you now.

Do 31: Vacationing Free While They Interview Thee

Since I conduct seminars, I work with meeting planners constantly.

If it's not fun and free, we don't do it. That's not a goal, it's a rule.

What if you could instantly arrange nonstop interviewing in whatever field you wanted while on a fully paid vacation at a world-class resort? Would life be a box of chocolates? The two-pound box? With many almond clusters?

That's what you get when you volunteer to help at the trade show of your choice.

How do you arrange it? Before lunch? (Yes, dessert first.)

Behold, genie (Do 1).

Pick a Resort Area

Pick any one your interviewing heart desires. Vegas is a great venue for trade shows (aka *conventions* and *conferences*).

Then google something like *las vegas convention visitors bureau*. (You can't make a mistake, since any variation of this will get you the list of hits.)

There's always a listing of the carnivals comin' to town. Sometimes you click a link, sometimes you write down the name of the group, sometimes you call the phone number given. Always look for dates, host hotels, and contacts.

This is a simple process since advertising on the Web is the major way resort areas attract visitors.

Next, you . . .

Pick a Trade Association

Any one you like. If you're a structural engineer, look for a building contractor or real estate developer confab. Or a coin convention if your hobby is collecting them. Whatever. The cybersky's the limit.

Then google the trade association or other sponsor. Get the phone number and call. You can e-mail too, but it's a little impersonal and takes longer to get a reply.

Ask to speak to whoever is running the show. Tell that person you want to volunteer to help with whatever they need done in exchange for an economy round-trip airline ticket, a small hotel room, and expense reimbursement of incidental ground transportation and fast-food meals. Talk about your passion to serve, your love of the business, and your expertise. Sell well. Their job security is tied to convention revenues.

Even the largest associations work on razor-thin budgets, and these events are usually the way they earn their keep for the entire year.

Often, associations outsource the event to convention planners. These professionals are high-spirited wheeler-dealers who negotiate comps and group rates from hotels and resorts.

Offer to record seminars, set up booths, make coffee, arrange cookies, change diapers—anything.

They're usually small businesses, so they can always use an extra. Someone happy and helpful? In exchange for a bulk-rate round-trip and a comped room? What's to lose? Print her a badge and send her a schedule. Does she have any friends? We're getting a percentage of the take. If it's free, it's me!

That ticket is your ticket to Nirvana. It's an endless Do 1 genie routine, complete with business cards.

It's hard to get turned down. But if you do, just ask for the vendor list and program, then . . .

Pick a Vendor

Same story, different sale. Just google the product or service for a minute first so you become an expert and all.

Use your best sales voice and smile while you're talking on the phone. Talk about ideas for getting people to the booth, greeting them, plastic sales incentives, balloons. Be creative and magnetic. You might be instantly interviewing!

The only downside is that you'll be bound to the booth and can't maneuver when it's open.

Or you can use the program to . . .

Pick a Speaker

There are three kinds of speakers: *Headliners, Keynoters,* and *Everyone Else.*

Headliners are the arena acts with their marquees selling motivation and moneymaking. Google, call, and sell.

They need security, setup, and sales help in unlimited numbers. Free works.

You'll need a large left front pocket. Thirty business cards per performance should do it.

Keynoters are tradeshow draws. Sometimes they get paid an honorarium. Other times, they just get expenses. Many peddle their wares (books, CDs, DVDs, whatever) in the back of the room, and they like to appear with a large entourage.

You just meet the keynoter there and do your thing. All expenses paid.

Then head for interview heaven—the vendor area.

In the *Everyone Else* category, you'll find a treasure trove of leads.

Industry-specific trainers, consultants, and other providers make their living by compulsively contacting. Becoming a free sidekick—willing to do grunt work with a suit and a smile—is a way to instant and incessant interviews.

Less-known business speakers also won't have a problem saying nice things about you. Most truly care about service and can always use a verbal fan touting their verbiage.

I've done everything from "name in lights" to "referee food-fights." I like low-profile workshops the best.

You probably will too. The demand is instant and insatiable.

When you're your hotel room, find the *Yellow Pages* in the desk, dresser, or nightstand drawer. If there's a free local call feature in the room (or if you have a cell phone with unlimited minutes), call around, and tell a few juicy prospects that you're here from out of town and would like to see the famous whatever-your-business-name-is. Arrange to meet that person when you're free. Do this many times and write down the name and contact information. That's why hotels have notepads and pens right there.

Otherwise, take the *Yellow Pages*, pad, and pen down to the lobby. Smile and politely ask for an open local line at the front desk. Most hotels gleefully accommodate, since charging for local calls makes guests angrier than paying for beer nuts.

As a last resort, use the lobby phone booth.

Then go back to your room (if you left), lie down on the bed, stretch, and dial the hotel concierge or front desk. Arrange to meet the hotel courtesy (read *free*) shuttle driver in half an hour outside.

Then call the toll-free number for the airline and find out the last flight you can catch home the day of your departure, with no upcharge in your ticket. Book it.

Now that you've rested, pack up. Be sure that your shoes match, your pockets have your I.I. kit, and go down to meet the shuttle driver.

Like taxi drivers, shuttle drivers are literally streetwise. That's because they're professional listeners. They're like nurses in pilots' uniforms (inside joke, Do 51).

Ask to go downtown to a shopping center or an industrial park.

Now back to the last thing to do before you leave . . .

Instant interview away.

Don't forget to turn in your expenses!

Do 32: Forming Your Very Own Job Club

. . . And volunteering to be the program director!

Job clubs are informal groups that meet to discuss help-wanted things. Usually at members' homes one evening a week. The members exchange leads, talk about their interviews, and practice interviewing. Some have newsletters and even participate in job fairs.

As a lead source, many are excellent. The members are out and about every day and get job market intelligence you can't possibly find by yourself. And sooner. Members learn about jobs while they're hot. By the time they're publicized, they're cold and old.

The members are intensely into local hiring trends. While some are career candidates who interview for fun (whether they're working or not), most are displaced middle managers actively reinventing themselves for today's jobs. There are contests and other incentives.

But many job clubs are less than a waste of time. There's a large sub-culture of people who (for a variety of reasons) dwell rather than do. Many are highly educated and have been effectively unemployed for years. If education without an occupation could make you successful, I'd never have taken the bar exam.

Get enough of them in a job club, and you can charitably substitute the word *job* for *social*. So ask about who's there before you invest interview time. Interviewing is not a team sport. It's an individual athletic competition.

Please run from those kinds of associations—whatever they're called. We're building your confidence back by direct, forward, positive, instant *action*. Anything else—and I include any advice from *anyone* else right now—will slow you down. If you keep doing what you've been doing, you'll keep getting what you've been getting. If that's not instant interviews, you're doing something wrong. Paint by the numbers. One hundred and one of them!

I mentioned becoming the program director at the top because that's the place for a savvy I.I. This gives you the opportunity of a livelihood to call, e-mail, and write hiring honchos.

Hiring has them participating in the community. It's the best PR and it's free. ("So buy our stuff. Let us build big buildings, make noise, obstruct traffic, and pollute.")

The program director of the Jobstown Job Club gets return calls.

If you don't have or don't like a local jobs club, repeat after me as you wave your magic pen: "Abracadabra!" (Can't find the pen? Check your left front pocket—Do 1.) "I am now the Jobstown Job Club. I vote for myself as Jobstown Job Club program director. I accept the position. I start yesterday at my usual pay."

Nobody knows what program director really means. High-level corporate execs don't admit to much. That's how they became high-level corporate execs. They don't ask, either.

Smile and dial. Here's how it goes:

Operator: Jobstown Bank. More bank for the buck. How may I direct your call?
You: Hi! What's the name of the head of Human Resources?
Operator: Patti Personable.
You: What's her title?
Operator: Vice president of Human Resources.
You: May I speak to her?
Operator: It's extension 437. I'll transfer you now.
You: Thanks.
Assistant: Human Resources. Ms. Personable's office. Clarabelle speaking.
You: Ms. Personable, please.
Assistant: Who's calling?

You: Ima Looking, program director of the Jobstown Job Club.

Assistant: Oh, hi, Ima! How are you?

You: Fine. Haven't we met?

Assistant: I'm sure—wasn't it at our Jobstown Banks On You event? Here's Patti.

Patti: Patti Personable.

You: Hi, Patti! This is Ima Looking with the Jobstown Job Club.

Patti: Hi, Ima! Are you calling to arrange for a speaker?

You: No, we're starting a new Value Added Inventory program, and I wanted to get your input. Thanks to your time and talent, Jobstown Bank is now on our preferred list. (Total honesty always. The *preferred list* is the Jobstown *Yellow Pages*. Write "preferred" on the cover of yours before you dare touch that dial.)

Patti: I appreciate that. We work very hard for the Jobstown community. What's the Value Added Inventory, Ima?

You: We contact the best, most creative businesses in Jobstown and ask them to give us something they need done. Then, we find someone to do it. It can't be any job that's currently available.

Then when the person starts, we prepare a press release and photos. It's picked up by TV, radio, and newspapers. The *Jobstown Gazette* is notified separately.

The only thing is, it can't be a current job opening. We're trying to show how our preferred-list businesses are really interested in solving their problems with local talent.

Patti: I really can't—wait a minute. There is one thing that comes to mind. When customers make a night deposit, the computer thinks it says right deposit. So it processes some of the craziest amounts you've ever seen. We used to have a day shift senior teller check the night deposits, but now he's on the night shift, so there's no day shift person. Do you understand the difference?

You: Sure, it's like night and day. I learned about things like that in night school. When do I start?

Patti: You? Serious? For real?

Let me see what I can do about having the chief teller offer a req for that job. I don't qualify for the free trip to Maui for referring you, but I'll probably get a raise. That's been bugging our operations officer for 83 days! Do you have a resume?

You: I do, but why don't I just fill out an application? (Your reason is that your rest-you-may (Do 5) is for an engineering job, and it would be easier to squish your background into a form.)

Patti: You can do that online.

You: I'd be happy to. (Scout's honor. You would—just not until you retire.) But I'll be near the bank on my way to a business meeting. (Word: You're meeting your kid's guidance counselor at school, and that's always risky business.) I'll just stop by and get it done! I don't like wasting time.

Patti: You sound very interesting, Ima. What's your background?

You: (Hooboy, gotta think fast.) I've been working with numbers for almost eight years. (If you haven't, don't say it, but of course everyone eight years old or more, has.)

Patti: I'll be in a meeting, actually with the chief teller. But my assistant Clarabelle knows all about the problem. She's received 83 calls about it from our OO.

You: Oh. (Good! You're learning. Always parrot back. Do 51.)

Patti: I'll let Clarabelle know to expect you. She's up here on the fifth floor, not down in the HR lobby.

You: Thanks. After I hire in, we can discuss the publicity. (All right! That alone will pop interviews like popcorn.)

I couldn't have handled it better if I did it myself.

Many lessons here. The best is that you never mentioned any salary. On the app where it says "Salary Requirements," you write, "Open." Otherwise the chance of your being too high or too low is approximately 100 percent (Do 89). We don't care what the job pays. Frankly, we don't care about the job at all.

But we always care about—say it loud—the almighty *interview!*

Do 33: Launching a *Proactive* Proposal

"Proposal writing" sounds so sophisticated! It's not. In this Do I'll show you how simple this instant interview device is.

Most business proposals should have a warning stamped on their plain vanilla covers. "Warning: Contents may cause drowsiness. Do not digest in a busy office. File under *B* for *Boring.*"

There are tons of books on proposal writing out there. Don't waste your money. The one that should be written is how to *accept* them! But that's not our problem. We just want an *interview*. A proposal is a device only, a way to get a face-to-face with the offeror.

If for some reason you are not able to connect with the offeror directly, it's time for a *proactive* proposal.

Notice I didn't say a volume of *Me from A to Z*. The offeror doesn't care about you. He cares about getting some work done. You just need to convince him that you'll do it.

The objective is not the proposal. The objective is the interview. *Instantly.*

With that little mantra, you already know more about proposals than the majority of jobseekers. This book is the only place you're going to find that information. If you go on the Internet, be prepared to snooze. And lose.

Let's review the steps to a proactive, *interview-getting* proposal:

First, know when you need it.

Is there a more direct path to the offeror? If so, take it. If not, consider a proposal.

The pitch letter from Do 9 and the proposal are very much alike. The pitch is written in the first-person—*I, me, my, mine*. The proposal is written in the third-person, *Ms. Proposa, she, her, hers*. You can guess which is more informal, can't you? Informal doesn't always cut it, though. The formal, "Ms. Jones" proposal works better in a nonservice business, such as an industrial environment.

Second, disregard the rules.

You've probably figured out that my approach to getting a job is unorthodox. Why? Because it works.

Part of the reason it works is because no one will get ahead following directions obviously designed to work against them. Most of the rules that unenlightened, scared, or lazy jobseekers meticulously follow are set up to screen them out, not let them in.

Rules like:

Send resume.

Applications taken online only.

You simply won't get an interview by following fools' rules to the letter.

That's true for proposals too. There's no standard format. Like resume writing, it's an art, not a science. Remember that *B for Boring* file? The fastest way to land there is to follow some textbook approach that won't get you any closer to the offeror than you already are.

So what can you do?

Interesting the Offeror

This is your first task. Write something that interests the offeror. You find this out by scoping out her web site, then targeting a phone call. Don't use e-mail, since you can't control the response as you can in an unexpected or returned-without-knowing-the-subject phone call.

Make the call.

Let's say your target is a small manufacturing company. Perfect for a proposal:

Receptionist: Getum Enterprises. How may I help you?

You: Is the owner in?

Receptionist: Who's calling Bruce?

You: It's personal. (That's why you didn't ask for the full name and title on this call. You do the same dance as in Do 1, like two kiwi birds at mating time. Sure enough, the offeror comes on the line.)

You: Hi, Bruce. I saw your web site, and it's not clear from the information exactly what your company does.

Bruce: We manufacture a variety of security systems. Our products are sold throughout the state.

You: Oh, that's great. I do web site design and thought I might send you a quick proposal about how you might be able to clarify the nature of your business and make it more inviting for people to use your services.

Bruce: That's fine. If you want to send it, I'll take a look. But we're happy with our web designer.

You: I understand completely. I just wanted to let you know how the site could be improved and would be pleased to give my suggestions to you in a proposal.

Bruce: Okay. I look forward to receiving it.

You: If you or your receptionist have a moment, I just would like to get a few details such as the official name of the company.

Bruce: I'll transfer you to my assistant, Robbie. He's out in the back cleaning off the company Splatmobile.

You: Thanks!

Write the thing.

Your proposal should include . . .

The Essentials

1. Identification of who you are
2. Contact information
3. Analysis of what the company presently has. (In this case a web site that's not communicating its diverse product range.)
4. Your suggestions for improvement, based on your experience and qualifications
5. How you would implement those suggestions

Do, Do, Do, and Don't!

1. *Do* include a single-spaced cover letter:

Dear Ms. Offeror,

    It was a pleasure speaking with you today. Enclosed is the proposal we discussed.

    I'll call you in the next few days so we can arrange to meet for a few minutes when I'm in the area.

    In the meantime if you have any questions, I've included my contact information. I look forward to hearing from you.

    Best wishes,

2. *Do* keep it to no more than three pages. Otherwise, it won't get read.
3. *Do* use lots of subheads and bullets.
4. *Don't* put a price or an estimate of what it's going to cost.

Getting It Out

The proposal needs a cover sheet: Blank and titled in the middle of the page: *Proposal for High-Visibility Web Site*. Don't say *slowposal* as the rest should. But it's tempting to say *goposal* because every syllable inside will *move*.

- Type C-O-N-F-I-D-E-N-T-I-A-L at the bottom of the cover sheet. (Too many people might read it, but one will be the offeror.)
- Staple one of your business cards (Do 1) to the cover sheet.

- Slip it into an inexpensive clear plastic binder (available at any stationery store).
- Mail it by regular mail in an oversized envelope.
- Have someone else just check the proposal for accuracy. Many successful proposers just find someone articulate at the store when they're making copies. Customers are fine, too. You say, "Excuse me. I have this proposal here. Would you take a minute for me and just tell me whether you see any typos?" Nobody says, "No."

I remember picking up some candidate after his interview with the CEO of a major corporation. As he was saying goodbye, the CEO commented to the candidate, "People respond exactly the way you treat them." I was very young. The CEO was very successful. I never forgot those wise words. May they guide your every move until you show up for that great interview in the sky.

That's why nobody says, "No." You just have to ask properly. It's so easy when you stop being self-conscious about being human. When you stop worrying about what total strangers think, and just appreciate them for being who they are. Everyone knows this but you. It's where that saying "You're your own worst enemy" must come from. You're much harder on yourself than anyone else could ever be. Does that make any sense to you at all?

Another absolutely wonderful source is any reference librarian at the end of any phone at any library anyplace. Those folks are savvy and they can spell. What they don't know they know how to find, and will do everything but prop you up during the interview if you ask. Never a charge, unlimited assistance, access to infinite resources. Wow.

There you have it. No long hours of research. No complicated books to read. No failures.

All you need to do is offer enough information to establish interest in the face-to-face. The proposal is a warm-up to the call that gets the appointment.

That proposal must *incite* the offeror to meet with you.

Incite and you're *in!* As in *in*-stant!

Do 34: Interrupting the Interview Intervention

Your confidence is at a lifetime high, you're interviewing with interesting people, and you're talking about job offers with your family and friends.

What an amazing transformation!

Your spouse didn't marry an egomaniac, though. Oh, he's been on your case about your lack of self-confidence for years. Your friends call you, and you're too busy running around to relax a little. Your kids are acting up because you're always talking about working here and there.

Of course, people don't change (Do 39). You're not changing. You're just using what you had all the time. Reprioritizing your values now because you've discovered your unlimited potential.

Your friends and family know and love you. So why would they not want you to succeed? Because they're petrified. Scared to death. They won't tell you that you're scaring them because they're afraid you'll bail if you discover your wonders. Or that they're afraid because you won't do what they want. Or that they're afraid because you "don't seem to care anymore." They generally will not confront you with the real reason. If they did, you'd counter with denial or statements they can't refute (like, "We gotta eat, right?").

The reasons you're likely to hear are that you're obsessive, compulsive, and (less clinically) crazy.

It's not that you can't take criticism. Of course you can. You don't think you're perfect. Only there's no such thing as constructive criticism. There's only *criticism*, and it's *destructive*. Constructive criticism isn't. It's a contradiction in terms. Designed to deride, derail, and destroy. Period.

They'll be ready to call an intervention—a forced confrontation with a severe interviewaholic. Maybe even call up a sympathetic social worker or psychologist friend.

It's all a natural part of your development. You can avoid all of this waste of time and negativism by understanding *them* as well as yourself.

I've studied the effect of instant interviewing on marriages (and live-in arrangements) extensively. This is because, without the support of a spouse, the process is not as much fun or as successful.

Kids adapt as long as you hug, explain, and thank. Give them as much time as you can, but your success is for them too. Never miss an event of theirs—that's a rule.

Your friends will probably not stick around. You'll be leaving them in the dust anyway. Sad but true.

Show me your friends, and I'll show you your lifestyle. When you look back after the dust clears, you'll wonder why you were stuck in the ditch with them for so long.

There are three simple techniques you can use to get your spouse on your side.

Here they are.

Moving the Ball

Later, we will talk about the benefits of parroting, or playing back, an offeror's words (Do 51). Using parroting, your answer or other reply immediately has you aligned with the other person and locks you into position to steer him into wanting you very badly.

When you're dealing with those who know you well, parroting doesn't work. You're just playing catch. They know how you throw. So repeating their words just makes them think you're playing a game (which you are).

Here's an example:

Spouse: Oh, you're going on an interview Sunday morning. Does that mean you won't cook breakfast?

You: Yes, I'm going on an interview Sunday, and I won't cook breakfast.

It's just a hearing test.
So you move the ball like this:

Spouse: Oh, you're going on an interview Sunday morning. Does that mean you won't cook breakfast?

You: That's right. I'm going on an interview Sunday to a dress manufacturer, and I'm really excited about the designer opportunity. I'll be no more than an hour. Let's go together. You can wait in the car and listen to your favorite songs, or go window-shopping for an hour. I'll call you on your cell if it will be any longer. Then we can treat ourselves to a brunch over there when I'm done. I'll tell you all about how it goes. And you won't have to clean any dishes!

Look at what just magically happened. Your spouse actually learned that you want to go out on a date with him. You welcomed him into your working world. He was lonely.

Depending on how the interview goes, you can decide how much you want to spend on the brunch. Be sure to insist. That's the deal.

If you don't, at least go out to eat somewhere. Otherwise you haven't moved the ball; you've *dropped* it.

He'll parrot *you*. Again and again.

Unclogging the Blockage

Unless you work with your spouse, he doesn't really know (and therefore can't be expected to appreciate) your pressures. He just knows you won't be cooking breakfast Sunday.

You unclog the blockage by recognizing what it is. This is what happens when you pursue your passion, and it's not him. He's alone, bewildered, shut out.

How about this:

You: I know I won't be home to cook breakfast Sunday morning. Why don't I do it Saturday morning before I go out on interviews? I really want to spend some time with you Saturday night. Let's spend a quiet evening at home together. Surprise me. I'll call you between interviews and be back by five. I just think this designer opportunity will be wonderful for our future.

Why does this one work? Because you're giving your husband what every lover misses with a working other—companionship.

You can do it. They can help!

Getting Participation

It's simple and painless.

The reason is that getting your spouse's participation doesn't require you to look down. You maintain your focus and just get someone else's perspective who has a stake in your success.

This *alone* makes you a better interviewer—particularly with members of the opposite sex. But it also makes you better because the buy-in has your spouse in that optimum you-and-me-against-the-problem mode. It's no longer "you against me." (Do 56)

Role-play in interviews. I wrote *The Complete Q&A Job Interview Book* specifically for this exercise. It sells well because it works well. There are a lot of imitators now, but none show you how to use the "actor factor" to nail interviews on those instant screen tests.

I don't usually recommend my books, but the *Q&A Book* will enhance your marriage as well as your interviewing skill.

Turn intervention into *interaction*!

What about the other amateur advisers in your life?

Advisers give advice. Simple enough. *Devisers* give *devices*. Simple, too, but scarce.

Boundless (literally, *no-boundary*) interviewing doesn't require anything more than the sum of *you* + *tools*. If everyone was the same, offerors would be even *more* confused! Why? Because they don't know what they want.

If I keep advising you to wear the yellow pumps with your chartreuse hoop skirt, will you do it? No. If your sister-in-law advises you to wear the orange pumps instead, you won't do that either. You're confused. A confused mind does nothing. You go barefoot.

So devisers don't try to change you. (It hasn't worked since the first egg cracked.) They boost *your* potency with vitameatavegamins.

Here are some clues about who to avoid like the jungle plague:

Someone who is less happy. Or who doesn't have what you want. Or who makes less money. Or who doesn't walk the walk. Or who says and does two different things. Or who lies. Or who breaks his word. Or who disrespects others. Or who can't do one single thing better than anyone else you know. Or who doesn't know the facts. Or who has some other agenda.

Does that leave only me? I hope not, but you could do worse.

Before we leave the subject of intervention, we need to address the professional advisers. These are my neighbors here on the bookshelf. Neighbors and friends in many cases.

I've read and written more books in the career field than anyone else. Done more and hold more certifications too.

This didn't increase my knowledge of how to get interviews. But it increased my knowledge of analysis paralysis even more. Accepting wrongheaded advice is far worse than accepting none. It reinforces bad habits and demoralizes by negative results.

Regardless of how much I like them personally, many authors and consultants in the career field are unqualified. Almost none have any business advising anyone about a subject so vital.

How do you know who's who in the zoo—er—jungle?

This is how:

The next time you're in a bookstore or library, do this little test. Pick six books from the career section. Most of the books either don't mention the background of the author or give only a few lines. The others have bios of freelance writers, salespeople, or career counselors. Virtually *none* have a background of systematically generating interviews for others. Yet they're instructing interview interns into internment.

I'm a great believer in trial and error. Sometimes thousands of tries and errors. It's the only way to invent a light bulb. Or to hit a baseball. Or to get an interview.

But you don't have to do it yourself. You can switch on a light, swing a bat to connect, and get an interview, if you know how.

Getting interviews and instantly morphing them into job offers doesn't happen unless you use a delivery that registers right then and there. You can only learn this from someone who has actually used the devices he recommends.

So consider the source.

What about making your own tribal trail mix? Pick how to dress from one, what to say from another? Do that with your diet if you must do it at all. You'll get fat, but you'll get interviewed.

Do what works. Otherwise you'll be getting ready to get ready until you get *retired*.

That's how you interrupt interview interventions and increase instant interviews!

Do 35: Arriving at Airports, Stations, and Depots

If you could find a free job fair with unlimited offerors 24/7, would you go? You just did.

When you're an instant interviewer—an incurable interviewaholic—your life shifts from chasing after teasers to identifying which rooms work. Airports, train stations, and bus depots are crazygood.

Some differences among them, though:

Attacking at Airports

The separate gate arrangement at airports gives you a perfect chance to instant from one to the other without the privacy problems of groups (Do 56). It's amazing.

Keep your carry-on light. Go to the first domestic carrier gate you see in a city you'd like, and look for a well-dressed business-looking person. You don't need to spot a laptopper like when on the plane (Do 38) because offerors are in plain sight. Always pick someone who's alone and doesn't appear to be guarding a companion's luggage.

Then, rest your recruited rump and say, "Hi! Do you have business in Boston?"

You might hear, "Yes."

You then say, "I hear it's a beautiful city. What's it like?"

Him: It is beautiful. I'm visiting my largest wholesaler to review our distribution system.

You: I'm waiting for a plane to Denver. What are your products?

The rest is exactly like any sitting side-to-side instant interview (Do 56). Fifteen minutes, eyeball, smile, say goodbye with a handshake, business card exchange (Do 1), and it's off to the next gate.

Stompin' at the Station

Train stations are a great place anyway. The security is civilized, the people are not as rushed. Being at the old ones is a blast from the past. Being at the new ones is a trip to the future. I love trains, and you will too.

There are fewer businesspeople, but they look much calmer. They are, and therefore you can approach them more easily than in an airport.

Since the gates usually don't have lobbies, the chamber method (Do 56) is used. If they do, follow the airport routine.

Doin' It at Depots

Public and tour bus depots are marginal places to instant. Businesspeople don't use them much.

But they're super places to meet savvy, helpful drivers and other staffers who know the area hiring trends better than almost anyone else. Follow the techniques to instant them (Do 36).

Do 36: Transforming Ground Transportation into Interview Information

People-drivers see and hear more useful interview intelligence in one shift than the average person does in a week. Run the numbers mentally and you can see why they're musters for your instant interviewing.

They're also very nice. You'd have to be. And funny? You'd need a sense of humor too. Approachable? An understatement. They're in your face.

You don't have to hop on a bus or ride a taxi if you're not going anyway. You just have to go where drivers go. Take bow-coo business cards. You'll be on the bow-coo interview route.

We have two bus terminals near our home. I discovered them when I was looking to take my grandkids on a field trip. I just called the bus lines and asked for the administrative office. They have tons of tools in the garage (like Bob the Builder would use). They even have ones that are 10 times the size of the tools used for cars!

Inside there are driver rest areas where you can visit with the staff. This alone is worth the trip. Helpers. Cool.

What's happening? Who do you know? What's going on at that corner with the fence? Why are so many people riding to that office building? Where are the people you drive working? Who's hiring?

The next places are taxi offices. Look in the *Yellow Pages* under "Taxi Services." Call and get the addresses (they're not listed).

How about airport shuttles? They're in the *Yellow Pages*, usually under "Airport Shuttle Services." Find out where they hang and go over.

Far more shuttle drivers than taxi drivers work part-time, and they have businesses on the side. Antennae up!

Check the *Yellow Pages* under "Limousine Services" too. Depending on whom you call, the I.I. inquiries can be done over the phone. The smaller, boutique services are frequently owner-managed. You may be talking to a businessperson who needs things done. A closet offeror.

On the others, get an address and go over personally. Limo drivers are super sources since they drive successful people.

When you're in another city (or if you want to be), look up these services. You can't find out more, higher quality, better interview intel faster than from them!

I've done these exercises myself. Drivers are so flattered anyone cares about them that they'll ask for *your* number!

Do 37: Tracking on Trains

If you ride commuter trains, offerors instantly are everywhere!

Train riding is a wondrous experience anyway. It takes people back to their childhood and a simpler time. They think of the amusement park. And it's predictable travel. This is a mindset found in no other place.

Couple that with the constant vibration that lulls passengers into a receptive state like a lullaby, and it's *instantime*.

Now for your train training. There's a specific way to sit and say in those seats.

Stagger Your Schedule

Pick times that businesspeople commute. Follow the briefcases and laptops like the undercover (job) security sleuth you are.

Take trips at different times so you find different offerors. Instant interviews require instant exits—no more than 15 minutes from hello to goodbye (Do 1).

Sitting next to someone (even if there are other passengers in the row) works fine. A little contorted because you're side by side, but you can adjust.

Avoid seats that face each other (Do 56).

Review the airplane techniques (Do 38) for side-by-side interviewing.

Go from One Car to Another

This is a great advantage in train riding. Seat, meet, greet, tweet, retreat, and repeat! It's like going to airport gates.

Three quality instants in a one-hour commute is easy, fun, and a sure way to shift your automatic offermobile into overdrive.

Stop at Stations along the Way

Try the ones in highly populated areas. Either ones where business travelers work or ones where they live.

That's where they'll be waiting and wishing for wonderwoman or wonderman.

The approach is basic airport gate (Do 35).

Stop at Stations Where People Are Getting On Rather than Off

Of all the predictability of train travel, nothing is more predictable than passengers rushing out of the cars. It's due to their energized state from the relaxing ride and anticipation of getting to work or home.

So unless you want to run and ramble simultaneously, find offerors waiting to board.

Make friends with the conductors.

Like all transpo people, they see all, speak all, and hear all. So they make the rounds collecting, selling, and punching tickets. They see the same commuters daily.

Friendliness is a railroad tradition. Don't be surprised if a conductor points out overactive offerors just by your asking. The words are usually deposited standing up: "Who on the train is a corporate executive?"

Don't wait for him to pass your seat.

We've got major moves of our own to do.

All aboard! Next stop, Interview!

Do 38: Taking Off in Business Class

Airplanes provide an unusually good opportunity for instant interviews with quality offerors.

You have a captive audience. You just need to captivate, then incubate. Capture, then release.

Why does every unpretzeled carrier have a fancy business traveler magazine stuffed in that pouch in front of your seat? Undoubtedly more business is conducted in front of airplane seat pouches than anywhere else.

So let's analyze, maximize, and *intervise*.

Fly with the Flock

The rush hours are weekdays from 6 A.M. to 10 A.M. and 4 P.M. to 8 P.M. Any earlier and you get world vacationers. Later, you're trying to interview in the dark. Other times are like weekends and holidays. You couldn't get an interview as a babysitter.

Call a Travel Agent

I use someone in Cleveland. It's as though she's right in my office in Los Angeles. One call to her is like a dozen calls to carriers, if I can even find out who flies where.

A dozen calls to carriers can waste several hours (time is money) and have me speaking with call-center agents who neither speak English very well nor hear very well.

Book Early

Thirty days before any flight usually will get you a refundable ticket and better seat selection. You want any *aisle* seat so you can move around. Early booking also allows you flexibility to change flights as the departure dates arrives.

I recently tried to change a flight from Shreveport to stop in St. Louis when my best friend became ill.

Booking on the very same nonstop flight had gone up almost five times as much! And only a few, less desirable seats were left.

Fly Business Class

Economy coach is fine too. But if it's no more expensive, try to get in that midrange between coach (usually in the back) and first class (always in the front). This is typically called *business class*. If you look around, you'll call it offeror class.

First class is not available on all flights and will become largely extinct as savvy frequent fliers discover that the various sections generally arrive at the same time.

Cost-consciousness on the part of airlines and businesses is making first class nothing more than a billboard slogan.

You don't really want it anyway. The seats are too wide, the drinks are too strong, and the price is too high.

Book Online

The phone recordings now tell you that there's a charge to book using a live person. Agents charge too. Paying a nominal charge is the least you can do to thank someone who's so wonderful. You can also go to any of the zillion travel web sites.

You can book online with the airlines directly too. The web sites are always mentioned on the recorded messages.

If you look through the sites, you lose the real-time depth and breadth that a live travel agent offers. You can also get locked in to nonrefundable tickets at times when business travelers are recreating or retiring. Keeping that in mind, booking online is a great way to save money, time, and to avoid those phones.

Wear Your Interviewing Uniform

Watch, pen, and business cards too (Do 1).

Bring Snacks to the Airport

It's much better, faster, and cheaper than taking whatever is close when you're there.

I usually end up eating when I'm walking, running, or shuttling to some last-minute changed gate. There's no way you can stop and eat or carry food when you have a laptop, briefcase, purse, or jacket. Often all of the above.

Nuts are absolutely perfect since the bags are stuffable everywhere and they're security-conscious nonbeepers. They have just the right amount of protein, carbs, fat, and salt to keep you going (without keeping you going). Truly the perfect interviewer's snack food any time (Do 3). High calorie though, so count like a baby.

Arrive Even Earlier

The airport obstacle course is a necessary evil to protect from evil. So practice your grin and bear it.

Arriving even earlier will enable you to use the self-check-in procedure that is replacing counter agents. It will also enable you to do it again and again if there's a terminal or system glitch. Glitches cause stress. Stress blows interviews.

Eventually you'll push, pull, and beep your way through the strip-search and walk, run, and ride to the gate.

Whew! Made it. Now, get over to a restroom and get yourself together.

We've already covered interviewing in airline terminals along with other mass transit holding areas (Do 35).

Look—they're calling for the C section passengers now. Let's get in line behind those pregnant ladies . . .

Plan A: Interviewing on Tight Flights

When the flight attendant says, "We've got a full flight today," we swing into Plan A. Basic tight flight mode.

As you're ducking, clunking, and bumping down the aisle looking for your seat, look for the bright laptop screens. Laptoppers tend to be either students (no) or businesspeople (yes).

Don't stomp on other passengers to sit on the laptopper's armrest, particularly in a window seat on a full row. Don't hold everyone up so you can find your pen to write the seat number on your palm either.

You'll find that laptopper later. She's a definite possible.

You can't accomplish much until the seatbelt sign is turned off, so read, look at that business magazine in the pouch, or just make a friend of your neighbor.

Using Your Takeoff Time

I have my MP3 player with meditation, self-hypnosis, and other brainfood that I play (Do 42) until the flight attendant announces to turn it off.

I also have a tradition of talking to my neighbor. People are so nervous at takeoff, and it takes so long these days. I just enjoy that human everyone's-in-it-together feeling you get when you're confined and terrified about the same thing.

Once the plane is at cruising altitude and the seatbelt sign is off, you can start walking around.

Go to the back of the plane and talk to the flight attendants. Niceness varies because many flights (and fliers) cause grumpiness, but they're sharp and helpful. I always ask about how long we'll be at cruising altitude and when we'll land.

Mentally compute how much time you have to I.I. It's cruising altitude time less 30 minutes to allow for carts in the way and fasten-seatbelt orders. If it's one hour, you can comfortably do two interviews. That's about the average.

Sitting Next to an Offeror

It's easy, even in a full plane. People get up and they switch if you ask. The seat assignment doesn't matter anymore.

Then find that likely offeror and either sit down or ask to switch seats with a neighbor. Open that business mag, look at one must-have travel item, turn to her, and say, "Hi! My name's Howard. What's yours?" Then when she says, "Amelia," you say, "Are you flying to Dallas on business?"

You don't need a contorted handshake here, and the words are not standard Magic Four (Do 1). But the eye contact and smile are SOP. You have 15 minutes to exchange business cards or to have her write down her contact info.

Then say, "It was a pleasure meeting you. I see that cart in the distance. I'd better get back in my seat before I become a human bowling pin. Have a great time in Dallas! I'll call you next week when I get home."

Go back to your seat, then take your pen out of your left front pocket and do the grading on the card. When the coast is clear, repeat the process or go to either end of the plane if you see any offerors there. Interview standing up. Then seat and repeat if there's time.

When you deplane, try to avoid seeing any of the offerors you approached.

Plan B: Interviewing on Light Flights

On light flights, you still follow Plan A, but the empty seats change your approach.

You can spot offerors easily. You can also be spotted by them and the flight attendants. So two interviews max, unless the cruising time is more than two hours. In between, be sure to talk to the flight attendants at the ends. It will help them know you're not drug dealing.

These conversations occasionally become instant interviews. Flight attendants have businesspeople in their lives, are natural networkers, and are caregivers. They fit the classic offeror profile.

Can you take off and interview? Can you *not?* The sky's the limit!

Do 39: Developing Your Persona

If you were to ask me the single biggest reason people get interviewed, I'd answer without hesitation—*personality.* Or *persona* for short and meaning a little more—the way you carry yourself.

Not qual-i-fi-ca-tions. Not ex-pe-ri-ence. Not cre-den-tials. Those are forethoughts in conventional interviewing, afterthoughts in instant interviewing.

Let me 'splain: In the conventional *pretend* world, you need certain easily learned, largely unnecessary features to be considered. If you manage to present those features through a printed resume or an online keyword play, you'll get a chance to get hired. You must then have a good per-so-na, or it won't happen.

In the *real* instant interview world, having a good persona is all you need. (Exceptions are artificially barriered trades or professions that require a specific ticket for entrance.)

You don't *get* a persona. You get what you got. Psychologists call this a *basic personality structure* (BPS). Let's look at your persona and see what we can do to make it more marketable.

Do you greet enthusiastically? Do you smile? Do you look people in the eye? Do you shake hands confidently? (Do 1) Do you listen with both ears or do you think about what you're going to say next? Is it next or is it at the same time?

How do you ask questions? Do you embarrass others with personal ones? Do you ask them about imperfections in their personal appearance? The way they walk, talk, wheel?

How do you answer questions? Are you open or defensive? Do you question why the question was asked? Or do you refuse to answer to prove your point? Does your jaw drop? How about your body language? Do you *say* and *convey* the same messages? Or do you say yes with words, but no with actions?

Are your ups and downs determined by events? Do you really, deep down, recognize your amazing, unique qualities? Can anyone or anything take that knowledge away?

Your answers will determine how fast and how often you get interviews. *Only* those answers.

If you see some bad habits there, change them. They're just habits—things we do over and over without thinking. You think, you stop, you substitute. It works.

Ask someone you trust and see whether she agrees.

Don't be too hard on yourself. Everyone rolls his eyes. Everyone complains. Everyone argues. Just be conscious of it. That will do wonders. (It probably already has by just reading this.)

Read it every day for a week or so. Repetition got you every negative habit, and repetition will replace every one.

If you are to succeed, *really* succeed—with peace of mind deep in your soul—please know one thing and one thing only:

People don't change.

Not *you,* not your *spouse,* not your *kids.* Not the people on a plastic surgeon's table or a psychotherapist's couch.

Don't spend another nanosecond trying to change yourself or them. It just frustrates you, and it annoys them. Period.

You don't get off that easy, though. Now it's time to substitute that changing habit with the habit of *growing*.

You either grow up or you grow down. You either blossom or you wither and die. There's really nothing in between, is there? If you've ever attended a class reunion, you should need no further convincing. They're either vertically the same, or they're horizontal.

Isn't what we think is change really growth?

Now we turn to improving your persona. We do that by something called a *sense of humor*. That's right—having a *sense* that things just happen and taking them *humorously*.

Let's look at something like being late. All mature adults try to be early or on time. You've instantly interviewed with a terrific offeror who has invited you back for a third time. You made a friend at the business, and know it's time for him to extend an offer for a dream job. You were to be there at 9 A.M.

Your daughter had a math homework assignment that was due today. You discovered it in her backpack an hour before she was leaving for school. She didn't do it and decided this was the morning she no longer needed to know math. By the time she figured out a few of the answers, you were already running late. Deep breath here.

It would be natural—appropriate and even what you want at some level (to punish her)—for you to show up late profusely apologizing, and at best looking weak.

But you're a member of the I.I. Society. We know what a job is (Do 1). Most important, we know how to get interviews today, tomorrow, always. We know this is a human experience that any parent in the civilized world encounters.

Now exhale. Fine.

Before anything else, you tell your teenage daughter to get her act together. You've got an important call to make. She complies because you have the car keys.

You call the office, and the receptionist answers. Smiling and using your most professional voice, you say, "Hi, Karen! This is Joan. I have an appointment with Andy at 9 A.M. Will you let him know that I'm on my way. I've been detained for a little while."

She says, "I think I saw Andy in the back. Would you like to tell him yourself?"

You reply, "No. That will just take longer. I'm on my way."

What did you do differently from every other sniffling, whining, weak jobseeking beggar? You *owned* the dialogue.

People are late. The world isn't going to wobble on its axis. You weren't there at *all* yesterday. The biz survived. And most important, Andy will only care *if you do*.

Will you apologize for being late? Of course! You'll smile, look him in the eye and say, "Sorry I was late. I was detained unavoidably. How have you *been?*"

That is a sense of humor. A sense of balance. A sense of self. Self-confidence. *That* is what Andy—and every Andy—wants. Someone who cares but doesn't care so much that she apologizes for being.

A sense of humor is rare in the workplace. Yet nothing *disarms* a *con-fronter* and nothing *defuses* a *confrontation* like a swift *quip* in the rear. What's the big whoop? It sure gets (and keeps) close friends. Gets (and keeps) people hired too.

Let's say you accept the job. (He'll offer it now for sure.) Your daughter decides to be a teenager again, and you're late the following week. Andy is trying to run a business, and it helps if he has people there during working hours.

So he says, "You won't make being ten minutes late a habit. Right, Joan?"

You smile, look at him and say, "It's not a habit, it's a *happening*. And it won't happen again!"

Make sure it doesn't, too.

I've used humor in open court during some of the most serious business cases imaginable. It's how you budge a judge and send a flurry through a jury. An eyedropper of humor can summarize a scoop of seriousness, too.

Your proper persona is a secret to getting interviews. The more you develop it, the more interviews you'll develop!

Do 40: Calling and Enthralling the Offeror

Your phone voice is going to be instantly perfect.

In your cold calls and follow-up calls, 100 percent of your image is conveyed by your voice.

Since I.I.'s talk quite a bit, they tend to become deaf to their own voices. For this reason, we use a four-step program of simple, proven voice-improvement techniques. Your voiceprint is unique but you probably don't really know how it sounds. This is because you hear your voice as it echoes through your head. Others hear it through their ears. How do you hear it through your ears? Record your phone conversations.

For a few dollars, you can buy a phone pickup from any electronics store to plug into your digital recorder. This is undoubtedly the most important training device you will ever have at any price. As long as the recorder is used solely by you, it's perfectly legal. You'll probably be surprised at how bad you initially sound. That's good. It only takes a few days of brutalizing to develop a more effective voice.

It's best to start with recording three segments of three minutes each in the morning, midday, and afternoon. Undoubtedly you will notice wide variation in the speed, volume, pitch, and articulation.

Here are the four steps.

Vary the Rate

The average jobseeker speaks at the rate of 145 words per minute. You can check your wpm by replaying the midday segment of the tape for 20 seconds, counting the number of words, and multiplying by three. Is your rate consistent? Do you pause for emphasis? Do your words run together? Do you gasp for air? Do you speak in a monotone? If you're trying to instantly obtain an interview, your rate of speed tends to increase.

If you're getting directions from an offeror, it tends to decrease. Since the phone doesn't permit the use of gestures and body language, a runaway rate of speech at closing time can cost you the interview. If you're up over 200 wpm at a critical stage, you're conveying more than *enthusiasm*—you're conveying *anxiety*.

Control the Volume

Do offerors ask you to speak louder? Do they ask you to repeat what you said? Do they hang up while you're still talking? If so, you're probably the only one listening. It's hard to interview that way.

And you know the other extreme. The offerors who think a telephone is a megaphone. This hangup is most common among those who work in a bullpen, where shouting may be a matter of survival. Check your midday segments. Is your volume level varied? Do you use a lower volume for unimportant words? (*A, an, and, but, in, into, the,* or *with* are examples.)

I learned the value of this on the talk shows. Changes in vocal power allow you to stress key words, especially *action* words. They also allow you to get a point across. Whether it's a scream or a whisper, be conscious of it.

Your recorder should be getting a good workout in your calling to help you develop an optimum volume level. Then you can work on varying it for emphasis.

Use the Right Pitch

Do your statements sound like questions with a rising inflection at the end? Do you sing rather than say? Does your voice sound like you're puppylicking the Cool Whip container while talking? Your basic walking kazoo?

Since most jobseekers have a range of only one octave, it's unlikely you'll be able to change the pitch. But reducing the volume will help you lower it.

Improve Your Pronunciation

The last thing that affects your phone voice is how you pronounce words. If you play back a familiar voice saying, "Du ya wanna," "gonna," or "interdukshun," it's time to correct the "prolem."

In surveying voices for *Instant Interviews*, I discovered that candidates over 40 tend to lose enthusiasm and dynamism in their speech. The result was a constant pitch with little difference in speed or intensity.

This boring pattern is just a symptom of the rejection shock that unstant interviewers encounter. They might as well call up the offeror and say, "You wouldn't want to interview me anyway."

Your voice conveys more about your feelings toward the offeror in the first moments than all of your words that follow.

Only four steps.

Call and *enthrall!*

Do 41: Reading the Offeror Like a Book

. . . Within a few seconds!

With remarkable precision. That way, you know exactly how to play the game.

Nobody knows how to do this but I.I.'s. That's you, and it's now.

You're appearing during your workday when the offeror could be expected to be frantic, overworked, and involved with things other than you.

So she's bound by an unwritten standard operating procedure.

Talk to someone who's like you.

In those first few seconds, she'll instinctively look for similarities between you and her. If she sees them, her brain flashes *go*. If not, it flashes *stop*. If it's go, the psychological alignment locks in as the instant interview locks in.

You should recognize by now that *all* interviews are instant interviews. We know it. The rest of the natives don't.

This was graphically taught to me in my first HR job. The company had outgrown its headquarters and acquired homes nearby to use as offices. Our HR department occupied one of the three-bedroom converted homes. It was in an *L* shape. As you went up the walkway toward the front door, there was a window on the wall to the right. That was my boss's office—formerly the master bedroom. His desk faced the same way as the front door. There was a window in front of the desk on the left side.

He had a convex mirror installed on the right upper corner of his office so he could look up and see who was approaching when the blinds were open.

I'd be sitting in my office (an inside bedroom) writing up some fantasy display ad. Suddenly, a loud voice would bellow out on the speakerphone, "Hire that one!"

It's all about that flash. It's all so sci-en-tif-ic.

You can instantly make the light flash green if you instantly know the three offeror types.

Here we go.

Outgoing: Type One

These offerors are sometimes called *socializers*. They're energetic, friendly, and self-assured. They wear flamboyant clothes or accessories.

Their offices have family photos, kids' artwork, and mementos. Their desks are disorganized and cluttered.

Don't be surprised if some of the books on the shelf are upside down.

You won't often see these offerors right away, since their schedules look like their desks.

But if you meet one, align by being upbeat and very friendly. Always follow the genie format (Do 1). They talk a lot, so be a good listener.

If you do it right, it's a "Hire that one!" situation. Probably not on your first follow-up phone call. (He won't call you although he wants to. He's just over his head. Good for us.)

Generally, great other-oriented people.

You can be funny and enjoy the ride. I remember going over to an outgoing offeror's bookshelf and turning my head like I was trying to read the upside-down spine.

That was my conversation with him, as he motioned for me to come in while he was on the phone.

I sat down. Standing was awkward, and he didn't motion for me to sit.

When he got off the phone, I said, "Hi! I'm here to see if I can help you with your hiring needs."

He smiled.

Loved that job!

Reserved: Type Two

Less gregarious offerors are likely the most successful.

Their clothes are predictable, not flashy, and they listen well. Their offices are neat, as are their desks. Look for expensive desk sets and custom-framed artwork. Maybe a family photo or two.

All business. So you be that way too. Let her know you need to get to an appointment, so the interview is short.

Stay and that green light will turn yellow. Stay longer and it flashes red.

So leave your business card, get hers, and get out.

Then get an offer from your follow-up in a week or so.

Analytical: Type Three

These are often technical or administrative offerors who rely on objective criteria in their decision-making. They think.

But they're just as impressionable as everyone else.

Their offices are downright sterile. Clean, neat. Few, if any, creative works. Perhaps a linear art work but no freeform.

The approach to analytical offerors is to ask more questions. It makes you sound like you know something. So, many people don't do it.

Clinchers in conversations are *how* you would improve their business, not just *what* you would do.

An example would be, "I'll contact the software vendor and work with the rep on updating the spreadsheet printouts."

There's rarely anyone whose face, dress, and office doesn't scream, "One!" "Two!" or "Three!". If you find one, he's probably got a split personality, anyway.

Try to leave the offices of a schizophrenic whenever possible.

You'll go from genie to *genius* if the offeror isn't in, but you can see her office. You'll know whether she's a one, two, or three immediately. You leave your card and know exactly how to handle the follow-up call. The glance is just as effective as a face-to-face.

It can be easily confirmed by checking out the employees. They pick up the dress, speech, speech patterns, accents, and mannerisms of the offeror.

This is called *company culture*, and if you're cultured, you're interviewed. The pop psychological word for this is *modeling*. We call it interview imitating.

Try this as you're arriving like a genie (Do 1).

There are really only three types of offerors. The predictability and the *ability* to control the outcome is nothing short of uncanny.

Read like that and you'll never interview the same way again!

Do 42: Increasing Your Interviewing Instincts

What if we could just heighten your senses so you'd just pick the best offerors, and close them on the spot? That'd be off the charts! It's all about *instinct*. That elusive sixth sense that makes our pets so much smarter than us mere mortals.

Dogs don't clog up their thought process with yesterday's history or tomorrow's mystery. You come home, they wag. You bug them, they growl. Someone knocks, they bark. You eat, and they're focused like a laser on your food.

This is because they don't read, write, or talk. They don't get confused. They live in the moment.

They *pounce*. With every ounce.

Let's see how we can awaken your instinct too.

Think from Digital to Analog

Forget *yes-no, on-off, go-stop*. That's digital decision-making. The world of work isn't digital. It's analog. It zigzags.

Have you ever instinctively had a hunch you'd get a job if you just interviewed with a certain business? Even if it wasn't hiring? You were right.

If you'd have just followed your instincts and instantly interviewed with them by appearing like a genie (Do 1), you'd be working there. You could do it now, in fact. You'll see you were right. Magic, huh?

Why am I so sure? Because in that situation, you're not operating *digitally*. You're an analog animal—all over the place, factoring in all the variables in that supercomputer between your ears.

That's why humans succeed and computers short out. We have a sixth sense in our mind that processes all of our sensory input. Computers have a brain that takes in a keystroke or a mouse click and processes it as a command.

Every successful jobgetter got the job by acing an interview. If you investigate, it wasn't some digitally constructed job. The person doesn't resemble the job specs (Do 26). The decision by the employer was based on raw *instinct*, pure and simple. But how did the jobseeker even know to apply? Why her and not you?

She recognized the choices (let's call that *awareness*) and then she followed her instinct.

Become Aware of Your Interview Options

Awareness is not the same as *analysis*. That's why career counselors are so dangerous.

They live in a world of *do-you-like* tests with *yes-no* questions, forms with plus-minus boxes to evaluate different jobs and resumes with rigid choices (*chronological, functional*, or a combination thereof).

That is a primary reason why so-called career counseling can't possibly lead to self-fulfillment.

So forget that stuff.

Instead, learn to really relax. Deeply.

Relaxation gets your conscious mind out of the way so your subconscious mind surfaces. This is a metaphorical way of saying that when you relax properly, daily static stops bombarding you, and you gain perspective.

When we talked about I.I. on planes, I mentioned that I listened to self-hypnosis recordings on my MP3 player (Do 38).

Every day of my adult life I have either meditated or listened to self-hypnosis recordings for at least 45 minutes.

My blood pressure is low, my energy is high, my age is a number.

This is what happens physiologically when you relax using either traditional meditation (repeating a word to yourself) or guided relaxation (listening to a self-hypnosis recording). In recent years, I've used self-hypnosis because it's *active*, not *passive*. It works wonders to help you improve yourself beyond merely heightening awareness. So you can lose weight, stop smoking, and generally self-improve while you're instanting better and better.

I'm absolutely convinced that whatever internal centering, creativity, and energy I have is a direct result of this disciplined relaxation. I interviewed instinctively where I thought I'd fit, totally ignoring job requirements. I nailed those interviews almost every time too, because I instinctively did what would incite an offeror to extend that offer.

I'll lay it out for you as I've done for so many megasuccessful jobseekers.

Know How Self-Hypnosis Heightens Instinct

You've undoubtedly found yourself parking in some office building lot to I.I. and didn't even remember driving there. Perhaps even actually interviewing with some excited offeror but thinking about an interview you just instanted.

These are two typical examples of how your conscious mind gets you through the day while your subconscious has a mind of its own. That mind is where the instinct often remains inactive because external noise literally overpowers those powers at the conscious level.

Self-hypnosis safely, effortlessly, and automatically causes your conscious mind to recede and allows your subconscious mind to tap into your instinct.

That's all you need to understand. That and how to awaken the giant within.

Instantly Tap into Your Subconscious

This is a huge way to increase important instants. The formula is:

Intent + Instinct = Instant Interviews

Intent gets your mind sharply focused. *Instinct* guides it; then your limbs and mouth are moving in the right way. The activity takes care of itself.

If you use a combination lock frequently, you don't think about the combo—you just do it. Same jukebox, different tune.

Now, write down one concise but very specific sentence stating three qualities of your dream job.

Best Manager: _____

Best Activity: _____

Best Pay: _____

Your subconscious is still sleeping. Be very optimistic. You're interviewing for a dream job. It doesn't know dreams from reality. It thinks everything you visualize is real.

We fool it when it wakes up. Ha! Ha! Now you made me a superstar!

Tape the piece of paper on your mirror where you'll see it every time you see your face. Leave it there for at least 30 days after you start using any self-hypnosis CD such as those discussed here.

Self-Hypnotize

Just go online and google *self-hypnosis cd* or similar headings.

Advising and *assisting* are usually much closer in the dictionary than they are in real life. You have many advisers (Do 95). This is a true *assistor.*

Many retailers also carry self-hypnosis CDs, and there are independent distributors at shopping malls and swap meets.

But the best selection, the best guarantees (almost always money-back), and the latest techniques are online.

Don't waste your time with personal hypnotists, and don't try to make your own recordings. (Let's get you the dream job first. By then, you'll be so together that you'll probably just stick with the CDs anyway.)

Pick any self-improvement thing, and there's a self-hypnosis CD or download on it. So start using your instinct right away. Avoid relying on self-hypnosis to cure any disease, but expect it to reduce or eliminate an undesirable habit. Regardless of the subject, all self-hypnosis will incite your instinct.

Many of the professional hypnotists who recorded the sessions will pick up the phone if you call the number on the web site. You will get a free consultation. You can also e-mail inquiries, and they generally respond promptly. They're not spooky like stage hypnotists and are people who have benefited from the techniques themselves. So they are knowledgeable, interested in having you succeed, and genuine caregivers. You'll be surprised at the dedication of many of them.

Self-hypnosis CDs are also available from your local library. When they don't have the ones you want in stock, they can order them through their system.

If you're not sure about the benefits, just order nonspecific relaxation recordings. They'll pop out your instinct in wonderful ways you never imagined! These CDs or downloads have exactly the same induction scripts as self-help ones. However, as in meditation, you only deflate the ball. You don't move it forward.

I record the CDs on my MP3 player for portable use, but you can download content directly from your computer.

I'm telling you to do this. Your eyes are getting heavy. You *will* be an instinctive interviewer. You *will* amaze yourself.

You *will* be the person you were meant to be!

Do 43: Bossing around Your Boss to Get You Interviews

The adjective *boss* means *cool*. That's *your* boss now—a *boss* boss!

You must tell your boss you're interviewing. (You genie, me wisher. Do 1.) If you don't, your boss will find out anyway. From you.

You'll smile more, you'll have a spring in your step, you'll stand up to the staff-meeting bully, and you'll start saying what you really think.

You'll also start getting more calls, having more "dentist appointments" and spontaneously singing in the middle of customer meetings.

Being upfront will ease your mind and force you to get out, *out*, OUT! It's really liberating and will energize your happinesshunt.

While you're checking that definition of *boss*, let me tell you what I did. It was while I was still in law school. I was working full time as an HR manager with family responsibilities and no money. My wife, Bev, was a key employee on her job. The facility relocated, so she commuted far on the company bus. That summer it was very hot, and Bev was very pregnant.

It was one of those times we all have when you look back and think: How did I ever do it? No—how did I ever *survive!*

The *HR* in my manager job didn't stand for *Human Resources*—it stood for *Heavy Responsibility*. As in, "If anything goes wrong, you're responsible."

I was responsible for everything from hiring employees to fixing the vending machines. It wasn't like I had a job as a systems analyst or a contract administrator. I had to be there, or the newsletter didn't get written. Or the operators didn't take a break. Or the assembly line didn't run because nobody called the temp service.

If I walked into the lunchroom, smashed the glass on the fire alarm, and aimed the hose, nobody would have missed a chew.

I had a few things going for me, though. I knew how to get hired. I just hadn't figured how to get *interviewed* yet. But I knew my boss, the vice president, could do that for me. A great guy, but tough as nails. A bodybuilder.

I remember walking into his office as if it were yesterday:

Jeff: Skip, I need to talk to you for a few minutes.
Skip: What now? I told you we submitted your tuition reimbursement request a few weeks ago.
Jeff: Thanks. Actually, it's about me leaving here.
Skip: What? I just wrote what a valuable employee you are in your performance appraisal. Besides, you're not a fancy lawyer yet.
Jeff: Actually, that's what I wanted to talk about too.
Skip: Okay, let's hear it. Sit.
Jeff: Wait—I'll tell Zelda to hold your calls. I'm going to have to resign *(closing the door)*.

(I didn't ask him to have his calls held or ask to shut the door. I now was the boss. If we'd had cell phones then, I would have told him to turn his off.)

Skip: Oh, fine. Just what I need. We're right in the middle of a big bid.
Jeff: Look, I have to study for my finals. Bev's doing the best she can, but our future's at stake. We've got the baby on the way, and I just made editor of the law review.
Skip: I know you, Allen. What's your plan?
Jeff: You *do* know me. So you know I wouldn't leave you in a lurch. And I know you wouldn't leave me in one, either. (*He really was a great guy, and this gave him a chance to prove it again.*) I won't be able to work full-time anymore, but I'll find, train, and job-share with my replacement for the next three months. You'll continue to pay me as usual. In

exchange, you'll arrange for me to interview with anyone you choose at least three times a week. I'd like something law-related.

Skip: So I'm doing outplacement now?

Jeff: Yes. Except that you're doing it because you can, not because I'm paying you.

Skip: I do know a lot of people. I could do that at the health club. (*He went there every morning with our* CEO.)

Jeff: That's why I'm so fortunate to have you in my corner—and in my life.

Skip: How are you going to recruit a replacement?

Jeff: My assistant, Agnes, can do this job.

Skip: She doesn't have the experience.

Jeff: (*Gulp! Better think of a zinger fast. Finding a replacement would take time I can't afford.*) I've got enough experience for both of us. You can keep her at her current salary for six months, and I'll even help you review her performance.

Skip: It sounds like a plan. But what will we tell everyone?

Jeff: I don't see any reason for a big announcement. I'll just make sure this all works out. That's the least I can do for all you've done and will do.

Skip: You know it's my pleasure. I'll just lie about you and get it done. (*He was only half-joking. I was no prize.*)

Jeff: I'll give you a background summary to keep you honest.

Skip: Three interviews a week, right?

Jeff: Yes, and I'll work around the clock if necessary to keep my end of the bargain.

Skip: Who's going to ask Agnes?

Jeff: Leave everything to me. I've got you covered.

Skip: I've got you covered too! I'll start making some calls.

I spent the next month helping Agnes learn what she already knew. I must have had 30 interviews. Skip kept me busy—I think he enjoyed his new mentor duties.

Something cosmic happened that day. I went from *desperation* to *inspiration*. What an empowering experience to just tell my boss what he already knew and to have more than his blessing—to have his guiding hand.

I interviewed with a clear conscience. Got a great gig. The next rung on an endless ladder that I've been climbing every day since.

As I said, I was no prize. But I had a gift (Do 1). Now I've given it to you. May it keep on giving for as long as you care to work.

That's my wish for *you*, genie!

Interview Insight

I've always made it my business to stay in close contact with former bosses. I learned from all of them, even though I didn't always like the lesson.

Many years later, I asked Skip why he had so much confidence in me. He answered, "You had integrity." He then told me something I'd never known.

I had a bad reference from my first career job boss. Skip ignored it and hired me anyway. I'd been interviewing under a cloud for years, but it never rained.

I called my old boss immediately and confronted him. He had a Ph.D., but that was the day he learned the other meaning of "professional reference." He became *really* professional.

I had every interviewer call him first. He was s-o-o-o helpful! That experience led to me writing the only book of its kind, *The Perfect Job Reference*.

Could integrity really be such a powerful component in getting hired? I found nothing about interview integrity anywhere. So I started studying it and using it as a basis for jobseekers to get interviews.

I started using *advancing adverbs* in instant interview training that would register indelibly with an offeror. I also mentioned integrity in resumes, cover letters, pitch letters, cold and warm calls, background summaries for references or referrers, and anywhere else for jobseekers.

Here are the dozen advancing adverbs you should look at, meditate on (Do 42), and live by every day.

competently

consistently

credibly

dependably

faithfully

fully

honestly

(continued)

honorably

immediately

reliably

responsibly

totally

These say, "Trust me"—not in the vernacular, but in the *viscera*. They say, "This is who I am. This is how I do things. So what I've done and where I've done it doesn't matter."

When you speak, let him hear, "He delivers!"

Do 44: Indemnifying an Offeror for Your Instant Dream Job

How about just going for the job you want? *Banzai!*

There's a secret way to do it (until now). It's called *indemnification*. Sounds so legal, huh? That's what we want. Something that shows sophistication. Seriousness. Supersense.

But you have to do your homework first.

Before you begin, google the business and print out any historical, philosophical, product, financial, and future plan information to study. Then google its product or service to find out its two fiercest competitors. Print out their information too. Study it and write down practical ways you can boom the biz.

Call the palace and ask the guard if the king of umbrellas is holding court. If not, when? Anonymously. Get a yes or a later time and you're almost there.

Then dress up. Your best. No perfume or cologne. (You showered, right?) Take a briefcase if you have one or can borrow one. Black with gold trim preferred. Pack it with your business cards (Do 1), a gold pen, your resume (Do 5), and a one-page indemnification agreement. I'll give you the template shortly.

You're off to see Mr. Mucho Macho Medicine Man. Bearing gifts. You and your business card.

If your junglejeep is a little wrecked, park its chassis out in the thicket. No need to blow your cover.

March your fine frame right up to that gate. Look the guard right in the bloodshot eye, smile, hand him your business card, and say, "I'm here to see Oscar the Offeror." (But use his real name.)

The guard thinks: "Hmmmm. Do I really want to hassle this important-looking person? But I've got to ask." Then he says his best professional phrase: "Do you have an appointment?"

Your response here is critical. You don't break eye contact. Continue smiling and say, "I'm here from out of town and will be leaving tonight. Just tell Oscar I'm here and wanted to stop by and tell him about what's happening at Competitor A and Competitor B."

The rest varies, but the result doesn't.

So there you are—nose-to-nose with Oscar. Much shorter than you pictured him.

You drop a Magic Four Hello (Do 1) on him.

Then it's Oscar and you.

Oscar: Do I know you?

You: Yes, but only in your dreams.

Oscar: What? Are you trying to sell me something? I thought you were from our external espionage—I mean new product research—group!

You: I'm sorry for any misunderstanding. I wanted to talk to you about Competitor A's and Competitor B's plans to move into the umbrella field. You risk losing the edge unless a few things are done.

Oscar: I already know about that. We've got our ways. But how do you know this?

You: I keep my head up. (*An instant winner's phrase, and not just to use with an umbrella mogul. Use it well.*)

Oscar: What are you proposing?

You: To give you a week of my services for a fixed, refundable fee.

Oscar: You mean like a consultant? We've tried that before and wasted our money. They told us to just fire everyone. We already knew that.

You: That's why I didn't suggest being a consultant. I don't want to *consult*. I want to *do*. There's a big difference between advising and assisting. (*Use that verbatim!*) I'll indemnify you against any loss you incur up to the amount of my fee.

Oscar: Let me get this straight. You're so sure you'll add value that you're willing to pay us back whatever we pay you?

You: Yes. But you've got to assign a project to me so you can see my capability. We'll meet at the end of the week and decide if this will work with me as an employee.

Oscar (*checking his wallet*): How much are we talking about?

You: Whatever you think is fair. At the end of the week, we'll talk. I
   brought an agreement for you to sign.
Oscar: Let's see it—I might have to run it by our lawyers.
You: It's not a major buying decision. Here it is.

Okay, now here is the template for your one-page document.

Worksheet

I, Oscar the Offeror ("Oscar"), on behalf of Worryworks LLC
("Worryworks"), hereby agree to pay Cleve R. Clever ("Cleve") the
amount of $ _____ on or before _____ (date). In exchange,
Cleve will provide services to Worryworks from _____(date) to
_____ (date) as an independent contractor. Said services shall
be on a project basis as requested by Oscar.

Cleve shall perform said services from home and shall spend
whatever time and effort he deems necessary at his sole discretion. Cleve
shall not hold himself out as an employee of Worryworks.

Cleve shall be solely responsible for any payment of taxes of any
services rendered to Worryworks. This includes but is not limited to federal
and state income taxes.

Cleve shall not use, disclose, or retain any confidential information
he receives in conjunction with the services provided to Worryworks. All
documents received from Worryworks shall be returned by Cleve on the
date the services cease.

Cleve shall indemnify and hold Worryworks harmless from any amount
up to the amount paid to him by Worryworks.

Oscar shall determine at his sole discretion the amount, if any, Cleve is
to repay. The request from Oscar to Cleve may be oral or written but must
be made within five business days after Cleve's services cease.

Cleve shall repay the amount to Oscar within five business days after
the request therefor.

Oscar and Cleve enter into this independent contractor agreement
to determine whether hiring Cleve as an employee after the week of
services would be in their mutual interest. Oscar shall decide this at his sole
discretion.

_____ (date)

_____

Oscar the Offeror, Principal
Worryworks LLC

_____

Cleve R. Clever

Before you use this little device, look in your local *Yellow Pages* under "Attorneys—Employment Law." Some advertise an initial free phone consultation. Call one or two and read the agreement to them slowly. If they suggest any changes, make them. Use the template as a guide.

We're not writing a formal release indemnification, a hold-harmless agreement, or an independent contractor agreement. Oscar is going to pay you a small amount of money. You're only presenting the agreement to get his attention and impress him.

When you thank the local lawyer, please tell her to send me a business card. I appreciate her helping me to help you help yourself.

Don't accept a postdated check, and don't agree to payment after you perform the services. You want to strike while the iron is hot.

Get your commitment *instantly*. It's now or never. (His love won't wait.)

Now let's get back to that conversation with Oscar. You've handed him that one-page agreement (the more pages, the less marketability).

You said absolutely nothing while he read it, and now the Great Offeror speaks:

Oscar: You've thought of everything! Where did you get such initiative? Where did you learn to write so well?

You: Just an instant inspiration, I guess. (*Private joke*)

Oscar: Why don't you work on rewriting our employee handbook? That thing reads like the back of my Rolls mechanic's bill! Here's one. (*Hands you the handbook.*) See what I mean?

You: I'll need to study it. Then I'll do as much as possible in a week. May I call you if I need more information?

Oscar: I'll leave instructions with our HR department to get you whatever you need. How much are we going to pay you?

You: This isn't a one-week project, and I'm only doing it so that you can see my capability. So you decide.

Oscar: Okay, Cleve. You talked me into it. You've got to be worth twice the amount my mechanic charged to fix the axle on our flex-stretch limo. There. I've written in the amount and signed the agreement. Are you going to sign it?

You: Okay. Oh, you forgot to fill in the dates.

Oscar (*filling in the dates*): You aren't afraid of me, are you?

You (*smiling with eye contact*): Yes, I am. Show me the money.

Oscar: Go up to accounting on the second floor. Have Bertha call me. We'll issue a check.

You: Fine. I'll make a copy of the agreement, sign it, and leave it with Bertha for your records. I'll have to fill out a W-9 form for the IRS. How about a new-hire packet too? I want to see how good a job I should do.

Oscar (*laughing*): You're going to cost me my reputation. They call me "Oscar the Grouch" when I'm not looking.

You: I can't imagine why. They'll probably call me "Cleve the Clown!"

Oscar: We should make a great pair!

You: Seriously, I really appreciate this opportunity. You won't be sorry.

Oscar: I didn't build this empire by misjudging people. You've got spunk, and it's a rare commodity these days.

You: Thank you. I won't let you down. Shall we meet next week at this time?

Oscar: I'll tell you what—I'll leave your name with Teddy the Terminator at the front gate. Go straight to HR, and we'll put you to work.

You: Now, that's what *I'm* talkin' 'bout!

Oscar: What did you say?

You: I was just saying, "How about that?"

Oscar: Have you ever ridden in a Rolls?

You: No, sir.

Oscar: Well, let's take a test drive. Meet me down by the heliport when you're finished with Bertha.

Be sure to fill out that IRS W-9 form before you start, get a check for payment in full up front, and remind Bertha to send you a 1099 form by January 31.

You did it!

There's another way to do this deed without using the indemnification and independent contractor arrangement:

Call a local temp service and explain you'd just like them to payroll you for a week. If Worryworks is already a client, this is easy. They might even tell you who services it. If not, you can help them sign up this new account.

Temp service people are flexible, creative, caring individuals who work on razor-thin margins. They're among the nicest people on the placement planet. So be grateful because payrolling one person for a week will never pay for itself.

You simply tell Oscar that Worryworks can pay the temp service the fee since you're its employee. Then you sign up with the service as a W-2 employee, they pay you what they agreed, and you go to work.

I don't recommend going the payrolling route because you don't want a temp assignment. It's too easy for Worryworks to simply keep you there on that basis.

Your instant power was demonstrated in the dialogue with Oscar. *You* were in control throughout. The Oscars of this world want people like that.

Being asked to do the employee handbook was a gigantic gift, even though you're a chemical engineer. It gives you a reason to learn all about the company, meet senior management, and learn the standard operating procedures like nobody else.

You're inside Worryworks, and really inside Oscar's head. Their worries are over—and so are yours.

Don't stop instant interviewing. Do the employee handbook in the evenings and catch up on your sleep another time. Keeping up your 16-a-day pace will keep your confidence up. And your options open.

Indemnification. If you can pronounce it, *go for it!*

Do 45: Networking Out at the Jobgym

Intense instant interviewing goes on at jobgyms!

You just have to know which are the jobgyms and when to networkout.

During the two years we were developing the basic genie technique (Do 1), I visited almost 30 gyms in Southern California. (I belong to one of the large chains.) I went from 5 A.M. through midnight depending on where my research led. I've logged well over 6,000 visits in 17 years.

I even instant interviewed at an independent gym while we were on vacation.

Run in place to warm up for a minute while I give you an:

Interview Insight

I went to the gym, walked up to the front desk, turned over an aerobics schedule, took my pen out of my left front pocket, and headed the page "Weekender Workout Welcome." Then I wrote down the deal I wanted (an annual prepay to use the gym periodically). Next, I laid a Magic Four Hello (Do 1) on the manager and showed him my offer. He looked at it, asked me for ID, and offered me a free smoothie of my choice to seal the deal.

You *know* I Magic Foured that goodbye with a smile!

A month or so later, it was advertised as a special to weekenders.

This technique was learned by slaving over a hot counsel table in court. Instead of jivin' with the judge, I would print out a Proposed Order in advance.

The judge glances, crosses out the word *Proposed*, and signs it.

Give an offeror a reason to offer, and he'll offer.

Okay, you look rested now. Let me check your pulse. . . . Good! You're ready for the heavy lifting.

Choose an Upscale Gym in a Large Chain

I'm thankful every day as I warm up walking to mine. (It really feels like mine. Nobody else in our 'hood uses it. Just like you'll start seeing all those inactive interviewers around you.)

It's so valuable that the price of our homes should be higher.

You need to find an upscale jobgym like mine that's used by executives.

Unlike choosing a Bigbucks for coffeeors (Do 74), find one that's convenient.

Look for a full-service gym with quality equipment, well maintained, a steam room, a sauna, a pool, and a complete class schedule (aerobics, yoga, stretching, spinning), a nutrition store, a juice bar, and workout accessories.

The place should be very active—teeming with upbeat staffers, trainers, and members. A popular gym has very distinct demographic waves from opening to closing, but it's always busy. You want to see *bodies!*

The lightweight strip-mall franchises serve largely crash dieters and retirees. If you see treadmills and free weights you could use at home with no shower facilities, see yourself out.

Take Advantage of the Free Trial Period

In the Interview Insight I showed you how I wrote my own deal with that independent gym.

You can do the same with the large chains.

Initially, always accept the free trial. The commissioned salespeople use that to get you in, but hate it because you discover it's a lot of work. So there's always some today-only special. They're high energy and frequently high pressure, so be very slow to sign up.

The deal you get locks you into a term, and you won't be able to lower the payments. A long-term contract gives you the best monthly rate.

There's a reason why even the specials are highly negotiable. Gyms have whopping fixed overhead. It costs them the same to maintain the place whether you're a member or not. The machines, the wet areas, the classes, the maintenance, the staff needed for service, safety, and security—it's all locked in.

Only a small part of the labor costs, utility costs, and disposable costs are variable.

Signing up new members while they're hot to trot is the only way to pay the overhead. So few people stick with a fitness program that new members are the primary source of revenue.

Recognize that you're in the catbird seat. Besides, you still need to find out if this is the right place for intense instanting.

When you do sign up, be sure to get privileges in all of the chain's gyms every day. You want flexibility to go wherever whenever as long as you're instanting about the countryside.

Go in at 7 A.M. and Leave at 9 A.M. Monday through Friday

Arriving at 7 A.M. sharp gives you two hours to networkout and then get out.

Right around 7 A.M. to 9 A.M. is when mentally fit execs are at the gym. After that, students, homemakers, bodybuilders, seniors, and all forms of unemployed persons sign in. Afternoons into dinner and beyond are 9-to-5ers with no offeror potential.

Avoid the classes. They constrain your time, and you can't instant interview in a class environment. Taking one or two members aside is just not a good use of this prime time.

Getting out at 9 A.M. has you pumped for a day of instant success.

I go seven days a week. There is every excuse in the workout world for not exercising every day. "Muscles need time to rest." How very clinical!

Start out slowly. You're there to interview and live longer.

Stick with it a month, and you'll love how you look and feel.

Working out regularly has the *flywheel effect*. This means your metabolism is revved up, so your increased energy and fatburning continue 24/7.

Truly successful people don't have to be told the value of *daily* no-nonsense physical exertion. Call it exercise, but it's exertion, and it keeps them sharp.

That's why every business hotel has a fitness center. If it doesn't, you don't want to check in (Do 60).

Stagger the Location of Your Locker

The locker room is an instant interview temple, but you need to sit in different pews.

After a few visits you'll see why. Members are territorial. Same faces. Same places.

You can't instant if you see the same person over and over. You can just become workout buddies. (That's *another* book you don't need. Do it alone or it doesn't get done.)

Bring a Small Purse

You'll carry this throughout your workout, so get a black one about 4 by 6 inches (canvas or leather) with a hand strap.

Pack it with a pen, 15 of your business cards, and a small spiral notebook (no register printers with paper around—Do 65). That little notebook will be worth an interview per page.

Head for the Free Weights and Resistance Machines

You're there to instantly interview. That's not possible on a treadmill or spinning bike. You're sitting alone for a long period.

Aerobic activity is important, but not for getting hired. The free weights and resistance machines are short-duration, and there's lots of interaction.

There are two ways to approach someone. The more effective way is to identify an offeror, then go over to where he's exercising and start writing in the notebook. He'll say, "Keeping track of your progress?"

You'll say, "I shore *am!* Howdy, podnuh! Whadya want done back at the ranch?" (Say it like a dude—a b-a-d dude.)

The other way is to go up to some businesslooking thirtysomething or older and say, "How do you use this one? How long have you been working out here? You're a regular here, aren't you? Can I work out with you?"

Then it's genie time, from Magic Four to Magic Four (Do 1).

There are very clear unwritten rules in a gym. You smile. You're courteous. You're all business. You don't gawk at the beauties. You don't point and laugh when someone's something pops out.

We have our rules too. We rotate our workout areas. We get two instants there. One following "huff" and one following "puff."

Then we . . .

Head for the Steam Room or Sauna

The steam room is the optimum place to instantly nail a mega-offeror.

When the steam starts, the privacy begins. You just sweat out your interviewin' pores together and offers shoot like the steam.

I remember doing a genie routine in so many saunas during that two-year beta test. It was "Poof, here's my steam—I'm your genie" (Do 1). By the time we'd dry off, we'd be trading soggy business cards and carrying on like Bert and Ernie.

There's just nothing like eyeing some icon in his birthday suit to give you a sense of sameness.

Get Out by 9 A.M. for Sure

You've got interviews left to instant, so head for the offerors outside.

Energized, ahead of the count—it's a brand new day with you in it!

Take the Magic Potion

Take the Magic Potion (Do 2) after your workout. It's F-U-E-L to *Find Unlimited Employment Leads* (Do 1).

Make Many Friends among the Morning Crew

The gym staff and the personal trainers know everyone.

They sign up the execs, see them every day, and must be vigilant. Their pay is far less than it should be for the safety, security, and member demands they have.

Let them know you want to meet successful execs. Give them your cards. If they're like the staff and trainers in the 30 or so jobgyms I have visited, they'll feel very good helping you.

Stay away from chatty members—many are there for the sole purpose of exercising their gums. They'll just slow you down. We have some that have been going to our gym for 40 years.

The staff tells me whenever a new exec is signed up at my gym. They like members to be friendly. It's good for business.

Visit Jobgyms While You're on the Road Instanting

Since you joined a jobgym that's part of a chain, get a list of locations and phone numbers.

During the beta test, I'd pick a jobgym before I left the house. Then I'd call and ask what office buildings, industrial parks, and shopping centers were nearby. Next, I'd get the hours and directions. Then zoom out the door and on the freeway ready to interview as soon as I got out of the car.

Networking out at the jobgym means intensive interviewing *instantly!*

Do 46: Renewing Acquaintances Instantly

Friends, former teachers, former supervisors, and former coworkers!

These and other acquaintances we'll discuss are right there—just below the surface—to more than double your interviews instantly. First, it's *who they know*. That doubles your opportunity. Then, it's *what they know*. Some manager who just quit, a new client who needs help, an office that's looking for a supervisor.

You always start with a phone call. Break the ice if it's been awhile. Smash the ice if it's been longer. Those cold calls are redhotter than you think.

Let's look at the unique advantages of each type of acquaintance.

Friends

The working ones have knowledge of job openings, and more importantly, potential ones.

However, they may not know about being eligible for an employee referral fee. Mention the possibility and encourage them to check it out.

So helping you with an interview may go even beyond friendship.

Besides, it's fun to work with friends.

Former Teachers

Make a list of your former teachers. You'll surprise yourself, because there are dozens.

It makes no difference whether the teacher liked you, whether you were a good student, or even whether the teacher *remembers* you!

Any teacher you can locate (start at the school or college) is likely to be flattered that you asked. One of the great rewards of teaching is to see your students succeed. Very few students stay in touch with former teachers, but the teachers think of them constantly.

There's a natural yearning to maintain the relationship and continue to nurture.

So even if you didn't like the teacher, your secret's safe with me. He'll still refer you and follow up on that referral. Neither he nor the offeror will ever know.

Students who keep in touch with former teachers will interview you when asked.

Count on it.

Former Supervisors

List at least two from every past job.

You already know that I consider former supervisors a precious lifetime interviewgetting necessity (Do 17).

Don't tell me about how they didn't know what they were doing. I'll tell you that's the definition! I don't even care if you were *fired*.

Former supervisors know of current openings, instant interviewing opportunities, and also qualify for bounties if you're hired.

You may be surprised at the reaction when you call them too. In fact, he might ask you to interview for *his* department. It happens often.

Former Co-workers

List them too. There should be many. Preferably ones with connections and ones you liked (in that order).

There's a unique opportunity with former co-workers that inactive interviewers overlook.

It's the big challenge:

I challenge you to get me as many referrals to interviews as I get for you.

Then when you meet (I discuss that conversation shortly), show her a copy of *Instant Interviews*. That's the only way she'll be able to compete.

Other Acquaintances

List anyone else you know, from former classmates to the person who runs a local restaurant. Give them each 20 or so of your callback cards (Do 14).

If possible, meet in person. It's too easy for these otherwise doing-something-else people to procrastinate and forget. The probability of them replying to phone messages, e-mails, or letters is low. The probability of them picking up the phone is high—so be persistent. One call every other day usually gets them within a week.

So if local, arrange to meet informally over coffee or lunch. Ideally while you're out interviewing anyway (Do 1). Bring an extra copy of your resume and at least 20 of your callback cards to the meeting.

Here's a former co-worker conversation so you can feel the rhythm.

Ann: How have you been?

You: Doing well! I'm excited about the interviews I've been getting and want to do more.

Ann: But I thought you loved working for the dress manufacturer. Weren't you doing inventory control or something?

You: Yes. It's been fine, but there's no way I can use my training in management there. I'm a people person and I deal with things all day long.

Ann: So you want me to help you?

You: That's half of what I want.

Ann: What's the other half?

You: I want to help you too. I've been reading this new book called *Instant Interviews* and it shows you how to explode your ability to get them. Here's my copy.

Ann (*looking at the book*): Now that you mention it, I'm getting tired of that 45-mile commute to work every day. I tried to carpool, then to work as a virtual employee, but it just didn't work out.

You: I just interviewed this morning for three jobs.

Ann: What? You had three employers call you?

You: Not at all. I just walked right in working from this little rulebook and got interviewed!

Ann: I'm in.

You: No, you're *instant!*

Ann: How do we get started?

You: Do you know anyone who's looking for someone with my management training?

Ann: Let's see—Hank, the new guy I'm dating, is desperate to fill a supervisor position right now. I'm not sure what it's about, but I know they're looking for people where he works.

You: Why don't we call him right now?

Ann: Okay, I'll use my cell phone.

You: Here's my resume. Take a look at my background so you'll be able to discuss it.

That's how you dig deep and wide into experience and a new career goal. When she calls Hank to tell him you'll be contacting him (or when he calls her to ask about you), chances are very good that she'll be repeating your words.

Reacquainting is a great way to do interviewing!

Do 47: Obtaining Publicity about Instant Availability

Publicity equals exposure equals interviews!

At no expense of time or money.

Are you part of a neighborhood watch group? Are you directing a school function? Did you recently receive an award? It's all publicity material, and it's all good.

You can frequently arrange to be interviewed by just calling the media. You can also write up a short piece about what you're doing and *why* (very important). That can be your e-mail to the contacts you receive by calling in first. It works for every TV station, radio station, and newspaper.

Be *absolutely sure* your phone and e-mail numbers will be mentioned. You do this by either *offering* your assistance or *asking* for assistance. Every one of the replies is a potential interview with someone who has a common interest.

A short Do to definitely *do*. So easy that unstants overlook it.

Try it and you'll see how fast you get replies from people who are like you.

That's what makes them want to interview you!

Do 48: Writing Letters to the Editor

Write in and ask for interviews!

We'll review some sentences to use in an instant.

I discovered the high profile of writing letters to the editor over two decades ago when our daughter Angel was in elementary school. One of her teachers was exceptional, and I thought it would be a nice way to thank her.

I was instantly inundated with calls from parents of classmates, school officials, and even the mayor of the city! All this without even having my phone number printed.

Since that time, I've suggested the idea to many jobseekers. The results were the same.

If you talk to the publishers of your local papers, you'll find that the most consistently, religiously read section is letters to the editor. Often even more than news items, since letters are topical and controversial. They often influence public opinion, so are must-reading for powerful, well-connected politicos (a dynamite interview source).

Letters to the editor almost always get printed too. That's because any censoring by the paper is very bad for business. Community newspapers survive as much on good will as on advertising revenue. Publishing the letters allows them to create controversy without taking a position. So few people write anything positive that the papers are instant about running the letters.

Short, focused letters have the best chance of being included. Be sure you have a single message. Almost everything else is backup.

There are two ways to use newspaper letter writing effectively.

Find an Offeror

Check the letters daily until you see one from a potential offeror. What's this person's stance? If it's serious and thoughtful, contact the paper or otherwise find out how to reach the offeror.

You'll have something to talk about before you talk about what you'll talk about! Say you agree and will be writing a short reply doing so. Ask to meet personally to review it with him. Don't say, "It's for our instant interview," but that'll be what it is (Do 1).

Be very busy, because these interviews can run over the 15-minute limit if you're not careful.

Discuss a Professional Subject

Try to connect the letter with what you've done or want to do. If you're in real estate or lending, discuss the housing market. Share trends, statistics, the latest information. Sound like the pro that you are.

Often hundreds of thousands of potential offerors will read it.

Letters to the editor are easy, fun, and highly effective to get quality interviews.

Rotate between offeror and professional subjects. One every three months.

Try it once and you'll see—instantly!

Do 49: Writing Articles or Columns

Freelance yourself! Why not? It's free.

If you write well (or know someone who does), write an article or a column for your local newspaper.

This works best with community newspapers, since they frequently need to fill up the space. Metropolitan newspapers have staff writers who are sometimes assigned, but if the article is good, it may be printed.

How do you do it? By actually being a *free*lancer. Just e-mail the article to the appropriate editor with a photo and bio. The content is whatever you think will attract offerors (Do 33). Just be sure to weave your contact information into the text for callbacks. *Give* something or *ask* for something.

We've been giving away answers to questions in articles, additional articles, and other items to readers of my columns for many years.

It's a way to generate instant interest . . .

. . . From people we call *offerors!*

Do 50: Using a Rent-a-Mentor

It's so slick that they don't even realize they're being "mented!"

Why wouldn't someone who knows he's older and thinks he's wiser *not* want to spend his life getting you interviews?

It happens.

But don't approach it that way. Don't *ask* him to be your mentor (Do 95).

Ask, *ask*, ASK—but just not that.

You can ask the rent-a-mentor questions in almost any environment.

You: Hi, Max!

Max: Hi, Tom. How've you been?

You: Great. I'm interviewing for a job right now, and am trying new approaches. *(Don't say 101.)*

Max: Good for you!

You: I sure hope I find a job like yours.

Max: Thanks for the compliment. But my job's got its challenges too.

You: I understand that. But I'd love something like it. How'd you hear about that job opening anyway? Did a recruiter call you?

Max: Nope. I was really unemployable. My sister-in-law told me about the job.

You: How'd you handle the interview? Was it tough?

Max: Not really. I researched the company online. Then, I just told them what they wanted to hear. I said, "If you want a 'yes-man,' I'm not your guy." The supervisor said, "We don't need any more yes-men around here." I was, they did. Things worked out well.

You: They actually hired you from that yes-man conversation?

Max: Of course! Nobody wants you to rock the boat, particularly if it's staying afloat!

You: Gee! *(Such a mentee word.)* How clever! *(Yet another one.)* Where did you ever learn things like that? *(I know it's not fair, but this mentor thing is for his own good.)*

Max: I know, I know. Just experience, I guess.

You: Do you have any tips about writing a resume?

Max: Make it brief and to the point. *(Whoop-de-doo!)*

You: Would you mind looking at mine with my cover letter?

Max: Well, okay. Just e-mail it to me.

You: Here's a copy of it. I'd love to see yours if you wouldn't mind. I'm open to any suggestions. Here's my business card with my e-mail address.

Max: Okay, I'll e-mail mine to you when I get back to the office. I see yours is one page. That's good. But I'd lose the pink paper. Take the bullets off and don't number over here.

You: That's great advice! Can I call on you for more as I'm trying to advance my career?

Max: Well, it looks like you're going to need my assistance, so why not?

You've just rented a mentor. Actually a long-term *leased* one! You did it by:

- Asking how he got the interview
- Asking how he prepared for the interview
- Asking for his resume

Ask, *ask,* ASK!
That's how you rent a mentor!

Do 51: Sampling the Sweets at Job Fairs

Most people leave job fairs with only a goodie bag filled with candy, cookies, and silly stuff. They're in a deeper funk than they were before they saw the ad. That's because they expected that the word *job* meant there were jobs, and the word *fair* meant they'd be considered fairly.

Not us. We expect you to be the *exception*. As in *exceptional*. Forget the little Paydays. (Really!) We want to find someone who's got the honeypot (both the honey and the pot).

So don your duds and let's go to the fair!

I want to get there an hour before it opens. That's when the management people are getting everything and everyone organized. It's hard to do instant interviews when everyone's grabbing the logo beanies or filling out apps at the table.

Good. Here we are. Plenty of spaces. Pull your junglejeep in right here. The fair's in that tent right next to the jobgym (Do 45).

The side entrance over here is open. Huh?—What's this? So many people in pilot's uniforms! They must have chosen a Halloween theme. That explains why there's so much candy.

No, that's not it. I just asked at the registration desk. They flew in from the mainland. They really *are* pilots. Attendance at these conflabs is in *their* job description. They are required to collect as much paper from the natives as they can, then they must pile it here and pile it there.

But there's a gray-haired lady in a Chanel suit with an LV briefcase over there. Look—she's the commander, ordering those pilots around. *H-e-l-l-l-o CEO!*

It's a Happy Health Plan booth. Here's what I want you to say. I'll be Edgar, and she'll be Charlie. (I know Charlie McCarthy's a boy, but it's a girl's name too. Besides, she's wearing a suit. We're just pretending, anyway.)

Edgar: Hi! I couldn't help but notice how impeccably you're dressed. I was wondering if I could give you a hand setting up your booth.

Charlie: Thank you. We're just waiting for the crew with the printed materials, so the booth is practically done.

Edgar: You look like an executive with Happy Health Plan.

Charlie: That's right. It's a happy day at Happy!

Edgar: I've been amazed by your success in attracting the large corporations to Happy. What's your secret?

Charlie: It all starts with our people. We pump laughing gas into our air handling system, so everyone smiles. It's contagious and incurable.

Edgar: I read about that. It's such a healthy idea. But I've studied your history, and you also have the best medical coverage for large businesses.

Charlie: That's right. I'm impressed with your knowledge! I was originally with Smile Medical Plan and learned the business there.

Edgar: Well, I'm honored to meet you! My name is Edgar Bergen. (Bingo! Magic Four Hello [Do 1] quick! Out with the right hand.)

Charlie: I'm Charlie McCarthy, Edgar. I'm the CEO of Happy Health.

Edgar: I'd never have guessed you're so, so . . . approachable!

Charlie: Why, thank you, Edgar! What kind of work do you do?

Edgar: Well, right now, I'm an independent contractor in the Happy Health brochure distribution business. Other times I'm a service representative for Tower Manufacturing.

Charlie: And what do you service?

Edgar: It's actually *who*. I visit our distributors and explain how to install custom bearings on racing bikes before they deliver them. Tower is a medium-sized bearing manufacturer located in three eastern states. Our corporate office and factory are here.

Charlie: How long have you been with Tower, Edgar?

Edgar: Well, Ms. McCarthy . . .

Charlie: Please, call me "Charlie."

Edgar: Okay, Charlie. I've been there four years, and I'm bumping my head on the ceiling.

Charlie: Why is that?

Edgar: I guess it's because I was so dedicated to the success of our distributor network that I trained the team too well. I've outgrown Tower because it can only sell so many custom bearings. With the system I developed, I could easily service ten times as many distributors. I'm a key employee at Tower and really enjoy the people I work with. I'm just someone who really wants to make a difference where I work. To increase the bottom line and make every day more successful than the day before. I've been fortunate to meet or exceed every goal we've made.

Charlie: Edgar, you're the kind of person we need at Happy. We're in a service business too. Success is all about serving others, don't you think?

Edgar: That's one of my favorite sayings. I say, "Service is the way to succeed."

Charlie: Oh, there's my driver over there. I'm late for a videoconference. Listen, Edgar, how can I get in touch with you?

Edgar (*reaching left hand in left front pocket genie-style*): Here's my card. I'd love to hear from you.

Charlie: Here's one of mine. My vice president of provider services, Donna Know, will be calling you within the next few days. I'm sure the compensation will be no problem. We pay in accordance with the value of our associates.

Edgar: Thanks! I'd like very much to talk with Donna. Would you mind if I help unpack and stack the brochures when they arrive? I'd like to learn as much as I can about your business.

Charlie: That's so thoughtful of you. Maybe I'll have you train our new hires too.

Edgar: Best wishes for success in the job fair!

Charlie: Thank you. It's already been a success!

Now see how easy it is? But it's not as spontaneous as it seems. I religiously followed the 10 Convention Commandments.

(1) I picked a mucketymuck. Very important. Otherwise you're just bangin' your gums on a non offeror's drums. So talk seriously only to those who can assist—and won't *resist*—hiring you.

That being done, (2) personal compliments are always the openers. Then, if there's the opportunity to (3) offer assistance, seize it.

Next, (4) demonstrate that you know and like the business. Ask (5) intelligent, nice questions that show you're interested. Then (6) introduce yourself with the Magic Four Hello (Do 1). Say just enough about yourself to demonstrate modesty and a compulsiveness to be the best at what you do. If you can paraphrase or even parrot the offeror's words, do it (like coupling "service" with "success").

Be sure to always (7) give and get a business card (or have the offeror write down her title and contact information).

(8) Nurse a commitment out of the offeror for the next contact (her choice). Then (9) show appreciation, and (10) do not be seen by the offeror again that day (unless an offer is extended on the spot).

Note that the entire instant interview took around five minutes. It could have been shorter or longer, depending on whatever. But never more than 15 minutes, or they've lost the urge.

In this case, the *offeror* left, so staying at the booth gave you time to hobnob with the pilots. Always with a smile, compliments, and offers to assist. No mention of the CEO or the conversation. You don't know the politics, and every business has them. Listen well to the company chatter, but don't react to anything negative. Max another 15 minutes.

Good—the CEO's still over there. Now get going. I'll be over here.

The offeror didn't ask for a resume, so why ruin a good thing? It doesn't get any better than what just happened.

You never wander around the fair where the offeror can see you, and you take as much company information as you can carry. Now, whenever Barbra Streisand sings "Have I Stayed Too Long at the Fair?" you'll be able to shout back the answer.

Great—now the CEO's over there checking out the Happy Health Halvah.

I'm going to find some Abbazabbas. Meet me at the junglejeep in 20 minutes or I come back to this costume party wearing my Streisand wig and singing falsetto.

Go get CEOed!

Do 52: Writing the Instant Bio

The instant bio (IB) gets interviews on contact!

It also sells your written words—articles, columns, even books. It can be used any time a publication requests information about you.

Friendlier and less formal than a resume, the IB hits only the highlights of your career.

An IB is always written in the third person (*he* or *she*, not *I*). It's easier to talk about yourself that way.

It's also very short, less than one double-spaced page.

The heading should be your name centered and in bold font. The subhead should be the same, and it should read:

Biography

An IB is different from a press release (Do 53). Use your letterhead. That will take care of the contact information.

Don't include generic superlatives like "amazing," "talented," or anything that sounds like hyperbole. Deal with specifics, primarily *how many years* you've been a *whatever you are*. Include attributes and accomplishments.

Something like:

Joe Bio has been a (profession) for (number of years). His specialties include (two to three examples). He has been awarded the (most prestigious award), has reached the (highest professional accomplishment), and is the (title) at (name of business).

If you continue to refer to yourself, use your first name. When you're submitting to media, use your last name. That's AP (Associated Press) style. It's what most newspapers use, and it makes you look very smart.

The class in salsa dancing you're teaching would require a different bio from the one for your service club speech on how instant interviewing changed your life.

Once you write the IB, you'll start feeling more confident too. It's positive self-talk that's reinforced every time you read it.

Use it and you'll get instants in ways you didn't expect!

Do 53: Writing a Press Release

You'll read it again in the most exciting places!

There are times when you need more than an instant bio (Do 52). Those times are:

- When you're doing something newsworthy
- When the release is for a specific event

The press release is not just a general fact sheet. It's focused.

You send it to TV stations, radio stations, newspapers, and news-letters.

You can usually use your letterhead. However, if you want a third-party look, like it's from a publicity or press agent, print out a letter-head using only your initials. That makes you an exclusive agent for y-o-u.

Centered at the top, in caps:

PRESS RELEASE

Like your bio, your press release should be one page double-spaced. Unlike your bio, it needs a headline.

That's easy. Just consider your focus. A current speaking engagement? Your latest promotion or recent award? That's where you start.

Your headline, in bold, no period:

Tim Harland to Speak to Valley Chef Society
Leona Patterson to Coordinate Chamber Mixer

Then move on to your accomplishments. Here's how you might do that.

Mr. Harland has 10 years of experience working with some of the most highly rated chefs in Connecticut.

Leona has worked as an events coordinator for high-profile conventions in Dallas for five years.

Did you notice something here? Right there in the Leona release. *Events coordinator* is not upstyle (Events Coordinator) the way it would be in a resume. It's downstyle (events coordinator).

That's how publications like it. AP (Associated Press) style. To be sure, call the publication if you don't have a current issue to review.

Speak the language of the media you seek.

Include information about what you'll be doing. Refer to yourself in the third person (he or she). End with this simple statement:
FOR MORE INFORMATION, CONTACT:
Use your letterhead information even if it's at the top.
Finally, proofread the release. Read it aloud. Did you catch any typos? Does it sound the way you intended it to? Did you give it to someone literate to double-check spelling and grammar? (Do 5.)
Do your press release well, and publications might even publish it verbatim.
Great free publicity in the most exciting places!

Do 54: Crashing Parties at Hotels

Businesspeople staying at hotels are there to improve their bottom line and to relax. What better place to permit them to interview you?

Like all travelers, they are there to experience new things. Away from office pressures, they listen more attentively and focus on change. Clear heads, open minds.

So let's get it done!

Most cities have around a dozen properties where your presence with business cards and a pen are all that's needed to interview instantly. (Call-back cards for additional penetration too. Do 14). You just have to time visits to coincide with major events.

Call the hotel or meeting center and ask who'll be holding an event there. The larger events are on daily schedules given to the operators. Ask about where to park (free, if possible) or where guest parking can be validated. If you're not sure whether you want to attend, park in the short-term convenience (free) parking near the entrance and scope things out.

As long as you stay in the common and public areas (hallways, lobbies, restaurants, shopping malls, or vendor areas), hotel security won't care. The security guards are actually quite helpful if you act as if you belong there. You won't be acting, either.

Many events encourage the public to attend. They include jewelry, art, and antiques. Every participant has a table, and you can interview freely. Follow the job-fair techniques (Do 51).

Private parties require a little more creativity. Blend in and mingle, using the chamber of commerce method (Do 56).

It's fun to discover an offeror! Could it be that nice lady ahead of you at the appetizer table? Offer to hold her drink while she serves herself.

What about the guy with the wild shirt and tan? It's easy to picture him in a suit and even easier to approach him.

People aren't scary. You're only scared of them. Just approach and say something like, "Hi, have you been to the pool yet?" Anything that starts a conversation. ("They don't have a pool here" is a great reply.)

I'm in hotels a lot and have stealthily crashed every size and shape of convention, show, and party imaginable. Sometimes because I was curious, sometimes to buy a gift, and sometimes I just wanted an apple.

I'm loose. I don't care what people think. My internal compass guides me, not what *they* think. I know—and teach daily—that true success is a journey guided by an individual sense of right and wrong. There's no other way to be successful because nobody else can do it for you.

Can I help someone be better according to his own measure? Is what I'm helping him do better for those around him? Is he better off by having known me? Is my word my bond?

Those are the four points on my compass. Adopt them without excuses, exceptions, or explanations. You'll interview well. Others will sense you're genuine. They'll want your help naturally because they know you'll figure out a way when nobody else can.

You'll learn why a call is often a calling. You'll find something you can do so well that the world will beat a path to your door.

I share this with you so that you can have the internal peace and zest that I have.

Instant interviewing is really just projecting who you are through showing what you can do. Crashing a party because you're the guest of honor. Smashing a mold that wasn't yours in the first place.

Crash and smash before it's too late.

Do 55: Granting Celebrities an Interview

How'd you like to work for a movie star? A TV personality? A real estate mogul?

You're ready, and so are they. It's a kick!

I know many of these folks, since I've lived and practiced law in the Beverly Hills–Hollywood area for many years. More shop at Target and Ross than all the upscale stores combined.

The big secret is they're just like any other working warrior.

It's just that *we're* not. We go gaga and they go anywhere else.

When they're anywhere else with nobody else, they become the most receptive offerors of all. Businesspeople trying to meet a payroll in an uncertain marketplace.

Connecting with famous people is really easy if you study them first.

Ironically, they tend to be introverted and insecure, wary of strangers. These things are understandable. Fame is earned by drive. Drive is fueled by fear (usually of failure or loss. Do 1.). Privacy becomes a way of life because celebrity attracts false friends.

They aren't a laugh happier and they don't live a day longer.

The story of Elvis is repeated in the life of almost every superstar. They hate being so public. It's called solitary confinement in the worst prison imaginable. Life in the fishbowl is equivalent to waterboarding.

For this reason, you never want to contact them directly. That's why paparazzi are so dreaded. They shoot more than photos. They shoot water guns at the waterboarded. Contact them directly, and you'll get instantly *uninterviewed*.

As always, you're most effective in person, so pick a local celeb. Let's say it's an actor who stars in romance flicks.

Google the name and click on the web sites. This will instantly give you biographical information, movies made, TV specials done, fan club contacts, and ways to e-mail or write the star.

Then loiter at the supermarket checkstand or even a newsstand. You can take 10 minutes before anyone cares. Reading magazines standing up is a national pastime. In markets, you can sit on a box and take notes too. You can get a pen from the checkers if you're not out on your I.I. rounds. Paper is all around. If not, find an unused register and press the printer button. (I once did it, anyway.)

Of course, you can just buy the mag. But why? We're not talking about a trig textbook here. Just take a few notes about juicy items concerning the celeb.

The objective is to get hot gossip, good or bad, so you can use it as a hook to communicate with him.

Assume one of the celebs' homes is in your town. Call your local newspaper office. Ask for the reporter who covers town happenings. He has his fingers on the pulse of the community. The reporter is often a free-lancer, not a staff reporter. Try to get a cell number, since these folks are out and around for a living. (Great contacts, incidentally. Upbeat, very sharp, and with more contacts than an automatic dialer. Always frazzled, never dull.) Try to meet that person *now*.

Ask questions like:

Who are the celebs' friends? Acquaintances? (Take names, numbers, and e-mails.)

Where does the celeb eat, drink, hang out?

Where does the celeb work out?

Where does the celeb recreate? The local tennis courts? Ball field? Golf course?

Who cuts the celeb's hair? Where? When?

Then, make your daily genie appearances for instant interviews (Do 1) near the places the celeb goes. You can even stop in, pop an I.I., and just ask when the celeb usually comes in. Ask what the celeb likes and anything else they know about him. (Mere mortals acquainted with celebrities are eager to brag about what they know.)

Then, target your time to grant them an interview. Happen to show up. Drop your Magic Four Hello (Do 1) on that awesome person, who'll be in awe of you.

Then:

- Compliment with your knowledge
- Listen well
- Exchange your card for contact information
- Follow up

You can pretty much take anything in their inner circle. It's a position of power and excitement at any level.

Almost all celebs are basically the same. They live in certain areas, eat at certain places, marry certain people, raise their kids a certain way, and send them to certain schools. Oh, there are exceptions. Ask them and they'll tell you they're one. S-u-u-u-r-e.

Different fishbowl, same shelf. It's called *circumstances*. They got what they wished and worked hard for, along with what they didn't.

It'll be a rollercoaster ride since they're capricious and crazy. But they'll pay you well if you show them your stuff. And you'll never be bored.

Definitely a *kick!*

Do 56: Mixing and Matching at the Chamber Mixer

Chambers of commerce have been around a very long time. That's because they work.

The lifeblood of any chamber is its *networking*. Without the interaction among members, a chamber's newsletter, lobbying, and advertising wouldn't sustain a membership base.

Call your local chamber office and speak to the CEO (various names but only one chief). Ask away:

Who's looking for people?

What do they want?

What's their business?

Whom do I call?

Who's your favorite? Why?

Take notes. Then, "When's your next mixer?" (if he hasn't already invited you, and invited you again). And, "Would you please send me a chamber directory?"

You shouldn't have to pay for the mixer. That's why it's called an invitation and you're called a guest. If you can't get in any other way, volunteer to set up or something. But don't get behind a table giving out raffle tickets and name tags. You're there to jump into the I.I. Mixmaster.

Look around for a table with thirtysomethings or older. It's more likely to have someone who's not starting a new business or looking for work and barter deals.

That's where you'll sit to eat, but you always interview standing up one-on-one in a room. Everyone's listening to everyone else. That's why they're there.

Work the room for a few minutes. Look around for a person alone. Ideally, well-appointed and professional looking. Not very chatty, but very at ease.

Walk up and do a Magic Four Hello (Do 1) at arm's length. (Don't invade her space, just her mind.) The big thing now is keeping other mixers out of the mix while you're matching.

After the Magic Four, drop a "What business are you in?" on her. Basic mixer talk. You might also try dropping, "Gee, this sure looks like the flamingo farm at the zoo!" on her.

If she doesn't laugh, stand on one leg. (We can live with no laugh if she interviews well.) But let's say she laughs. You've moved from mix to match.

Say "I just overheard that you're running a good jewelry business." (It's a mixer, so you're listening. Everyone does at a mixer.) Say something like, "I'd like to share an idea with you. Can we step outside for a minute?" This is what is known in Sumo interviewing as the "Mix 2, Match 2, Mate" maneuver.

It's virtually impossible to interview when some yahoo in a cowboy hat is standing between you and an offeror eating a bowl of chili with a handful of Saltines. So you do-si-do (she leads—it makes her feel like she could be the boss) out into the hall.

If there are chairs side by side, sit. People in facing chairs are psychologically conveying "It's you against me." (Standing face to face—sans a cowboy in between—is fine.) People in chairs side by side convey, "It's you and me against the problem." You're just starting to mate, so anything but facing chairs, *sit*. Facing chairs, *stand*.

You found out she's in the jewelry manufacturing business. Forty-five employees and growing. Say: "I wanted to know what you thought about my reviewing your necklace inventory. I'm told I have an eye for fashion and enjoy designing jewelry. I wouldn't charge you or anything. It's just my passion, and you seem so dedicated to producing the best."

What's she going to say that won't make her look like a chambermaid?

Why is she there if not to build her business?

Whip out a card from your left pocket, then your pen (Do 1), and get her card. (She'll have one unless she left it inside while the junior high swing band was playing "Flamingo Serenade.")

Going back into the mix is okay for a few minutes, but now you can't stay. Forget the raffle. You didn't really need a fruit basket that badly anyway.

Getting instant interviews at a mixer is better than standing on one foot all night.

Thank her as you escort her back to the talkfest, shake hands, look her in the eye, smile, and say, "It was a pleasure meeting you! I'll call you next week." (Don't say anything about an appointment. The walls in there have ears.)

Then find your host (the CEO), give him a handshake, eyeball, smile, and thanks (Do 1). Then ask him if there's anyone special he'd like you to meet. "Yes," you stay and work the same routine; "No," you go pronto.

Then there's the chamber directory. Call the phone numbers only to find out when the member's in the office. Confirm the addresses so you can appear like that very magical genie you've become since Do 1!

Do 57: Learning to Play Ball from the Blue Crew

This Do is an interview incentive for you.

Relax for a minute and I'll tell you a story.

Bev and I recently celebrated our thirty-sixth anniversary. (I'm still working on it—second marriage and all.) Bev had never been to a baseball game, so I drove up to Dodger Stadium to get the best seats and scope out the place for the big day. (Advance sleuthing is optional for instant interviewers but mandatory for lifetime lovers.)

Calling or e-mailing the Dodgers is like calling or e-mailing any business these days. If you want to get anything done, I don't suggest it. Basic information (like office hours and directions), fine. But I didn't know any first or last names of execs, and certainly couldn't penetrate deep enough with a cell phone or laptop.

Phones are better for interrupting than interviewing. Don't try to phone an interview in. You've got to be there. Show up.

So I took down the office hours and directions and drove down to the stadium. I was surprised that on a weekday in the middle of the season, nobody was there looking for work.

I overheard the receptionist giving callers instructions on how to apply for a job either in person or online. So I asked her why nobody was applying in person. Her reply: "They just apply online, I guess, and we send them an automatic e-mail confirmation."

This is why opportunity is smashing down your door. Employers don't expect walk-ins because there aren't any. Jobseekers don't venture out.

Then a short, elderly man hobbled in wearing a Dodger uniform and cap, carrying a Dodger bag. He sat down next to me and we started talking. He spoke in broken English.

I got the whole nine innings. But the conversation was interrupted by him jumping up and calling out to passersby things like,

"Hey, Don! I followed your career. Would you please sign this ball for me?"

The players weren't in uniform. They were just walking by randomly.

That guy must have had a half-dozen balls in that bag. Then I went over to buy my tickets. As he was leaving, he showed me all the autographed balls!

I asked a few people how they got their jobs. One met someone informally at an electronics store. Another at a bar. Yet another at a sporting event.

I decided to validate my study and survey some important-looking people the night of the game. One was referred, then instantly interviewed with a manager, another was an HR walk-in and instantly interviewed with the first person she could find (using Dodgerspeak), a third was at a game and got creative by instantly interviewing someone apparently in charge of Dodger Dogs.

The people who work at Dodger Stadium are outstanding. Knowledgeable, courteous, and enjoyable to be around. How do they pick such winners? It's called common sense. These people showed initiative from the first pitch. *Interview* initiative. They instantly interviewed!

I met not a single person who applied online.

This experience reminded me of a summer job I had one year when I was still in college. I hired people at Universal Studios. We'd sit there all day adhering to our mechanical interview schedules.

Then we'd get a call from some exec and hire the person they met at a polo game. This happened so often that we'd keep one line open just to receive management calls.

I wish you could have been there, genie (Do 1). The disconnect is so obvious that everyone out there in Lalaland misses it.

If you don't step up to the plate, you can't hit the ball out of the park.

Take a lesson from the world champion Blue Crew.

Play ball!

Do 58: Promoting Interviews Using Postal Centers

New information about instant interviews goes on in private postal centers every day!

In this Do, I'll show you how to get that information. You must know the right places, find the right people, treat them right, and ask the right way.

Follow this formula.

Pick an Independent Postal Center

Almost all postal centers are either independently owned franchises or independent.

There's a big difference for interviewing lead purposes.

Franchises have detailed privacy procedures they must follow. Therefore, don't expect to learn of any box holders looking for help or expanding.

Independent postal centers are just the opposite. The owners are usually on the premises and have other businesses there. These businesses vary from dry cleaners in office buildings to storefront operations that do photocopying.

They see, hear, and talk to a large volume of people every day, and they know what mail comes in. From past-due notices to checks.

They gladly put customer flyers, brochures, and cards in all the boxes to help customers promote their businesses.

I had an independent for years. He'd call me up and say, "You've got an overnight package. Two checks came in. And this letter looks like it's from a new client."

I thought that was so comical. He said it like he had opened my mail. It never occurred to him that maybe I didn't want him to know what I was receiving!

He became a valuable partner.

I'll discuss how to do that shortly, but first . . .

Pick the Location Carefully

If you were here in Los Angeles, you'd want a postal center in Beverly Hills, Century City, or downtown.

The upscale addresses would be Rodeo Drive, Avenue of the Stars, or Wilshire Boulevard. That's where the rich, famous, and up-and-comers have their so-called offices.

Regardless of where they *really* have their businesses, these people understand the importance of a successful image.

So find a postal center that's convenient, but stay away from ones in residential and low-rent areas.

It doesn't have to be fancy or even clean. Look for flyers from box-holder businesses, a bulletin board with business cards, and an open atmosphere.

Establish Your Expectations

Bring a box (maybe 1,000) of your callback cards (Do 14) and your check-book. If possible, meet with the owner-operator personally.

If you can't, qualify the manager. How long has she been there? Does she plan to stay? What is her background? These are not personal questions. They're serious business ones.

Tell the person in charge about yourself. Let her know that you want the least expensive box but that you want it long-term and that you'll pay in advance.

This is very important. Most independent operators in high-rent areas have the box service to help pay their rent while they run another business.

Collecting monthly or even annually from box holders is a royal pain. Your full-payment offer will improve their cash flow and underscore your seriousness.

However, you want the lowest possible rate—and you want every single interview lead they hear about. Starting right now.

Tell her you'll call at whatever time she likes every day. You're interested in any interview leads more than your mail. You really need her help, and she can feel free to refer you to any box holders, other customers, business associates, or anyone else who can use an excellent employee.

Call the Postal Center Every Day

Just ask about whether you have any mail. If the attendant is busy, call back. You're not her only customer.

No need to drive her crazy about interview leads. She'll tell you because you're her favorite customer.

Unless you're really using it for mail delivery, personal visits can be once a week or so.

If the postal center is far away, you can arrange to have your mail forwarded too.

My guy used to deliver ones he thought were important on the way home!

Remember the Postal People at Holiday Time

Candy, cookies, perhaps a gift basket.

They provide a great service and deserve special treatment.

Show your appreciation. They'll call you with leads, pass out your cards, and run your very own interviewing sales office.

If you find the right postal center, you'll be getting quality instant interviews while you're out instantly interviewing.

Your very own personal recruiter "running with a most placeable candidate" (Do 26.)

Do 59: Targeting Interviews with the F-O-C-U-S Principle

I'm about to show you how to instantly target the interviews you want most. A method shared only with the I.I.'s I've helped.

Napoleon Hill was the first person to observe: "Whatever the mind can conceive and believe, it can achieve." It was in the most popular success book ever written, *Think and Grow Rich*.

Now, six decades later, I'm going to show you how to harness that great discovery. It's my lifelong secret to tapping into the power of human creativity. A mental thought process that effectively sequences thought into action.

Thoughts alone are stillborn. Action alone is "Ready, fire, aim!"

Presenting for the first time anywhere in print:

The F-O-C-U-S Principle

Each of the letters in the mnemonic *focus* stands for an element of the technique. They are:

Framing
Objectifying
Creating
Unleashing
Starting

This is how it works.

Framing

Framing is what happens when you get an idea.

Let's say you want to work as a research chemist for a pharmaceutical manufacturer. The thought is *a wish*: "I wish I could work as a research chemist for a pharmaceutical manufacturer."

It's one of thousands (actually tens of thousands) of abstract thoughts that aimlessly pass through your mind every day.

You start transforming those thoughts into action by *framing*. Be realistic but *optimistic*. In this case, just playing with your kid's chemistry set isn't enough experience (familiarity) to get the gig. But the chances are you have a lot more or you wouldn't have the wish.

In normal adults, the conscious mind only processes things it thinks are doable.

You just consciously force the framing by writing down on a piece of paper: "I am going to instantly interview as a research chemist for a pharmaceutical manufacturer."

That's really all there is to it.

Keep that piece of paper near where you do your relaxation exercises or self-hypnosis (Do 42). Look at that sentence just before you start.

Objectifying

Objectifying is a way of giving energy to the thought captured in the frame. It's the beginning of automatic goal-setting.

Google *pharmaceutical manufacturers* and your city.

Print out a list of all the ones you can find, along with their addresses, phone numbers, and specialties.

Keep the list but don't use it for a day. Give your mind a chance to complete the focusing cycle.

Creating

Creating is how that amazing computer between your ears connects the framed thought with the objective object.

In this case, interviewing with pharmaceutical manufacturers on the list. That computer of yours will try to do what it always tries to do—match. It scans, sorts, discards—scans, sorts, discards—24/7. Waking and sleeping.

You can see this clearly if you meditate (Do 42).

As if by magic, you'll watch a movie of yourself interviewing at some local pharmaceutical manufacturer. At first, it will be a very short preview. And after a few days, it becomes a full-length movie—an accomplished fact.

But there's mo' yet to our spelling spell . . .

Unleashing

Unleashing happens when you consciously decide to act on that matched mass.

Master motivator Tony Robbins calls this "unleashing the power within." We call it "instant interviewing."

You're now ready to take on the workingworld.

Your mind whirs. Whether you have all the ingredients left for the Magic Potion before you leave (Do 2). What to wear (something just like the offeror since you know—or can find out by an anonymous call—how she dresses). What she'll ask (get *The Complete Q&A Job Interview Book* by yours truly. No imitators-but-not-duplicators). How you'll answer (in the *Q&A Book* too). What *you'll* ask (Yep, there too).

And how you'll say, "When do I start?" (with no help from anyone).

Now you, the ingenious instant interviewer, get to . . .

Starting

Starting is not to be confused with "Starting to get started."

Starting to get started is what your basic inactive interviewer does. You see them behind every starting gate greeting the gatekeepers.

But you? YOU?

You're starting *instantly* and definitely *indefinitely!*

I could write an entire book on The F-O-C-U-S Principle, but it wouldn't get you any more instant interviews than what I just revealed.

If you want to target like a machine gun, look at the Framing and Objectifying pages before you meditate or self-hypnose (Do 42).

Targeting specific interviews is simple—just *focus* on them.

Do 60: Outerviewing There and Now

Outerviewing is interviewing away from home with your expenses paid by an offeror.

Picking a place you'd like to be, finding someone to invite you there, and instanting like a magical maniac on a mission.

You just have to get an outerview with the anchor offeror.

Let's say you want to live in Boston. You're in Dallas and don't have the money to make a scouting trip to the Boston area. You need to find an anchor offeror in Boston to host your coming-out party.

There are 10 steps to doing it.

Google the Area, then Contact the Local Newspaper and Chamber of Commerce

It might be a metropolitan newspaper or a suburban one. Type *newspaper* and the name of the city. Look for help wanted, advertising, and editorial department phone numbers.

Call the newspaper office and speak to a supervisor in each of these departments.

Google and call the local chamber too.

Tell the person you reach that you're looking to relocate to the area. Ask who they think would be a good contact for job interviewing.

Write down the business name, contact name and title, phone number, and e-mail address (if they know it) of each contact.

Google Each Business

You must do this step or you won't have the talking points you need to sell them on your knowledge and capabilities.

Print out a few pages of history, products, and future plans. Write in the margins how you can benefit the business. Nothing elaborate, just to shift your mind from idling to overdrive.

Write Down Your Talking Points

Print a form for yourself. Head it with the information from your newspaper or chamber calls: the business name, contact name, contact title, phone number, and e-mail address.

Now type these words on the left, with a line across the pages:

appointed _____

appraised _____

assessed _____

assisted _____

bargained _____

budgeted _____

built _____

coached _____

communicated _____

completed _____

conferred _____

consolidated _____

consulted _____

coordinated _____

corrected _____

designed _____

determined _____

directed _____

drafted _____

educated _____

employed _____

enlisted _____

explained _____

facilitated _____

finalized _____

found _____

(continued)

handled _____

hired _____

identified _____

influenced _____

instituted _____

instructed _____

interfaced _____

interviewed _____

led _____

maintained _____

managed _____

modernized _____

motivated _____

negotiated _____

organized _____

prepared _____

promoted _____

qualified _____

raised _____

refined _____

resolved _____

reviewed _____

revised _____

scheduled _____

selected _____

served _____

showed _____

succeeded _____

supervised _____

supported _____

systematized _____

taught _____

trained _____

Then think of a sentence that states an accomplishment of yours that directly relates to the specific business.

This is an *absolutely essential* exercise, since it will force your mind to do the matching I discussed with The F-O-C-U-S Principle (Do 59). When you do your relaxation or self-hypnosis exercises (Do 42), glancing at the talking points will indelibly fuse them into your delivery.

Now you're ready to make the outerview calls.

Rev Yourself up to Call Each Contact

There's concentrated power when you call from out of town honing in on a single person at a single business.

Before you call, play your most rockin' backbeat music. For me, it's always been Jerry Lee Lewis. If you know his story and ever listened to his boogie woogie piano playing, you know why. For you, it's any song that gets your juices flowing.

Then make that call.

This is a high-pressure "gotta-see-you" wham-bam hard sell.

Think of a reason to be crazed about working for the business. How about the climate for your health? Monetary health qualifies.

The awesome goods or services of the biz? You can't raise someone else above the level of your own enthusiasm. So it's enthuse or lose.

Your unique ability to contribute to the business? You have it. You know it. They don't. They want. They'll pay to get.

Then . . .

Use Your Talking Points

Try to mention as many as you can. Check them off as you talk. You can repeat, but cover the bases. Listen too. But this is one time you can do most of the talking.

Offer to Fly at the Lowest Fare, Any Time Day or Night, and Stay at a Budget Motel

The only requirements are there must be an *open return ticket* and the motel must have a *courtesy van* (Do 31), and preferably a *fitness center* (Do 45).

You'll submit your expenses for ground transportation and fast food. Later you can negotiate another day or two of lodging and meals.

If that doesn't work, then . . .

Offer to Sign an Employee Payback Agreement

Use the initials *EPA* so it sounds like something everyone uses. Say that if you're hired and you don't stay 90 days for any reason, you'll reimburse the business for your expenses.

Accept whatever terms are offered. This is not about the offeror. It's about *you*. Anything is better than what you've got.

If two or more offerors go for the idea, negotiate for an upgrade in the flight, lodging, and food.

Google Trade Associations for Members in the Area

Just type in *trade associations* and the kind of business (or the title of the job) you want and the city.

Call each of the members there. Let them know you'll be coming in for a scouting trip and want to meet. Ask them for their help. Let them help you just as you would family and friends (Do 17).

This will blow up your list of contacts and your self-confidence. You'll have friends waiting for your arrival.

Get Tons of Interviews Following the Guidelines for Interviewing while Attending Conventions

You do this from your motel room (Do 31).

If there's no courtesy shuttle, consider the expense a legitimate part of your ground transpo. It is.

Submit the Expenses

Airfare should be prepaid. When you interview with the paying offeror(s), pick up any required expense reimbursement forms.

Of course, save *all* receipts, copy and total them when you get home, then submit them.

Get outed. There's no expedition in the jobjungle more fun than all-expense-paid *outerviewing!*

Do 61: Uncovering the Office Building Underground Instantly

You don't find job postings on the building directories.

They're in the brains of the security guards and parking attendants. That underpaid, unappreciated underground who make the buildings safe and accessible.

This is an invisible interview intelligence network that unstant interviewers overlook.

When you know their cover, you can *uncover* them instantly!

Security Guards

Most uniformed guards are hired by a security service that contracts with the building management. If you pay attention to their uniforms, you'll see this readily on their emblems.

For security purposes, the guards are often rotated to different sites. Much like temporary employees (which some are), they develop a great knowledge of interviewing activity in the area.

Walking up to a guard and asking about job openings for large tenants isn't the way to find out. For one thing, uniformed guards are normally there to keep a high profile—to act tough as a deterrent. For another, they're usually being video recorded on their rounds by the cameras.

So the only question to ask is, "Where's the security office?"

Find out and go there.

Security Offices

You're now in the jobjungle war room.

There's usually a panel with split-screen, panoramic, and close-up monitors that track the common areas and sensitive spots. There are chairs for holding suspects, work schedules, extra uniforms, handcuffs, locked cabinets with security devices and firearms, first-aid items, and other police paraphernalia.

There's a sergeant or other CO ("commanding officer" and sometimes "closet offeror") in charge at the console. That's the person to know.

Walk in and introduce yourself with the Magic Four Hello (Do 1).

Tell the CO that you're looking for job interviews with businesses in the building.

Unlike a typical instant, this is not a private conversation. The security office is also a lounge. Guards report for duty there, clock in, clock out, eat, stretch, and talk.

There are only four subjects that security guards talk about constantly. (No, not that one.) In order of frequency, they're: (1) weirdness on their watch, (2) job openings, (3) other jobs they have, and (4) jobs they'd like to get. You don't hear a whole lot of talk about families or social lives because that's not professional. These are rent-a-cops, and they take their duties very seriously.

So when you give a CO your card, ask for his and actually show respect. He wants to earn his stripes. He does this by telling you what he knows about interviews, what he's heard about interviews from his lieutenants and officers, and what he thinks are likely places for interviews.

Depending on the amount of rotation on the schedules (and therefore familiarity with the tenants) the guards there might help with leads.

Ask for some paper, take your pen out of your left pocket and write down the names of tenants, floors, and suite numbers.

If there's one thing every private security guard can identify with, it's interviewing for a job. It would be hard to find one who hasn't done more than her share of them.

From every walk of life and with much footwear wear, these dedicated folks will dedicate themselves to helping you.

Leave 10 callback cards (Do 14), get their business cards, and go to whatever businesses in the building they suggest. Stop back in before you leave to smile, shake, and thank.

Call or visit that war room once a week.

Parking Attendants

You drive in, you drive out, you self-park, and hardly even notice the uniformed caretakers.

You couldn't know more about hiring trends, job openings, and interview possibilities if you knocked on every door in that big building every day.

From valet parking to detailing cars, these people earn extra money by knowing the VIPs—the *very interviewing persons*.

They're busy but approachable. You may be running after them as they get into a car or look for one, but it's worth doing.

Then if you don't see the office, ask where it is and go in. Give the attendant a callback card and a quick, "Thanks!"

The parking office might look very much like the security office, and the technique with the dispatcher is just like the one you use with the CO.

Office Lunch Counters

These are usually run by owner-operators who know everyone.

They're typically very friendly. Buying any item is all that's necessary to obtain high quality building offeror information.

Buy something small while you're on your weekly visit and ask a lot of questions.

Before or after your instants in any office building, these stops are must-sees for must-do's!

Do 62: Running the Routes with the Jobjungle Scouts

"Hey, y'all!"

That greeting was inspired by Food Network's Paula Deen. Her honorable mention is my honor.

Paula started The Bag Lady with $200 and the idea to deliver lunches to office buildings. One by one every workday. From those humble instant interviews, Paula's become synonymous with delicious Southern cooking.

Her personal transformation from the early shows is beyond description. Yours will be too. Smile—one foot in front of the other. Use Paula as your "roll" model.

Nobody knows the innards of office buildings like the hardworking people who wake up early, load up large, and push elevator buttons for a living. They're the modern-day jobjungle scouts. Heightened senses—flying below the radar. Savvy supersleuths with instant interview information every day.

Think of the incredible instantness of someone like Paula. Get up at the dawn of dawn, make your lunches, wrap, pack, sort, store, and do a hundred or so other things before you ever look in the mirror. Then out with a smile, a good memory, and off you go.

When you get back home, you go to your day job. Figuring out and ordering all the supplies and food you need for your fickle pickle friends. Then rushing in your order before the suppliers close.

Wouldn't you like to know someone like that? You do! I'm talkin' 'bout *you!* The classic profile of an I.I.

Someone who understands that interviews don't *happen* any more than sandwiches happen. You *make* interviews happen. You read a recipe (as you're doing this instant), you get the ingredients. You follow the recipe to the letter. It works. You work.

This is how to run the routes with these jobjungle scouts.

Google *office sandwich delivery cleveland* and you'll get 38,300 or so links. That's about average. You don't have to relo to Cleveland. Just go on a local scouting trip.

Then click on the web sites, write down the phone numbers, go over there, and instant interview! Many will allow you to design your own route. If so, pick areas where hiring is highest.

Do whatever you can to get a route. They're always looking for people who'll go the distance. Your Magic Potion will power you there (Do 2).

If food can't get you in every door and have you interviewing with every person in every lobby, every elevator, every hallway, and every office, start a route of your own. As a "mobile eating stopper." It's definitely one of those jobs of the future.

Of course, ask like a banshee for leads too. Scouts will have them in abundance.

Another less-voluminous way is to google the many roving suppliers who deliver to specialty markets. These deliver everything from tools at construction sites to surgical supplies at medical offices.

Law firms use attorney services that pick up and deliver daily. Accountants use tax processing services that do too. Many payroll services work like that. The list is infinite. The instant interviews are infinite.

Paula's autobiography is entitled, *It Ain't All About the Cookin'*. It sho' ain't.

Yours will be *It Ain't All About the Job*. And you're writing as you're reading.

Let's start it out with: "It ain't all about the job because there's *never* a 'job.' It's just you and the offeror."

Do you see the endless possibilities here?
A famished forest awaits.
Run to help run those routes!

Do 63: Banking Personal References Instantly

Think of this and the following Do as being two huge do-posit slips!
Because references properly selected are like *money in the bank*.
Let's write the slip.

Selecting the Right Personal References

With all the legal and business restrictions now limiting what a business can say about a former employee, personal references are far more important than before.

The interviewer receives an enthusiastic response that can't be equaled by professional references.

Each of your personal references should:

Formally consent to give a reference about you, have a different surname (even if related), and work in an office where she can receive calls during regular business hours without distraction. Someone who can discuss you knowledgeably, intelligently, and enthusiastically.

Begin by listing 30 options as possible. Then cut the list down to the top five.

Where do you get a list of 30? Personal friends. Casual acquaintances. Then, add business advisers such as your attorney, accountant, or banker. Maybe you've recently purchased a house—your real estate agent is a natural.

How about community leaders, members of your service club, or buddies at the gym? Are there teachers at your kids' school with whom you have a special rapport? Jot them down.

What characteristics do you need in each of your top five?

- A successful business or professional life
- A self-confident, outgoing personality
- Good verbal skills

Although personal references can be located anywhere, it helps if they're in the community where you're conducting your job search. You can leverage their favorable reputations.

In picking the top five from 30, choose those most likely to be receptive immediately, accessible, and properly positioned to help turn calls into instants. Personal references will be complimented that you think they're so important. You *know* it!

Try a script similar to the following between Betty, a jobseeker, and Harry, an attorney who lives in her neighborhood:

Betty: Harry, this is Betty Bono.

Harry: Hi, Betty. I've been meaning to call and ask you what you're using on your roses this year. They look great.

Betty: Why, thank you! I'll have to refer that question to the family gardener. Frank takes care of the yard.

Harry: I'd really like to know. I haven't had any luck with mine. What can I do for you?

Betty: Well, I just passed the CPA exam, and I want to make a career move now. It was convenient to work in town while the kids were young. But now I'm ready for a larger organization. I thought I'd target the insurance industry.

Harry: Sounds good. Congratulations on your certification. That was a lot of work. I wish I knew someone to recommend. I'm afraid I can't be much help.

Betty: Harry, you can be a big help. I'd like to use your name as a personal reference. We worked closely together on last year's school budget campaign. I was impressed by your energy, your effectiveness, and your ability to communicate. I trust your observations of me were equally good and that you wouldn't mind saying so to a prospective employer.

Harry: I'm honored to be asked! I couldn't have done all I did without your assistance with the numbers to support our arguments. Talk about analytical skill! The Board of Ed. is still talking about your accuracy!

Reassuring Reluctant Personal References

There may be some personal reference who says:
    I've never given a reference before.
    I'm not sure how to go about it.

I'm afraid I'll say something wrong.

To overcome these objections, reassure them that you're going to pro-vide them with a sample application, your resume, and a list of questions typically asked. Tell them you'll go over the key points that you want them to cover, and if they'll just review the materials and answer natu-rally, it will all be fine.

Express the importance of their help and how much you appreciate it. If they still seem hesitant, thank them and allow them to decline grace-fully. You want references with genuine enthusiasm. The last thing you need is for your future employer to sense that someone is doing this only as a favor to you.

Preparing Personal References

Your *personal references* need

- Your rest-you-may (Do 5)
- The reference summary
- The personal reference questions

The Reference Summary

For personal references, this summary is simply a one-page list describing your attributes and activities that (1) the reference can authenticate and (2) are relevant to your target job. Here's the summary that Betty Bono gave to Harry, her personal reference.

Name: Betty R. Bono
Phone No.: 555-555-5555
Fax: 555-555-5555
E-mail: bettybono@gotmail.com
Position Desired: Accountant for an Insurance Company
Attributes:

- Determination
- Accuracy
- Thoroughness

- Commitment
- Follow-through
- Energy
- Enthusiasm
- Competence
- Positive Attitude

Job-Related Skills:

- Compiled financial data and developed complete, accurate forecasts
- Presented concise, understandable financial reports for budget projections
- Demonstrated knowledge of accounting principles and procedures

You should prepare a similar summary to give to each of your references. Be sure your references understand and agree with its contents. Don't be shy about your attributes. Your references would rather have correct information on what to say than risk messing up.

As you review the summary for each reference, make sure that he understands:

- Your job search objectives
- Specifically what you want him or her to say in a reference call
- The proper tone of voice for maximum impact

If you're targeting more than one job, the reference should be given two or more summaries. Each should be clearly marked so your reference knows what to say to whom.

It's important that each reference have a slightly different summary, even though it means more work for you. Otherwise, they may all come out sounding exactly the same about you.

Canned responses won't get you the job; you need each reference to answer with the appearance of spontaneity, candor, and enthusiasm.

The Personal Reference Questions

Your personal references should be given a list of probable questions. Each should get two copies—one with suggested answers written by you, the other blank to let your references mesh your preferred answers with their own personal versions.

The answers should help refresh your references' recollections about the dates and details of your relationship and to make sure that what you say is verified by what they say.

Personal Reference Questionnaire

How long have you known _____?

How do you know _____?

What is your opinion of _____?

Does (he/she) get along well with others?

_____

Is (he/she) usually on time?

_____

Is (he/she) absent from work very often?

_____

Does (he/she) bring work home very often?

_____

Does (he/she) like (his/her) job?

_____

What are (his/her) primary attributes?

_____

What are (his/her) primary liabilities?

_____

Offer Assistance to Personal References

What is said to the reference checker is too important to be left unsaid by you. Even well-meaning references can reply inappropriately when they're unprepared.

You can help them handle the questions equally well. Let's take that last question about liabilities. Here are a few answers that can transform liabilities into assets.

> Well, the one liability that comes to mind is that Betty considers herself last. She's never too busy to help someone or volunteer for another position. She's one of those people who proves the truth

of the phrase "If you want it done, give it to a busy person." It's funny, though. Betty never seems to get ruffled about it all. She's organized, efficient, and goal-oriented. It seems the more she does, the happier she is.

Betty's liabilities? Oh, I guess you could say she's a workaholic. She's canceled our Saturday morning tennis game on several occasions because she wanted to work on her projects while the office was quiet. Completing her work has consistently been her top priority. She's very dedicated.

Always end the script about a liability or weakness by turning it into an attribute or strength.

Arrange for enough time to explain your objectives and show your references how they'll help you achieve them. Meet personally over a quiet lunch or dinner (your treat) and let them know how important this is to you. Give them your carefully prepared information, and review it in detail.

Resist the temptation to give in when a personal reference says: "Hey, I don't need your resume or any of this paperwork. Don't worry." Worry for an instant. Then explain that it's important to give them *facts* rather than just *opinions* (spins on facts) and *conclusions* (clusters of facts).

Debriefing Personal References

Ask your references to accept telephone calls or to return them immediately. Of course, you'll offer to pay any toll charges. Have them notify you of the details the moment they hang up. You need the feedback *now* so you can instantly impress in your next interview.

Using Personal References for Job Leads

Once references get involved with you, they feel as though they have a vested interest in your success.

Your background information can get this reference to see you in a new light. Previously a friend or acquaintance, now you are a professional with credentials. The reference may have contacts that can work in your favor to secure additional job leads.

You don't want to push your personal references too far, since they're doing you the great service of speaking on your behalf.

If you can work your way around to the subject, however, or if they say, "You know, after looking at your resume, I've got a friend you should talk to," then by all means follow up.

This is how personal references are turned into career cash.

That's your *first* huge do-posit slip!

Now we'll write the next one . . .

Do 64: Banking Professional References Instantly

Here's your other huge do-posit slip!

Because references properly selected and prepared are like *money in the bank*.

Now let's write this slip.

Selecting the Right Professional References

Stay away from using current supervisors.

Review your career history and current business contacts for the names of the most potent references.

Consider:

- Former supervisors at past employers
- Your boss's boss and other high-level executives at past employers who know your contributions
- Coworkers at present or past employers who also know your contributions
- Subordinates who can verify your management ability
- Colleagues who served with you on committees or task forces
- Members of trade associations or professional groups who like you
- Managers of support departments who assisted with your projects (finance, management information systems, communications, sales, marketing, market research, purchasing, or inventory control)
- Members of consulting firms and other vendors who worked with you

After you've assembled a comprehensive list, pick up the phone, smile, and begin calling them. Cross off all the people who greet you with

"Bob who?" Cut the call short if the person sounds unenthused. You want at least five professional references who are glad to hear from you, and whose words and *word skills* will help you land that job.

Your reference must mention attributes that get you hired. Say a job requires the ability to supervise. You roll out the five references who can attest to your managerial skills. Another job might require analytical skills. Contact the staff accountant from your last job. Call the professor who gave you an A.

Think ahead to all the possible attributes you need, and keep a list of references to backstop them.

This is how it goes:

You: Tom, good to hear your voice again. It's Karen Condito. Did you get the article I sent you last month on semiconductor research?

Tom: I sure did and I really appreciated it.

You: My pleasure. I wasn't sure if you subscribed to that journal. Anyway, I have another reason for calling. I'll only keep you a minute. I've decided to move on. The reorganization here has led to limited potential for advancement, so I've decided to look for a director position.

Tom: How can I help?

You: Since we worked together in the past, I'd be honored if you'd provide a professional reference. Your reputation in the industry should help verify my credentials. Will you assist me?

Tom: I'll do my best.

You (*Briefly mention the objective of your search and the businesses you're targeting. Then finish with*): I'll be sending you a couple of items that'll help refresh your memory of our work together, and I'll call you back once you've had a chance to scan them.

Tom: Good talking to you!

Preparing Professional References

Your phone calls should get you the top four to six colleagues from your past or present. Now, you're going to talk with them (if they're geographically distant), give them their scripts, and coach them into an award-winning performance.

Why bother? Because most of the time your references are anything but professional! They've been caught off guard or may not remember the highlights you'd like them to recall.

You need to give (or send) four items to each of them:

1. A sample completed application (You can either request one from any employer or buy a form from a stationery store.)
2. Your rest-you-may (Do 5)
3. Your reference summary (an example follows)
4. The professional reference questions

The Reference Summary

A reference summary is a brief, neatly typed one-page summary, using short headings, that reviews the facts that your reference will verify. Concentrate on traits, skills, and accomplishments that apply to the target job.

Be honest, but not modest. Few references will overstate your attributes; most will understate. So give them every word you want them to say, and they may actually develop some good words of their own. It's all in the preparation and careful prompting.

Name: Karen A. Condito
Phone: 555-555-5555
Fax: 555-555-5555
Email: karenacondito@gotmail.com
Former Title: National Sales Manager
Attributes:

- Effectiveness
- Goal orientation
- Motivational skills
- Reliablity
- Enthusiasm

Job-Related Skills:

- Supervised and motivated a field sales force that grew from 12 people to 20 during three-year tenure. Managed and led in-house support staff of six.

- Accomplished sales objectives by product, resulting in an average annual increase in sales of 30 percent, with an overall three-year cumulative increase of 120 percent.
- Installed computerized sales reporting system.
- Used customer feedback to help create five new products, which are consistently among the top sellers produced by the company.
- Established a sales incentive program that increased sales across the board, and more than doubled them in the two lowest performing territories.

Professional Reference Questions

The final item to give each professional reference is two versions of a list of questions they are likely to be asked in a phone call. The first will have suggested answers completed by you to help them remember.

Perhaps they never knew you that well when you worked together or the specifics of your job responsibilities. Then give each of your references a copy of a blank list, so they can use the completed one to fill in the blanks in their own words.

Professional Reference Questionnaire
How long have you known _____?
How do you know _____?
When was he/she hired _____?
When did he/she leave _____?
What was his/her salary when he/she left _____?
Did you work with him/her directly _____?
Was he/she absent from work very often _____?
Did his/her personal life ever interfere with his/her work _____?
What were his/her titles _____?
Did he/she cooperate with supervisors _____?
Did he/she cooperate with coworkers _____?
Did he/she take work home very often _____?
What are his/her primary attributes _____?
What are his/her primary liabilities _____?
Is he/she eligible for rehire _____?
Can you confirm the information he/she has given us _____?

Overcoming Sensitive Areas and Objections

Review any sensitive areas with the reference. Assume you were going through a divorce when you worked with your reference and he remembers that it interfered with your work. Don't leave his or her response to chance. Say something such as:

> I was going through some rough times during that period. I wouldn't have made it without you. How will you answer questions about my productivity?

Confront a ghost and it vanishes. Fear it, and it haunts your hunt. People don't tell the truth, even if they try. People tell their *perception* of the truth.

If a reference objects to something you wrote in your materials or remembers it differently, listen and make changes. It's rare, but you might hear:

Reference: I don't know about this computerized sales reporting system you say you installed. I know you were involved, but the controller was really responsible. Could we just say you participated in choosing and installing a system?

You (*graciously*): Of course. It's more accurate, and sounds good. That's fine.

When your review is finished, summarize the key points, and tell your references you'll notify them who'll be calling, when, and why.

Notifying Professional References

If you know that you're getting close to a serious offer, call your references and alert them. Make sure they have your materials on their desks.

Communicate with your references throughout your job search. Don't call without a reason, but make brief, time-conscious calls to inquire if they received expected calls and how the conversations went.

Press gently but firmly for any key points of discussion. You may want to work them into presentations with other potential employers if this job doesn't work out.

Check to see if they'll be available for future calls too. You don't want to give the name of a reference who won't be there. If one is traveling on business, ask if he'll be checking in with the office for messages and returning calls before he returns.

Using Professional References for Job Leads

When you contact all your references, you advertise your availability. One might say, "I know Ron Davis, who's in charge of manufacturing at Nexus Instruments. Maybe I can put you in touch with him."

Never refuse an offer like that. Even if your references don't offer, ask. If they can't help directly, maybe they know someone who can.

Here's an example:

Amy was stalled in her job as a writer of technical manuals for a small software manufacturer. She'd been with the company for three years and had been promoted to supervisor of her department of four writers and a technical editor.

Although her undergraduate degree was in computer science, she studied at night to complete an MBA in marketing. Amy believed that her education combined with her knowledge of user needs prepared her for a marketing manager position. But her company had only one such position, and it didn't look as if it would be vacant soon.

So Amy decided to review her contacts to find a few superstars who could become superreferences. She wanted them to supercharge her into a bigger company where she could maximize her marketing education. She decided on:

- Joseph, a former co-worker who left to start a small software company. Although Joseph's company only had a few products, one of them had recently been successful and was getting loads of industry attention. His letterhead read "Joseph Porter, President, Specialized Software Corporation" with a prestigious address.

- Glenda, a marketing manager of computer peripherals who Amy had met at a conference.

- Dr. Lawrence Potter, an adjunct faculty member at the graduate school of business where Amy studied, a former government official, and the director of competitive intelligence for a manufacturing company. Amy took Dr. Potter's course in marketing. They became friends and she helped him prepare a proposal.

Amy's three primary references had a wealth of contacts in the software marketing business who could help her target marketing directors of manufacturers. The letters they wrote to introduce her and direct attention to her resume won her instant interview after interview.

She had four reference-influenced offers and today she's rapidly climbing the marketing ladder at one of the world's biggest software manufacturers.

You may not know any highly placed officials or company presidents. But somewhere among your contacts there is someone who'll write a credible cover letter to get your resume read, your interview set, and your job offered.

Consider your professional references as a lifetime lifeline. Advise them when you get your desired position. Express your appreciation in a phone call (a letter is even better) and promptly send a tasteful but not too expensive thank-you gift.

Be sure to let them know you'll willingly serve in the same capacity when they mount job searches. Keep in touch and tell them of your progress. If it worked once, it can work again as they become sources for future job advancement.

Essentials for Professional Reference Letters

You want to ensure that the writer is able to do you some good. He or she should be a *preference reference*. A preference reference:

- Knows the recipient of the letter
- Knows someone the recipient knows
- Is known to the recipient
- Has a letterhead and a title that will add credibility
- Holds an equal or superior position to the recipient

Here's an example:

AMERICAN FOODS COMPANY
2204 Mercantile Building
Chicago, Illinois 60626
555-555-5555

Stacy P. Edwards, Director
Market Research

Date

Margaret O. Blaine, Product Manager
Convenience Foods Division
American Foods Company
1667 Commonwealth Avenue
Boston, Massachusetts 02210

Re: Allison F. Harston Reference

Dear Marge:

I hope all is going well with your new product launch. Last month when my department gave you that revised market research you needed, you asked me to let you know if you could return the favor. Now you can.

My associate, Allison Harston, is applying for the product manager position at the breakfast division of American. In addition to great credentials, Allison has the energy, insight, and dedication needed to be an outstanding product manager.

As the enclosed resume shows, Allison recently enhanced her ten years' experience in product marketing at United Foods with an MBA from Bentley College. She graduated with honors in spite of a sixty-hour-per-week job that required travel.

Although she has moved up steadily at United Foods, now that she has experience and graduate credentials she'd like a larger environment.

I know John Lawson is hiring for this position and that he'll interview Allison if the request comes from you. It won't be a waste of time. In fact, John will probably owe you a favor once he meets Allison.

Please pass Allison's resume along to him. She'll call John for an interview by the end of the week.

Thanks in advance for your assistance.

Best regards,

Stacy P. Edwards

cc: Allison F. Harston

Enclosure

This is how professional references are turned into career cash too. . . . And that's your *second* huge do-posit slip!

Do 65: Getting Your Foot in the Store Door

Working retail—with its new items, bargains, and socializing—can be truly exciting!

But before you sit down at that store employment terminal . . .

Write These Keywords on a Piece of Paper and Put It in Your Right Back Pocket

communication skills

customer care

customer service

leader

leadership role

leadership skills

led

led team

management development

management skills

motivational skills

partnering

retail management

service driven

service oriented

store management

team communication

team effort

team leadership

team management

team productivity

team results

Instant Interview the Store Manager

Go over to a checkstand, smile, and say, "Would you please page the general manager of the store?"

If the checker says, "What's it about?" say, "I need to ask him how to find something online." This stops any further questions cold, and you'll hear the page.

Then you might hear, "The GM's not in. I can get you the LOD" (leader on duty—it just makes you want to salute). You answer, "Great!" We don't care, since we're all about instant.

During that instant, go over to a vacant register, push the little button on the printer (love that button! Do 55), and tear off a strip about six inches long.

When the manager answers, look serious and say, "I need to speak to you privately for a minute." He'll follow you as you walk away from the checkstand.

Then you execute the Magic Four Hello (Do 1) with the store sentence: "I'm *really* interested in being a part of your team!"

He'll say, "You have to go over there and apply online." You say, "I know, but I want to talk to you first. What are the management positions at the store level?" Note you don't ask about openings.

Be sure to *write down* the exact titles he gives you. Then say, "Is that the exact title?" He says, "Well, actually, 'Guest Services Manager' is 'Head Honcho, Complaint Department.'" Write that down.

When he's done, demonstrate the Magic Four Goodbye (Do 1) and thank him profusely like you've got the job. Ask his full name, exact title, when he'll be on duty, and the store phone number. Write all these things down with your list of job titles.

Then hop on the electric shopping cart and drive over to the terminal.

Enter the Keywords in Your Responses to the Application Items

This will embed them indelibly into the computer database (Do 15).

So remove the paper with keywords from your right back pocket, place it next to the paper with the titles the manager gave you, and plunk away!

The application says, "List your most recent job activities." You plunk, "Used communication skills in customer care activities as a leader in obtaining team results."

That's okay—I don't know what it means, either. You have to be a computer to know. But some "human development sourcing specialist" in

Zimbabwe will send the app electronically over to HR, and you'll get an e-mail inviting you to call a toll-free number.

Don't wait for that, though . . .

Call the Store When the Manager Is Supposed to be Worcking

Ask to speak to him and say, "Hi, my name is Christine. We have stock in Bullseye." (You do—that paper stock from the register.) "I wanted to stop by and speak with you for a few minutes about joining your successful team."

He might say, "You just have to come in and enter your application online—or you can do it at home."

You say, "I did that yesterday at your store. George was very helpful."

He says, "I'd be happy to meet you."

Understand How Store Managers Think

Store managers spend long hours on their feet with a job description that would bewilder anyone.

The pressure from district managers, the employees who don't show up, the complaining customers (happy ones don't wait around to praise), the scheduling, the inventory that doesn't arrive, the sale that wasn't known, the spill on Aisle 5.

When you're in the store, notice where it needs improvement. Are the aisles cluttered? Which ones? Is the return line too long? Are the checkers rude? Don't ask anyone—just observe objectively.

Career retail managers are no different from any other offerors. They're looking for any way to get off the treadmill. The only difference is they must look good to often-unreasonable bosses who aren't even around. This is why it sometimes seems they're more concerned about the customer complaint than the complaining customer.

That's why the genie technique (Do 1) is so phenomenal to get them on the phone to HR for I.I.'s.

Managers have ultimate control over hiring in their stores. They just don't exercise it because there's nobody to pitch. So they let the digital door closer do it for them. HR sends them bodies. They check for a pulse while worrying about the spill on Aisle 5. And they wonder why "nobody wants to work anymore."

Don't let that computer terminal stop you—it's just a way to get past the beeper at the front door.

Check Out the Store Online

Go to the "About Us" section. Click it and print the puff page. You want growth hype, number of stores, company philosophy, mission statement (great to memorize for I.I. playback), number of employees, and future plans.

This instant information is your instant *in*.

Know Where You Want Your Instant Interview to Go

Your objective isn't a job.

It's an opportunity to contribute and to help in any way possible.

Follow the classic genie technique (Do 1).

He'll remember your call. It's the first time in his long career that anyone has ever respected him enough to set up a short meeting to help.

Oh, he gets asked about job openings all the time. All he has to say is, "You need to apply online." That gets him back to the spill on Aisle 5 and his daily inventory tracking report.

He'll be impressed by your knowledge of the company (from your instant Internet investigating), your knowledge of the store, your togetherness. You'll be so memorable! You'll be blown away by what is done when a store manager wants to hire someone. He'll create an opening if necessary, and HR will be very obedient.

Calling a group of workers team members doesn't make them a team. MVPs like you, yes. If he's got any deputies worth their name badges, he's worried about losing them to another store.

No more than 15 minutes, even if he wants to sit down in the food court and treat you to a cup of coffee. Sorry, instant business is business.

If you'd applied online—without going up, down, and sideways—you'd never get an interview. You'd get a very nice, customer-friendly PR e-mail.

That's not because Bullseye doesn't want the most talented, dedicated people it can find. It's because the rules become the lowest common denominator.

Occasionally, someone motivated dares to be creative.

A perfect example just happened.

Interview Insight

Bev and I were at a clothing store. She wanted to look around, so I sat down to wait for her. Across from me were two individual restrooms marked "Men" and "Women."

I decided to use the few minutes to try an experiment. I walked over to the checkstand, pushed the button on the register printer (can't resist—Do 55), tore off a strip of paper, borrowed a felt pen from the cup on the counter, and wrote in big letters "OUT OF ORDER." Then I asked the security guard for some tape (the checkers were busy), received it, and taped the sign on the Women's room door.

Now, before I tell you what happened, surely you know the restrooms are basically the same. Oh, there are a few differences. But nothing to get constipated over.

So I sat and watched. You know what happened!

A Keystone Kops routine: "Aw, shucks," a quarter-turn right, a few steps, a quarter-turn back, push, enter, and lock. People sat next to me waiting, so I walked over and pulled down my sign. Back to business as usual. Doin' their business following the signs.

Rules. Always rules. Some make sense, others are just signs. You decide for yourself. Ignore rules for fools. You don't need a case of the runs to figure out what works.

You just need to follow *Instant Interviews*.

Getting an interview is just not urgent enough for the herd of hunting hyenas. They don't know the law of the jobjungle either (see Introducing Instant Interviews!).

For retail fun, you only need to get your foot in the store door. Now the rest of you's in *without a beep!*

Do 66: Newspapering on Your Route for Instant *Ins*

Interview *ins* will pop off the page by the time you're done with this Do!

The very best printed source for instants is the community newspaper. Usually these interviewing treasure maps are free and available on racks in supermarkets, walkways, and other high-traffic places around town. Most are weekly. Get the latest ones instantly. Newspapering should be a part of your routine as you're out the door doing your daily appearances (Do 1).

Pick up the paper and scan it as you mark the areas with your pen. Then tear off the pages with what you marked, discard the rest, put them into your left back pocket, and go on your next interview. You should be able to do this in around five minutes. While you're walking and interviewing, your subconscious mind will be filling in the blanks (Do 42).

By the time you get home, you'll have ideas on hooks to use when you stop into the places mentioned.

I'm walking in a nearby city right now, so I can show you how it works.

Here's a rack outside a convenience store. There are two local papers.

First I go right to the masthead of one—that part of the paper with the names of the publisher, editors, address, and phone number.

I'll use that address to stop into the office and interview (Do 1). I may also use it to write a letter to the editor about something that might have people calling me (Do 48).

Let's see what news they printed. This is great! Here's a headline about a skills center that's opening and it gives the names of the companies sponsoring it. I'm circling that one as we speak.

Next there's some VP who just got a promotion with a real estate company. I'll circle that too.

Here's a piece about a campaign to clean up graffiti. Four local businesses are involved. Circle that.

Not bad for the front page.

Now turning to the inside—I've already circled the masthead—there's the editor's column. She mentions the annual fiesta that's coming up in a nearby town. I'm circling the first date and will get there early. I'll follow the job-fair technique for sure (Do 51).

Then the editor mentions that some developer is trying to take over a whole block of stores that have been serving the community for years. The merchants' association has asked other businesspeople in the area to attend. Circle that one for sure.

I could go on, but you get the idea.

I never close these papers without looking at the page with the little display ads from the entrepreneurs who provide services. I look for the "no job too small or too big" words. Those are my kind of people. Junkyard dogs.

So here we have two or three pages I zipped through, circled, folded, and stuffed in my right back pocket. I could have spent a full day at the library reference area when better information was right there screaming "Here I am!"—instantly!

If you do that a few times, you'll find that there are 10 categories of news you can use:

1. A job promotion (a job opening and a contact)
2. A retirement (a job opening and a contact)
3. A site is purchased by a business relocating to the area

4. A local business announces it is expanding

5. A contract has been awarded to a local business

6. A new product is being introduced by a local business

7. A local business is acquiring another business

8. A city ordinance or other law has been passed requiring a change in the way local businesses operate (parking and smoking bans are perfect openers to meet every business in the area)

9. A business expo, convention, job fair, chamber of commerce meeting, city council agenda item, marathon, or other gathering is being held

10. A notice indicates a business is growing

Newspapering once a week for a month will convince you the local paper is the in thing to read!

Do 67: Remembering Your Lines Instantly Like a S-T-A-R

You make your entrance. There's a hush in the audience. Here comes the star!

There are only four things that get an offeror's interest. Say them and you're fast-forward interviewing.

Remember them with the mnemonic of who you are—a S-T-A-R. The letters stand for:

Spot something

Talk about it

Attribute and accomplishment

Result

Your remarkable brain will take what you see and hear, then signal your smiling mouth to say the words naturally.

Once you're past the Magic Four Hello (Do 1). . .

Spot Something

Let your eyes do that signaling to the brain.

Say you spot an old photocopy machine in the office area, but there's a roomful of blank paper ream packages and many copies. You upgraded the copier for an employer in an earlier life.

(Sometimes the offeror will mention something first—like hassles with copying. If so, consider that spotted by your ears.)

So, you . . .

Talk about It

Say briefly (two or three sentences) something like, "I see you're using a Zero 32 copier with an automatic feed and five-tray collator. We had one when I was at Paperpusher. How do you like it?"

Simple enough. Just wait for the offeror's reply. He'll probably say, "I don't, but we've had it for so many years that I haven't done anything about it."

Now you show starpower . . .

Attribute and Accomplishment

"I seem to have this ability to increase cost effectiveness in routine business activities. At Paperpusher, I was able to reduce our photocopy costs by 60 percent while getting copies three times faster."

Then you segue into . . .

Result

"We improved productivity, reduced cost, and had proposals out to our customers faster than we dreamed possible!"

The offeror will ask you for details if he's interested. It doesn't matter because you've moved further toward the goal.

Then just keep using the STAR technique whenever you spot something you can improve.

A star you *are!*

Do 68: Turning On Off-Offerors

You open the door. There's no gatekeeper. It's face to face with an offeror. Not even one outstretched arm.

Just a two-eyed stare.

He's your basic off-offeror!

We can finally use the I.I. switching technique. Let's turn him on instantly.

There are only six switches. They may be coated different colors, but they all say, "Instant On." They're hotwired.

We'll number them, and I'll show you how to flip the switch.

Flipping the Switches

You'll smile very naturally when you're greeted with . . .

Switch 1 Off

"I'm busy. What's it about?"

Switch 1 On

"I can see that you're busy!" (Agreement.) "I'm busy, too." (I'm as impatient as you.) "How about if we meet at 5 P.M. tonight or 8 A.M. tomorrow at the coffee shop?" (Make a decision, big shot!) "I want to talk to you about helping you get less busy and increase your business."

He'll say, "How?"

That's our instant invitation, but you're just a little too important to accept right away, So say, "Look—you're busy now and so am I. See you downstairs at five?"

He'll say, "Fine—have you got a business card or something?" (They're programmed to say "or something." Isn't this fun?)

You reply, "Sure. Give me yours too."

Drop a Magic Four Hello and your card, then leave (Do 1).

If he doesn't show up, you go up to his office (or call if the meeting place is not right there). Now you've got an even *better* switch than you had before!

Be very nice when you convey, "Where were you? I was really looking forward to meeting you!"

He's going to want to make it up to you. It's called the *Important Instant Interview!*

Switch 2 Off

"I've got a meeting in five minutes and I can't deal with this right now."

Switch 2 On

"Here's my card. Give me yours and I'll come back later. I really want to get your ideas about something."

With this encounter, offerors are never too dormant to ask, "About what?"

But you're too ready to answer. So you say, "I'll stop by later. Have a good meeting!"

Switch 3 Off

"If this is about a job, we're not hiring now."

Switch 3 On

"I know that. In fact, that's exactly why I wanted to get your advice for a few minutes."

He'll reply, "Advice? What kind of advice?" (Every business owner or manager has free advice. When someone asks, they can't resist.)

"I just wanted to ask you about where you think I can use my talent."

Magic Four Hello him now (Do 1).

Switch 4 Off

"All of our hiring is done through HR. Here's the web site where you can apply."

Switch 4 On

"Thanks, I'll do that. But first I want to talk to you directly. I'm not looking for an HR position."

This slight tug of the rule-rope is a *huge* power play. The offeror instantly knows you're not easily intimidated, understand that HR won't get you hired, and want to work *now*.

You're wedging yourself right in the center of the endless tug-of-war between HR's interminable inertia and the hiring manager's instant intentions.

The most successful managers interview whoever they want, take the flak for doing it, then walk candidates through HR once they've decided whom to hire.

The most successful recruiters don't deal with HR because that's not how placements are made.

If you haven't done the Magic Four Hello yet, it's probably because the offeror Magic-Foured you already!

Switch 5 Off

"We're in a hiring freeze."

Switch 5 On

"That's what I was hoping. I wanted to discuss consolidating or outsourcing some activities and using the savings for your procurement budget."

Offerors are very impressed by this. They know every hiring freeze has its share of ice crushers. If he thinks you're one, he interviews instantly. (The words "procurement budget" echo throughout the jungle.)

Switch 6 Off

"Business is slow."

Switch 6 On

"I have some ways we can speed it up! Sometimes just a small change can make a big difference. What have we got to lose by just talking about it?" (The words "procurement budget" echo throughtout the jungle.)

Note the "you and me against the problem" technique (Do 56).

It works because it checkmates the offeror. If business really *is* slow, the offeror will be very receptive. If it *isn't* slow, why doesn't he have time to interview?

Big psychological power.

Flipping these switches works just like I said.

A bright sign lights up that reads "Instant Interview!"

Do 69: Demonstrating the Instant You

Now that you see offerors only bite with an offer (hence the word *offeror*), let's take your show on the road!

There's nothing like having an offeror walking up to you.

Doing demos can be done these ways.

Do an In-House Demonstration

Find a product or service you'd like to demonstrate where offerors will watch. Go to an appliance store, an industrial supplier, a distributor, or a manufacturer's representative.

Choose a high-end commercial item. Just pick a freezer, prefab building, or maintenance service.

Tell the highest manager that you'd like to publicize and demonstrate the product or service.

If the manager tells you she can't make that decision (or any other excuse), just smile and say, "That's fine. I understand. How do I reach your district manager?"

This gives the manager *apoplexy*. She either tells you she'll check your request and call you tomorrow (count on it), or gives you the name and phone number of the district manager.

Let's assume she tells you it's fine, but they can only pay you a percentage of the sales from the product. This is usually the difference between the purchase price and the employee discount. However, you might also be hired as an employee to do this and be paid a draw (a fixed amount against your commission) or an hourly wage.

Then it's a simple paperwork signup including filling out a W-9 (if an independent contractor) or a W-4 form (if an employee) with the HR department (Do 44). And you've got your deal.

It's all very instant.

In some cases, the store even has the table, tablecloth, microphone, extension cords, and other items in the back because it's done in-house demos before.

Since you're there and loaded for bear, let any friendly manager instantly interview you too. Straight genie talk (Do 1).

You've shown creativity, initiative, and guts. Those commodities are in short supply there, regardless of how much the shelves are stocked.

Get your card in her hands and yourself in her head.

You'll get a very good return call!

Contact a Demonstration Company

You can google *product demonstration* and the name of the city you want. Then write down the phone number and apply.

A much better way is to simply ask the demonstrator at the place where you'd like to be. Do an instant on him! Ask him to refer you, get his company name, address, phone number, e-mail address, and the name of the hirer. Get the hirer's contact information too.

Some demonstrators work for these services, others are employees or independent reps with the manufacturers or distributors. The routine is the same.

Call, sign up, and let them know when and where you'd like to be assigned.

Make Up a Flyer

. . . With your name, phone number, and e-mail address prominently displayed.

We wouldn't want to disturb the retailer.

A one-page, simple advertisement or announcement.

Work with the store and the source (manufacturer, distributor, or representative). Use a product brochure as your guide.

Did I mention with your name, phone number, and e-mail address *prominently displayed?*

Set an optimum date and time for the demo (worthy offerors are attracted early on weekdays).

Have the store and source send it to their mailing list, post and stack flyers in the store, and generally be sure everyone in sight whoops it up.

Ask for a large banner (bought by the store) outside and posters inside. With your name, phone number, and e-mail address *prominently displayed.*

When you're driving to your instants, stop and leave flyers wherever you think offerors will read them.

Cars parked in VIP parking definitely need windshield-washer covers.

Get the Retailer to Arrange for Announcements in Trade and Local Papers

Almost all manufacturers have a cooperative advertising program. If not, suggest a co-op ad with your name, phone number, and e-mail address *prominently displayed.* They cooperate, you demonstrate—your interviewing self!

Learn as Much as You Can about the Product, Price, and Competition

Ask the store, call the source, and google the product for competitors, ratings, and user comments.

Hold Your Demonstration

. . . Of *you!* Leave business cards out, *pass* them out, and instant on any-one you can get alone!

Have a signup sheet with name, affiliation, and contact information. We call it I.I.-ing!

Demonstrate at Trade Shows

You can have a table or booth at any trade show you like. Just reread Do 31 and Do 54.

Then follow those guidelines.

Interview Insight

Speaking of flyers, our granddaughter Gabby is a wonderful, creative crayoner. I once gave her a coloring book and asked her to draw out-side the lines. She did some of the most beautiful, colorful, whimsi-cal masterpieces! In school, they'd grade her down for that.

The lesson in lifelong learning is to know where the lines are drawn, but know as well that they're only on one page of a whole book. There's a library full of learning in Gabby's instant illustrations.

A fulfilling life is out there beyond the job description.

Do demos right, and offerors will watch you work. They'll be instantly impressed. And want the demonstrator more than the demonstrated.

Just demonstrate that instant *you!*

Do 70: Auctioning Yourself Off to the Highest Bidder

Once you're deluged with instants, offers start.

You get so thrilled with the chase—seeking out the jobjungle jewels—that you don't think to go *back* to offerors you turned down. They're dis-appointed, so make their day!

If you don't, you're missing the dynamic of an auction. It's fun, makes you feel very wanted, and can increase everything about a new job. Pay, vacation, responsibilities, power. All because the process itself takes on a life of its own. Ebay built an e-empire on that fact. Only we use the phone.

Assume you just got an offer from Olivia, and you turned down Curtis yesterday. (I'm setting it up this way because it's more awkward than if Curtis's offer was still being considered.)

Assistant: Curtis Counter's office. Dora speaking.

You: Hi Dora, this is Sally Instant. Is Curt the flirt in? . . . Oops, sorry! I used that to remember his name (Do 82).

Dora: Hi Sally! Sorry we won't be working together.

You: Well, that still may happen!

Dora: Great! I was looking forward to you doing the monthly sales report. Here's Curt.

Curtis: Curtis Counter.

You: Hi Curt! This is Sally.

Curtis: Well I'll be . . . to what do I owe this honor?

You: Well, I've been reconsidering your offer. I just received one for twenty-five percent more from one of your competitors (true—every offeror is a competitor). But I would really like to work with you and your team.

Curtis: I've been thinking about it, too. The fact that you had the courage to call me back says volumes about you. I appreciate the call.

You: I was thinking that we could reconfigure the job so that I'd contribute even more. Why don't I just start and within a week I'll have a job description for you with creative new duties?

Curtis: But what if we can't continue to pay you that amount?

You: I always want to be paid what I'm worth. There's a lot we can do to increase your profit. The competitor really wants me, and I'll just tell her it's going to be another week before I decide.

Curtis: You would really do that?

You: Yes . . . it's the honorable way to handle this, eliminates your risk, and enables us to really look at this opportunity from the inside out!

Curtis: Sounds like an offer I can't refuse!

You: What time do you want me there tomorrow morning?

Curtis: Are you busy now?

You: Yes. I have to call a very excited competitor of yours.

Curtis: How about if I meet you at 7 A.M. and we start talking before everyone arrives? Then you can fill out the paperwork.

You: I'll be at the front door at 7 A.M. sharp, ready to help.

Curtis: Looking forward to getting you on board!
You: Thanks. Have a good evening.
Curtis: You too, Sally the savior!

Counteroffer counterattack calls (better than e-mails) are great fun when you're instanting, because you just drop the counteroffer on the offerors. Then watch them slosh around in the mire. They gasp, grasp, and outbid the phantom competitor.

When you have multiple offers (an I.I. occupational hazard), it becomes downright exhilarating. You need a scorecard to keep track.

Here's one instant interviewers use:

Name of Offeror	Phone Number	Date of Offer (or Counteroffer)	Amount of Offer (or Counteroffer)	Other Benefits Offered

This is not like going to your boss with a counteroffer, because you don't have a vested interest in either job. You're also not considered a traitor, since you have no obligation to either side.

It's like going to an auction and watching yourself on the block.

Just instant interviewing away while your stock price is rising.

Now we'll end this Do with a fable.

Interview Insight

I worked my way through college playing drums. Worked with some incredibly talented musicians, too. One was name Jedediah. He was one of those remarkable people who could play any instrument in any style, and had perfect pitch. (That means you'd say "E flat" and he'd hum, then walk over to the piano, plunk the E-flat key, and it would be the same—if the piano was tuned.)

Those piano keys were an extension of his fingers. Playing piano was as natural to him as writing a sentence. He was like an electric player piano. Brahms to boogie woogie. He also composed brilliant R&B music that would give you goosebumps. Jed played, recorded, but never really shared his gift. He would go from label to label. Every label wanted his work—but he would never sell it. The better the offer, the more he thought the recordings were worth.

One day I received the news that Jed died. I remember thinking that he must have had two graves—one for him and one for all those masters. His funeral was the last time that music played—forever. The world will never know what it missed.

The moral: Don't Jedediah jobseek.

Let that auctioneer bang that gavel and shout it proud "Sold to the highest bidder!"

For now.

Do 71: Lowering Your Interview Age Instantly

Let's show offerors age is just a number—*one!*

I wrote *Finding the Right Job at Midlife* in 1985 and have been working with seniors since that time. When you appear like a genie (Do 1), there's no time for you to be screened out. You're *there*, granting a wish. It will be done! Age isn't even a thought, let alone a number.

But let's lower your age just to boost your confidence. Your " hire" self will do it.

Your Looks

Find someone in your family who's one or two generations down from you (daughter or granddaughter, for example). Someone in her thirties, the same sex as you, and professional.

Hip too. If you're gonna boogie down, you gotta know what is hip (title of a Tower of Power song). I play drums, so this is serious.

Clothes

You probably won't have to buy that much, but front and back pockets are essential (Do 1). You can get the clothes you need from outlets anywhere. It's business casual (not like when you were younger) and the variety you can wear is endless. Just show some class.

Men should lose the suit, white shirt, and tie on the basic genie appearance. Women can leave the suit and fancy jewelry home. Pick comfortable shoes with good support. You can buy one of a dozen orthotics for them at any drugstore if you want to cushion or support your feet more.

Check for frayed clothes, scuffed shoes, gaudy jewelry or old glasses, and other midlife memorabilia.

Then have that thirtysomething double-check your work. You'll tend to be too practical.

Face

No facial hair where it doesn't belong (including nose, lips, and ears). You don't need cosmetic (or dental) surgery to have more interviews in a week than you had in your long lifetime.

Hair

In spite of all the hype about hair, too few older folks care for theirs well.

Most older jobseekers treat and comb their (less) hair the way they did when they were young. Wrong.

Tell your stylist that you're reentering the job market. Let her be the judge of what looks good. It's called reinventing yourself!

Dyed hair must look natural. If you're using a black dye and you have a very white face, use the magic potion instead (Do 2). It's not a shampoo, but anything's better than that dye.

No hairpieces, unless they're very small and really match.

Hands

Hands are really important and frequently show the signs of cooking, gardening, and hammering (ouch!).

Your nails should be trim and clean. Women should wear nail polish.

Perfume or Cologne

None.

You're out there on the route, so are already glowing from the inside.

These tips will enhance your success.

So on the subject of your looks, be spiffy. You'll be doing a lot of moving, and I want you to be comfortable. Instant interviewing is great fun, and you deserve to enjoy every minute.

Your Speech

Your interview delivery is the same as for any other I.I. Avoid these phrases. Only old folks use them.

At my age . . .
Back in the days when . . .
It used to be that . . .
I remember when . . .
When I was younger . . .
When I was your age . . .
Years ago . . .
Nowadays . . .

Ask your kids and grandkids to nail you whenever you start saying something freaky like that. It'll get you their support, and therefore increased instants.

I love working with seniors because they are such great people to be around. Offerors feel the same way instantly.

You have one thing that younger I.I.'s don't.

Your number—*one!*

Interview Insight

Here are some excerpts of an article that a magazine wrote about my exploits with our grandson Jonathan when he was three. I share it with you because this is the kind of thing that will make you young (and very happy).

Supergrandpa Jeff Allen shows what can be done
Supergrandpa Jeff Allen spends every Thursday morning volunteering at his grandson's preschool.

Jeff commented, "The teachers want to know why I don't get up off the floor. I tell them, 'That's where the kids are.'"

The mornings at the preschool came about naturally because grandson Jonathan spends every Wednesday night at his grandparents' home. "Grandparenting is not a cameo appearance," says Jeff. "There are an endless number of things you can do with grandkids to help them explore their exciting new world the *right* way. Few cost anything but love and time."

While Jeff describes the things he and Jonathan do together as "goofy," most of the activities are learning experiences.

One time after they read a *Curious George* book set at a train station, they rode the Metrolink to Union Station. When Jeff introduced Jonathan to the engineer, they were invited to sit up front. Jonathan was in charge of the microphone, calling "All aboard!" on the loudspeaker at every stop.

Jeff has found that people in charge are very willing to share what they do.

"At the UPS office, they weighed Jonathan on one of those big package scales, and put a '49 lbs.' label on him.

"After we finished some ice cream cones, Jonathan asked me where the ice cream came from. I soon learned that cows no longer lived in L.A. There were no dairies. But I finally located a herd out at Pierce College in Woodland Hills. When I explained our purpose to the guard, we were invited to go past the no-entrance signs to see the cows up close."

Jeff finds that offbeat adventures like following a trash truck to see where it goes are more fun than an amusement park. "There's almost an inverse relationship between what you pay and the benefit the kids get from something like that," he says.

"Our very favorite time was one day after visiting Krispy Kreme (strictly for the educational purpose of seeing how donuts are made). We spied a truck rental place and I drove in.

"We walked up to the manager, I introduced Jonathan and asked if he could ride on the wheeloader with a backhoe (we knew every kind of construction truck). The manager said, 'I never had a father. Hop on!' That day, we drove every type of truck on the lot, went on every scissorlift, used every kind of jackhammer, and had the time of our lives."

I could give you hundreds of things like that we do. It's no different from instant interviewing. You just go out and *do it!* Nobody minds. In fact, they welcome the opportunity to share what they do. We just have to get out of our own way.

Nobody says no to a smiling grandparent with kids. I'm nobody special—I just *did it!*

Now at nine, Jonathan remembers everything we did together.

Grandkids are such a precious gift that keeps on giving. They make you more than young—they make you immortal!

Do 72: Partying Early at the Offerors-Only Warehouse

There's an offerors-only party goin' on at dawn—and you're invited!

How thoughtful to have businesspeople over for coffee, muffins, and pastry!

With a host at the door cheerfully starting conversations.

You don't have to be a member to look—only to buy.

If you can't knock out a half-dozen instants there, you must be in the returns line.

Just look for a likely offeror over in the paper goods, bakery, or beverage area. They often have the larger flatbed loaded with supplies or food. These are typically merchants who resell the things or people stocking up their offices. Both are perfect victims.

A few offeror openers are:

It looks like you're gonna have one heckuva party!

Are you in business for yourself?

Have you tried these coffee stirrers before?

Then s-l-i-d-e right into the Magic Four Hello (Do 1) and you're one stand-up superstar! Grade her business card, sample some green eggs and ham, then on to the two other areas.

Warehouse stores are wonderful places for unpretentious people to get down to business. The managers at ours told me they encourage as much networking as possible. One suggested I might try the food court outside. You don't even have to be a member to be served (Do 74).

If breakfast samples are given out at offeror party time, ask a sampler, "Who hired you?" Get the name and contact information. Call to see if you can do sampling only during AM party time (Do 69). If not, pass.

Welcome to the club.

Greet the greeter with, "Sam I *am!*"

Do 73: Generating Instant Revenues and Interviews

Can it be? Making money while instantly interviewing? If everything happens for a reason, this is *it!*

Become an office-area measurer.

How I Got the Idea

My roommate in college was a real estate agent. He and his brother used to pick a residential area, knock on a door, and offer to appraise the homeowner's house for free.

They'd walk in like the Blues Brothers. Then they'd whip out a tape measure and start writing down the square footage. The homeowner would follow them into rooms, closets, and bathrooms watching and wondering as they wrote down numbers.

They'd then sit down, appraise the house, and get the listing.

I always remembered the impact of that. You can see why we were roommates!

Then when I was an HR manager, I was asked to look for a new site since our lease was up. In doing this, I discovered we were grossly overpaying for our space.

The reason? The square footage was overstated and nobody ever questioned it. The measurements were from another lease and we were only subleasing part of the space.

Then we started checking the listings for commercial and office buildings. We discovered that square footage was inflated on the listings over a *third* of the time!

How I Did It

I needed to take a leave of absence to study, and it was harder on an empty stomach.

So I bought a tape measure from the hardware store bargain bin, asked a real estate agent friend to show me how to do the measuring, and became an instant "lease payment lowerer."

I hardly had enough for stamps—let alone enough for a mass-mailing campaign. So I just drove around to industrial and retail areas and wrote down the names of businesses on the buildings along with their addresses.

Next I stopped at the office buildings, walked in, and wrote down the names of the tenants and suite numbers for that address.

When I got home, I opened the phone book (pre-Internet) and wrote down the numbers of the businesses. Then I drove over to the chamber of commerce and asked for the free directory of members.

That became the direct mail list I used to send a flyer to a few hundred businesses. It read something like:

ARE YOU PAYING TOO MUCH RENT? WOULD YOU LIKE TO PAY LESS WITHOUT MOVING OR LOSING ANY SPACE?

WHAT ABOUT GETTING CASH FOR RENT YOU OVERPAID?

CALL TODAY!

I photocopied them at work, with the permission of my boss. He gave me envelopes too. I just needed one more thing—a short letter agreement for the tenants to sign. That night I was in my law school library preparing it. Photocopies courtesy of my employer.

The deal was I'd survey the premises for free. If the lease square footage was more than the actual square footage, the owner would pay me half of the refund. Future savings were theirs. No cost, no obligation, no advice. Just a quick meter reading. They instantly signed my simple one-page agreement.

I appeared like a genie (Do 1). I surveyed the premises all right! Spoke to anyone I wanted. It was *quite* the instant interview experience!

Predictably, a third of the premises were smaller than the leases stated. The landlords fell all over themselves to make the refunds. "Instant" was an understatement. Today, the phrase is "All over it."

I made valuable business contacts in the community and ate valuable food.

But I turned down dozens of job offers from grateful tenants.

You Can Do It Too

This little business turns you into an electromagnet. Offerors are attracted to your magnetic field.

You immediately attract businesspeople who have large facilities, with many offerors in them. You drive by their businesses every day and just need to get inside to instant on them.

Writing the Agreement Letter

The letter format is more signable and just as enforceable as a legalistic document (Do 44). It all depends on what message you want to send. Here are the six things the letter should contain:

1. The exact name of the business and any principals to be bound. (Usually parties who signed as tenants and guarantors on the lease.)

2. The square footage set forth in the lease with the date, title of the lease, and names of the parties.

3. A promise by the tenant to pay you half of any refund you determine is due from the landlord within 10 days of its receipt (or any part thereof). You agree that the tenant can retain all future rent savings. (This is an instant closer.)

4. A promise by the tenant to use their best efforts to obtain the refund. All attorney's fees, litigation costs, and other expenses are to be paid solely by the tenant.

5. An understanding that your role is strictly to inform the tenant of the objective determination regarding the actual square footage. You are not providing legal advice or representation and are not an attorney (unless you are).

6. A release holding you harmless from any miscalculations or repercussions from negotiations with the landlord (like eviction), and any other acts or omissions.

Rough it out yourself and look in the local Yellow Pages under "Attorneys—Business Law." Call one or two who offer a free phone consultation and read it to them slowly, making any changes or additions they suggest (Do 44).

Wave Your Magic Measurer

Home improvement stores have a device known as a "true laser distance measurer." It's an inexpensive battery device slightly larger than a TV remote. It looks really impressive. You place the measurer in the corner of the room, aim it, turn it 180 degrees, aim it again, and press a button.

Earn While You Instant

With that magical measurer and your simple letter signed by you and the tenant, you're in business. (Almost—don't forget a business license at city hall.)

You'll be amazed at the effectiveness of the marketing. Owners or managers just don't take the time or have the little bit of knowledge necessary to save themselves a fortune. It's mind-boggling when you see the multipliers of months, years, and decades of overpayment.

This little business costs you almost nothing. It instantly generates revenues and *interviews!*

Do 74: Grabbing the Bigbucks Instant Offerors

Coffee places are designed for sippin' and hangin'. But where are the bigbucks coffeeors? Not sitting at the tables.

Lets go grab 'em!

Go to the Bigbucks Locations

There are only around 25 in any major city, located near large office complexes in commercial areas and industrial parks. Downtown has more than its share of Bigbucks locations.

Only a few locations because that's where top execs stop and bop. The volume of sales in these outlets is staggering, and so is the volume of instants you can do.

Find them by calling a few stores of the major chains. The managers are rotated constantly and will tell you where to find the Bigbucks locations.

Then instant interview with them daily. Many who started at Bigbucks are successful coffeeors today. I have two in my family who used the coffeeors as offerors.

Go at the Bigbucks Hours

They're not the ones posted on the door.

They're from 6 A.M. to 9 A.M. Monday through Friday.

Any other time, you're just lookin' at laptops. Students, social networkers. The customers at the tables? They're either not networking or their net's not working.

Stayin' and Playin' or Stoppin' and Boppin'?

Bigbucks coffeeors don't stay and play. That's for workers.

They stop in, order, and bop out. Moving targets who take the coffee and the newspaper to go.

So the action's not at the tables. It's on the lines, at the condiment bar, at the door, and in the parking lot.

Take a Cup and a Lid

If you can't afford or don't like coffee, just take an empty cup from a table. You need a prop to look like you belong. It's a quick way to boost your self-confidence.

You can also ask the barista for an empty cup and lid. She'll gladly give it to you. Or you can take ones from the stack in front of her. I should caution you however, that this is neither ecologically nor environmentally sound. Nor very nice, since the least you can do is clean up in exchange for a Bigbucks interviewing office.

Hold your hand over the handwritten name.

You can do this. Yo mama wud jes laff!

Execute the Grab

The classic genie technique (Do 1) still works. You just have to appear magically. While they're standing in line, shaking the sugar, or running out to their cars. You grab with a little offeror opener:

Hi, I've seen you here before and wanted to introduce myself.

Excuse me, but I wanted to ask what business you're in . . . you look very successful!

I see you're in a hurry, but I just have to ask you . . . how do you like your beautiful Maserati?

In the first example, you go straight into the Magic Four Hello and proceed with the Full Monty. In the second two, you wait for an answer.

Be Fast but Firm

This Do is verbal Quan Do. You're talking to someone who has major responsibilities (he thinks), hasn't had his coffee (you know), and hasn't read his paper (now probably won't get the chance).

So be fast but firm. You want to say something like:

> I'd really like to be around someone successful like you. Is there anything you can have me do to show you how dedicated I am to succeeding? I just need a chance.

Stop and think about this for a moment now (not while he's instant interviewing you).

You're a bigbucks bigwig. Someone wants to learn from you. Wants you to be her mentor. Isn't afraid to approach a total stranger because she's comfortable enough with herself.

What do you say? "Sure. Give me a call."

You think you're still dreaming.

So give and get business cards.

This is how you can grab those Bigbucks coffeeors. And how they'll grab *you!*

Do 75: Interviewing as an Intern Instantly

An offeror doesn't *really* know what interns are but he instantly likes them. So our unofficial definition of an *intern* is the perfect opener to get instant interviews!

He thinks it's a student, there to learn—always helpful, reliable, humble, grateful. I used this hook to become a "legal intern" (law clerk). The employer had a hiring freeze but that thawed instantly. I just started an internship program!

The official definition of *internship* we'll use for offerors is *fixed-term employment.* Only they have to *ask* first. That's why the intern device is so powerful.

Before I show you how to clinch interviews every time with this device, let's look at only three questions an offeror *really* asks. Three numbers that open the combination lock in his mind—and *click,* you're in.

Will You Be My Pal?

This is by far the most important question.

It's not asked that way, of course. It's asked by:

What types of books do you read?

What are your hobbies?

Where did you go on your last vacation?

By now you've learned to pick up cues from the office, then the offeror, so you always answer with what he reads, what he hobs, and where he vacates (Do 41).

Will You Help Me Relax?

We discussed this in reviewing preparation of the rest-you-may (Do 5).

As with the first question, this is not asked that way. It's just not socially acceptable to admit you're lazy.

So her questions are:

Do you think you have the experience to do this job?

How would your skills be an asset here?

What areas of our business would you improve?

You counter with some genie (Do 1) version of:

Not to worry. Whatever your little palpitating heart desires.

Now we get to the final question that instinctively grips every offeror.

Am I Taking a Risk with You?

That is rarely verbalized. But every look, every introduction to others is a yearning for that warm, fuzzy, no-risk signal.

Here's how you warmfuzzy an instant offeror using the basic genie technique.

The Magic Four Hello is followed by the intern intro of:

You: I'm looking for an internship and would love to work here.

He: What do you mean?

You: I'm looking to stay three months and help you in any way I can that will give me the experience I need with a highly successful business. The *Opportunity News* is looking to feature prominent businesspeople and this would be free publicity for you.

He: That's something we can always use. But only three months? What if we want you to stay?

You: Let's see how it goes. You're under no obligation. I'm here to help and learn!

He's in forest fuzzyville.

The fourth question he might ask but doesn't care about:

He: Do I pay you?
You (*smiling*): Yes, you pay me.
He: How much?
You: Whatever you think I'm worth.

Pay is a relative term, counterbalanced with the answers to the other three questions. It's a tax-deductible afterthought.

That's why we don't obsess about pay or negotiate it with the instant approach (until we're deciding between multiple gigs). If we don't like the deal, we instant interview out.

Since offerors naturally want who they can't have—and you're irresistible—they ratchet up the offers.

Whatever he offers, you say, "I'll have to think about it. I have other offers pending." (You do if you're an I.I.)

Now you know what *intern* really means.
Instant interviews!

Do 76: Zipping Through It All at City Hall

You can zip through any city hall within a few hours. It generates an average of nine interview leads.

I learned the way to do this in courthouses. Respecting and learning from the clerks wins cases.

Go on a weekday afternoon when you're done with your 16 instants for the day. You'll get more news than you can use in a day. Replenish your supply of business cards from your car. You'll make good use of them.

Look at the directory, and make a few notes about the rooms where you'll find . . .

Business License Department

You'll see the people applying for licenses milling around the counter. These are usually startup business enterprises.

Be friendly and ready to assist a likely offeror. Maybe she needs a pen or help with the forms. General genie gifts (Do 1).

Get excited for her. People starting a new business hear "It'll never work" very often. You're about to have a magic moment.

Go from Magic Four Hello to Magic Four Goodbye seamlessly. Then when she turns in the forms and leaves, grade her business card or paper, go up to the counter, and look for the most likely person to tell you everything he knows.

Ask:

What new businesses have filed in the past week? (Take notes. There's always paper around.)

Where is your list of filings?

Do you know anyone who could use assistance?

Business licenses are public records, so the clerks talk freely. They see everyone who's opening, changing ownership, changing business names, or moving.

A big source of information. Leave your card for sure.

Building Inspection Department

Inspectors are usually back from their rounds in the afternoon. You can set your watch by their discipline.

With the exception of home-based businesses, every new, remodeling, or expanding business deals with these cops.

They can be brutal in enforcing the codes and—like police—off-duty they make up for lost friendliness.

When you meet inspectors informally, they're basic taxi drivers (Do 36). Very knowledgeable, down-to-earth, people-people who will help you in any way they can.

Try to get an invitation to go behind the counter into his office. Say, "Would you mind if we talk in your office for a few minutes?" He won't refuse—it's his office. He can sit and relax with someone who actually *wants* to talk to him.

If you're looking for interviews with any building-based business, it's hard to envision a better lead source.

Parks and Recreation Department

This is usually a very open, informal place where people sign up for activities.

There's a wealth of information available.

You'll probably also see flyers and calendars that include business meetings, company picnics, and expos.

Take whatever information looks promising.

Then ask a likely offeror, "Who do you know that's looking for someone to help with any of these things?"

Your list of names and numbers will be rather long.

Tack your callback card on the bulletin board too (Do 14).

City Manager's Office

Whatever the title, a city manager is the civil service equivalent of a chamber of commerce CEO. (Many are called chief administrative officer—CAO.)

He's a person you should meet, and who may be an excellent lead source. If he's in a meeting (most are all the time), his next-in-command is fine.

Very often an assistant knows more because he's *not* in a meeting all the time.

Public Utilities Department (Water, Electricity, Gas)

These offices are very much like the business license ones, but the records are not public.

Ask a likely clerk what businesses have signed up for new service.

If you find someone who'll talk, write down the business names.

Police Department Community Service Office

If the police department is nearby, stop in.

Police do everything possible to polish their image. They expend considerable resources in community outreach programs to reach people like you.

Find the reacher and reach (slowly) in your left front pocket for your pen.

Police are everywhere all the time. They know what's *really* happening in the city.

Be friendly and ask. He'll be friendly and answer.

Instant yourself on any offerors you spot, and leave your card with every person you meet.

Within a few hours you've zipped through a valuable series of lead sources.

You can't find this instant-intelligence information anywhere else!

Do 77: Accepting Temporary Assignments

It's natural to instant while you're on a temp assignment!

Temp services have historically sought jobseekers interested in short-term or part-time employment. Many are actively interviewing for regular jobs too.

Office support and factory openings were the original temp market. But their services have now fully expanded to filling technical, executive, and professional openings everywhere at every level. It's not unusual for these temp assignments to be full-time for years.

Most of the services dispatch their employees and charge the client on an hourly basis from the time cards submitted. The temp is paid an hourly rate too (obviously lower than the billing rate).

The service is responsible for all payroll deductions. Many offer additional benefits and bonuses for their employees. To some clients, the temp markup is worth not having to interview even for otherwise full-time employees.

A temp assignment gives you a no-obligation look at offerors that no other way can provide.

Here's an example of an assignment that worked into a direct hire:

A business decided to upgrade its computer system so a large accounting department could be reduced. The manager of IT called a contract service (another name for a temp service that places nonclerical employees) for a three-month systems analyst assignment.

The jobseeker was at a regular gig. He learned the instant interviewing techniques and was having so much fun getting offers that he wanted to do that without hassles from his boss.

So he registered online with the contracting service, filled out the payroll paperwork, and was dispatched.

Free of the worries about losing his job, he was a different person on the temp assignment. Everyone loved him, and within 45 days the offeror decided our friend should run the accounting department!

So he instantly interviewed with the director of finance and was hired.

He literally *made* his own opening! (Don't we all.)

The contract service graciously waived their temp-to-hire conversion fee when the temp transferred to the client's payroll. They knew the client would want more temps as the transition was completed.

It did, and still does.

Whether it's staffing down to automate jobs or staffing up to add them, temp assignments are a great opportunity to instant.

You can also interview for other jobs posted internally by the client (Do 30).

Accepting temporary assignments means accepting instant interview invitations!

In the next Do, I show you how to leverage that powerful temp advantage . . .

Do 78: Temping Differently to Interview Instantly

Temporary services—from clerical to interim executives—are instant interview incubators!

Until now, temps didn't have access to this remarkable benefit because they didn't know how to do it. Now we'll turn up the heat on those incubators and see what hatches.

Forget temp-to-hire. It's temp-to-bow-coo-interviews time . . .

Decide What Specialty You'd Like

Temp services specialize in every field imaginable. You're interested in law? Accounting? Health care? There's a local temp service for you.

They also specialize in certain levels within that specialty—support staff, midmanagement, professionals.

Google *temporary help services,* the specialty you'd like, and the area where you'd like to interview.

You can also use a general temp service if you're not sure.

Let Each Temp Service Know Your Intentions

Tell them that you're available as a temp and will go out on assignments.

If a full-time position is offered by the client, however, you expect them to waive any immediate placement or temp-to-hire conversion fee. In exchange, promise they can count on you to represent them well and do everything possible to increase their business.

Many temp services waive conversion fees as a matter of policy for good clients or after a certain period. Whether they'll waive an initial placement fee depends on the service.

Respect their decision. It's their business.

Register with a Dozen Temp Services

Since you're turning up the volume on your future, you'll want to maximize your reach. Local, where you'd like to relo, whatever.

You can do this online. Pick ones from various specialties if you like. Register online and interview by phone. This will save time.

Go Only on Those Assignments that Mean Interviews

The temp service will discuss the client, duties, and pay with you. Make it clear that you can and will do the job, but that you're going on the assignment for the purpose of *interviewing*.

There are only two types of assignments for you. Those that *are* instant interviews and those that allow you to *do* instant interviews.

Of course, get the name of the client, its address, phone and fax numbers, and e-mail address. Then directions, dress requirements, and length of assignment.

Use the Assignment to Interview with as Many Offerors as Possible

Go much wider than internal job postings (Do 30) and jobs that are being advertised (Do 19).

Use your incredible instant skills to *make* job openings as you do whenever you appear like a genie (Do 1).

You can probably sleepwalk through your temp job. Clients don't usually give nonemployee, short-term strangers responsibility for major things. Temps don't usually want those jobs either. They want flexibility and freedom.

That's you right now.

Think of the Temp Service as a Partner in Your Interviewing

Temp services work all day (and night) to find and fill employer needs. Often frantically and very competently.

One minute they're picking up a temp to take him to the job, the next they're trying to get a time card from someone who's left the country.

So your little business about instant income while incessantly interviewing is—well—*incidental!* Now you see why I call temp services *instant interview incubators.*

So turn on your computer and turn up the heat!

Do 79: Igniting Intense Interview Interest from Competitors

When you just show up at a competitor of your last employer, you'll know the meaning of *intense interview interest!*

Every business has competitors, and every one wants to know their secrets. Many have intricate procedures to protect them. Preventing their disclosure and use is often the highest priority of the business.

I have experience here. I wrote the only trade secrets law for the placement industry, testify as an expert on the subject, and litigate these issues.

So, when you appear like a genie and announce, "I used to be with Worst Enemy, Inc.," the natives scurry around, find the chief, huddle, and invite you to the war tent. Blowdart shooting instructions follow.

Be careful not to get lipstick or eyeliner on your interviewing uniform when some scout sits you down for a face-painting. You're getting your 15 minutes of fame—no more—so go through the wartime recruiting ritual. Smile, eye contact (Do 1).

Avoid a group interview. The interview interest is so intense that note-takers and minions of all stripes will attend.

Resist the temptation to disclose anything proprietary. This is not only wrong, but two other factors will undo the deal. Initially, the offeror will be concerned that she's doing something illegal by discussing the information with you. (This is true even though she asked—they instinctively *ask,* then *reflect* and *regret.*) Then she'll wonder what you'll tell some other competitor about *their* secret sauce.

So use your competitor background for what it is—an instant interviewgetter.

Competitors are frequently located far from your last (or present) employer. If so, the answer is to call. Fax or e-mail won't work. The instant impact is gone. The competitive offeror will start reflecting, calling an employer lawyer and otherwise losing the intensity of the interest.

Here's how the call might go:

Operator: Hello, this is Competitive Company.

You: Hi! What's the name of your director of engineering?

Operator: Louis Lookout.

You: Thank you. Would you transfer me, please?

Operator: Please hold.

Receptionist: Engineering Administration.

You: Hi, Louis Lookout, please.

Receptionist: Who's calling for Louie?

You: Archie Archrival from Worst Enemy, Inc.

Receptionist: I'm sorry. . .I dropped the phone. Give me a minute to find my upper bridge. Oh good. . .thought I broke it there for a minute. A-h-h-h. That's better. Now where were we? Oh yes. . .you wanted Louie. Just a minute. He's in a closed-door design meeting with his senior design staff. I'll interrupt him.

You: Gee . . . thanks!

Louie *(catching his breath)*: Hi, Archie! How're things over at Worst Enemy?

You: I left a week ago. It was a RIF *(Reduction in Force)*.

Louie: That's great . . . I mean awful . . . I mean great! What kind of work did you do?

You: I was the director of technical support and interfaced with the senior design staff. *(Note the words* senior design. *You picked up the words from the receptionist.)*

Louie: Where are you calling from?

You: Enemytown. I was one of the few nonvirtual employees.

Louie: Really? We'd like to meet with you. How does tonight sound?

You: Well, considering we're three hours later than you, it might be a little tight.

Louie: Okay. I'll get over it. Why don't I have Harry Handshaker, our Director of HR, call you and arrange a jobjungle ambush . . . er . . . scouting trip.

You: I've got other opportunities I'm considering. (A *classic take-away close*.)

Louie: You want to talk to us first. Just hold tight and I'll see if Harry can arrange a videoconference.

You: No . . . that won't be necessary. (*Good for you. Get in their face and s-m-i-l-e!*)

Louie: Okay you're hired . . . sorry, I meant "You're on!" See you in a few days.

You: I'm looking forward to it. Competitive Company has a great product line.

Louie: We'll have a limo pick you up at the heliport!

Igniting? You're *cookin'*!

Do 80: Bonding Instantly with Immigrant Offerors

Instant interviewing is immigrant interviewing.

We instant all over. We deal with what *is*.

You'll meet offerors from another country every day. Many are very successful. Many more want born-here U.S. citizens at the front of the business. If you're one, you qualify.

Successful immigrants know what you know—people like people who are like them. One either whines or one works. That's the way the workingworld works in any language.

There's another reason even more compelling—and troubling. Immigrants are not usually treated very well. Those who succeed in spite of language, racial, or custom barriers are extraordinary. They *overreact* to kindness.

So bond with them like this.

Welcome an Instant Clue

If you see a foreign language newspaper or a religious symbol, check yourself. What was your instant reaction?

It was probably something like, "This place isn't for me," or "Why do they have to impose their beliefs on everyone else?"

Not so fast.

Hear yourself. You're instigating internal instant intimidation. Externally, there's just no issue here.

Think more than positively—think *possibility*, as my friend mega-author Wayne Dyer would say.

If you do, you'll be thinking *probably* before you finish the Magic Four Goodbye (Do 1).

How about if you hear a foreign language?

You might think a thought like, "They shouldn't let employees talk so nobody else understands," or "They're taking over!"

That's the wrong thought.

A great way to forcibly wrench your thinking is to pretend you understand every word.

Do this, and they'll ask, "Did you understand what we just said?"

Your answer *(smiling)*: "Basically!" (Tarzanic translation: "Me friend!")

Smile wide. You're going to be a great asset.

The offeror just has to meet you.

Ask Where the Offeror Is from

That bulge in your left back pocket is offeror contact information (Do 1). So this is no time to hide behind a bush.

Say (silently count 1-2-3), "Where is your boss from?"

The reply will show you you're instantly interested in someone else, and give you instant insight into the environment that influenced the immigrant.

It's not stereotyping to know that a person is from a dictatorship country, a war zone, or a newly formed nation. It's instant intelligence. His land, your turf.

If you're waiting, use the time to ask even more, like, "What country is that near?" or "What is it like there?"

Instanting is all about *aligning*. Mirroring. Magnetizing.

Do the Magic Four Hello with an Immigrant Finale

As you finish the Magic Four Hello (Do 1), get the issue out of the way with: "It's so interesting to hear you're from China! When did you first come to the United States?"

Then listen. He's closer to offering you a job with every word.

Discuss the Offeror's Background During the Interview

That's what he really wants to talk about.

It's called *psychological buy-in*. He talks, you listen. He realizes there's actually someone from the United States who cares about *him*. V-e-r-r-r-y big score.

Embedded in the instant interview technique is the reality that the job has nothing to do with shaking loose an offer. The jobseeker's job-ability does.

Jobability is defined since the first printing of *Instant Interviews* as simply *your ability to get the job*. That's not the same as your ability to *do* it. Doing is a done deal.

You still don't exceed 15 minutes, even if you have to extricate yourself from his hug. If you can't reach, try sidestepping with him over to the intercom and buzzing for a paramedic.

As a last resort, just shuffle to the next instant with him still bonded.

Do the Magic Four Goodbye with an Immigrant Finale

Follow the Magic Four Goodbye (Do 1) with: "I'm absolutely amazed at your perseverance and am thrilled you succeeded. It would be a privilege to learn from you. I look forward to seeing you again soon."

Write the Offeror's Country of Origin on His Business Card

You can do this as you assign the grade. Just "From Nairobi" is fine. You won't have much room and you'll remember. (I know the card's crushed and the pen's broken. But it was worth it.)

Google the Offeror's Country

You can find all kinds of information (history, maps, places of interest). Print out one good page just so you have something to talk about.

Then click on a news update and print that page.

You may already have an offer. If not, mentioning positive things you researched will clinch the deal on your follow-up (Do 1).

Visit a Restaurant that Serves Food from the Offeror's Country

Take one of your loved ones and reward yourselves.

A local authentic restaurant is a terrific learning experience. The place is probably owned by an immigrant from the offeror's country. Tell her you want something tasty and fun. Tell her you want to sample everything you can.

Restaurateurs are an outgoing bunch. Customers and staff will help too.

Food is all about customs, so ask whatever you like.

Take her aside and instant on her too. Why not?

I'm so excited to discuss immigrant offerors for the first time anywhere. They're such terrific people—truly Ameri-*cans*. Tap into their abilities and let them tap into yours.

Don't be surprised if you get an instant *invitation* with your instant offer. To a welcoming celebration you'll never forget!

Do 81: Disabling a Disability Instantly

In doing the research for *Successful Job Strategies for the Disabled*, I started appreciating the wondrous way disabled jobseekers compensate.

Strap yourself in, up, or whatever. I'm now going to show you how to go, *go*, GO to incessant interviews—laughing all the way.

Don't Disclose Your Disability Before the Interview

Whether to disclose a disability is always the first issue. The thinking goes, "I'll have to disclose it eventually, so why not just get it out of the way now?"

Don't do it. Not in your resume, a cover letter, a reference letter, or any other pre-interview correspondence.

If you're out and around on I.I.'s and use a cane, walker, wheelchair, or other obvious assist, just *ignore* that you aren't walking in like the others.

This is *absolutely essential* to your interviewing prowess. You won't interview as well acting or thinking disablement.

Do you need me to tell you that you have attributes I'll never have? If you're blind, can't you hear, smell, feel, touch, and taste better? Don't you *really* see better?

If you're in a chair, don't you maneuver it as though it was an extension of your body? Isn't a walker just something to move you faster? A cane to either keep your balance or help you see?

The offeror can't consider this, so you're just helping her comply.

So let's be real clear on this business of disclosure prior to the interview.

Don't.

Disclosure During the Interview

The shock value of you tapping or wheeling into an interview is really quite comical. Receptionists scurry back with the news, assistants call the employer lawyers, offerors stammer.

But this initial shock wears off quickly when you take it good-naturedly. You're a genie (Do 1), you've appeared in a puff of smoke, and you're gone in 15 minutes. So, smile, and make eye contact (yes, even if you can't see). Sooner or later, you'll get to the rest of the Magic Four Hello—the handshake and greeting to the offeror.

Disclosure on an Employment Application

The app usually asks something like, "Do you have any physical or mental limitations that would interfere with working for us?" Always answer "No" (Do 89).

Of course, you'll answer it if your disability is serious. But it's not. So pay attention to me now. *Don't!*

Not for you, not for them. That so-called disability doesn't exist unless doing the job would be impossible even with a *reasonable accommodation.*

Defining *Reasonable Accommodation*

In *Complying with ADA*, I went through the Americans with Disabilities Act chapter and verse. It requires employers to make that reasonable accommodation for disabled employees.

Like most laws, the ADA is subject to interpretation. The words *reasonable* and *accommodation* are patently ambiguous.

There's not a single EEOC or state administrative ruling, judicial decision, legal treatise, career book, Internet site, or other place you'll find a definition of *reasonable accommodation* you can use.

Here's why: What's *reasonable* in law depends on the *circumstances.* They vary with each case. Let's use lifting weight as an example, since even jobgenies have a weightlifting restriction.

The offeror wants to hire you as a computer systems analyst. This requires lifting containers of data storage records that are too heavy for you. The records can't be stored in lighter containers. However, a long table with a conveyor belt can be purchased for less than two weeks of your salary. Other employees can easily be assigned to lift the containers onto the table.

That's a pretty reasonable accommodation. If you telecommute from a virtual office, an electronic lift with the conveyor belt table in your home might work. Might not. That doesn't make it unreasonable, just impractical and maybe impossible.

So nobody in Congress, the EEOC, the state compliance offices, an employer lawyers' office, or a library knows. Except you and me. We're absolutely certain of what *reasonable accommodation* means. It means, "I can do it. You can adjust."

We don't ask, and we don't check. We don't beg, and we don't apologize. We just "J.D., C.P.C." (Do 1) through this little boogaloo break-dance and *ignore* any objections.

Defining a *reasonable accommodation* is a little out of your line. Doing so is the offeror's problem, and she'd better be right. If not, she'll know the definition of a *relentless accusation*.

What to Do if You're Not Accommodated

Let's assume you've had your I.I. and you really want to work in that systems analyst gig. It will be as a virtual employee (doable in our scenario). The offeror doesn't seem to know how to handle this because you'd be the only telecommuter.

Follow me to your keyboard and we write:

Dear Ellen,

It was a pleasure meeting you this afternoon and discussing Dontgetit's need for a systems analyst.

I am looking forward to starting immediately from home and just need that conveyor belt and lift. If you like, just deduct the cost from my first two weeks' pay and you can reimburse me in 30 days if everything works out.

This should ensure your compliance with the ADA.

Please give me a call as soon as you receive this letter so we can finalize my compensation and arrange for me to start.

I'm really excited about working with you!

Thanks for your consideration.

Very truly yours,

Larry

You can't legally be required to pay for a reasonable accommodation unless it's a hardship on the employer. But there's no law against offering.

It has such a nice ring to it—like, "Checkmate!"

Use the ADA as the Disabled's Device for an Interview

Citations to the law and cases are all you need. You can find books with them at your local library. Or look in the Yellow Pages under "Attorneys—Employment Law" and call someone who offers a free phone consultation (Do 44). Mentioning the ADA is just another device we use to get so-called disabled instant interviewers undisabled.

You're not in this Do because you want to sue anyone. You're not interested in retribution. You're interested in *contribution*. You want to work now and you will interview and get hired like anyone else.

Don't get in your own way. Don't disable *yourself*. Truly you're the only one who will if you don't devise with the device.

Why I'm Telling You

An unwritten "You Can't" sign doesn't mean what it says any more than a help-wanted ad or an offeror does. Don't accept self-imposed rules blindly because rules take on a life of their own. They go from artificial ideas to absolute restrictions.

Rules restrict. Life begs to be lived fully.

Interview Insight

We have a wonderful home over a lake in the mountains. We call the area "Beverly's Hill" (named for its famous resident). I'm writing to you from there as we speak. When we arrived, we thought the nursery had delivered a potted plant at the top of the stairs.

The plant turned out to be an ailanthus "tree of heaven" that had grown from under the carport. It only knew to grow through the planks right in front of the steps that led down to our front door. We left it there because it was so naturally beautiful with its yellow flowers. It also caused passersby on our mountain road to do a double-take—reason enough to leave it.

It just naturally followed the sun. You can too.

The Beatles sang, "For tomorrow may rain, so I'll follow the sun."

Think about that song when you're instanting. Sunlight is everywhere. Yet too many jobseekers think they're walking (or wheeling) around under a cloud (Do 43). Tomorrow *may* rain.

But today, you're *enabled!*

Do 82: Recalling Offerors' Names Instantly

Instant recall!

Here's how to avoid saying something like, "Thanks, 'offeror.'" Tell me your name and I'll consider your offer with the others I got today.

Assume you're busy on your rounds using the basic genie technique (Do 1).

This is what you do.

Rivet and Rhyme at the First Mention of the Offeror's Name

The name is usually mentioned when you greet the receptionist. She might say, "I'm sorry, the supervisor is busy right now."

You say, "What's his name?"

She says, "Nat Langer."

She might introduce you to Nat or he might introduce himself. You'll still rhyme. Think instantly, "Nat, bat, cat, flat!" More words aren't necessary.

Now we move on to the face-to-face.

Parrot the Offeror's Name in the Magic Four Hello

Follow the Magic Four Hello (Do 1) but don't say "Pollywannajob."

Use "Hi! *Bruce*. It's a pleasure meeting you."

Not only have you helped your busy brain recall, but Bruce feels like you're his very own African gray.

Think of Someone You Know with the Same Name

If you can, do it *eo instante*.

The first name of anyone in your brain will do.

"Mary" might be from the Virgin Mary to Mary Poppins.

Think of the Offeror Doing Some Activity that Rhymes with his Name

There's usually a moment to do this while waiting, walking, or hugging.

If it's "Herbert," think of him eating a bowl of sherbet.

"Herb," think of him executing a burp.

"Herbie," think of him slurping a Slurpee.

"Bert," think "You Bert, me Ernie."

Unless you're interviewing for a poet gig, don't worry about *precision*. Just instantaneous *speed*.

Say the Offeror's Name During the Interview

Don't overuse it. Just something like, "Merv, you sure have organized the territories well!"

Do the first four exercises before you try this. Otherwise *Maxine* becomes *Justine*.

Getting corrected instantly is not our thing. We prefer getting an offer.

You probably still will, but you won't know who it's from.

Use the Offeror's Name in the Magic Four Goodbye

Conclude the Magic Four Goodbye (Do 1) with "I look forward to speaking with you soon, Natalie!"

Think of an Association Using the First Letter of the Offeror's Name

When you're out of sight grading, picture "Donna the dancer," "Sam the sander," or "Joe the hobo." No need to write it on the card unless they really look like that.

Instantly Remembering Names at Events

When you're at a job fair (Do 51), chamber mixer (Do 56), or other event, here's a way to recall names instantly.

Rather than lose your laser focus, just think *initials, names,* or *words.* Most lawyers would literally still be practicing if it weren't for *mnemonics*—initials, words, or names that use the first letter of a series you're trying to remember (Do 59 and Do 67). "I-R-A-C" is the law student's writing guide: "*I*ssue, *R*ule, *A*nalysis, *C*onclusion." Definitions, theories, answers. There are even preprinted legal study aids using mnemonics! Making up your own is like fighting your way through your own resume—it's far more effective.

So if it's "Shirley, Oscar, Nancy, and Yul"—in the order you met them, they work at "SONY." If it's "Sol, Oscar, Shirley," they're sending you an "SOS." You don't have to be Daniel Webster, either. "Nancy and Sol" are driving in a "Nissan."

We're just firing neurons in the noggin neighborhood.

Now tell me—are we stallin' or *recallin'?*

Do 83: Swap Meets for Top Greets

"Go to the swap meet and shop." Reasonable enough, if you're not looking for instant interviews.

But if your focus is, "Go to the swap meet to *greet,*" you're at a place that couldn't be better if you designed it yourself.

Excitement is in the air!

The open atmosphere, the open people with open minds, and their open businesses. Probably the optimum optimism venue.

Review and do with your front pockets full (Do 1).

I'm writing this Do as we arrive at a swap meet that's been around for 50 years.

We showed up at 7:45 and walked right in. The ticket booth was still being set up. They allow early birds to come in free with the vendors until 8 a.m.

We stopped by the information booth. The signs said, "Ask us. We're here to help. Apply here. We refer applicants to our merchants. Find a merchant." A big business card display was there with several hundred cards to take for leads.

What an oasis in the jobjungle! A large tribe of happy hunters, all networking with the goal of having fun and making money. Nobody's better than anyone else. They meet before the meet every week, exchange leads, talk about what's hot, laugh, and sing. Working wonderland—and yours free.

All swap meets are not this established and well organized. But even local flea markets have motivated owner-operators. They're high-spirited and always looking to capitalize on a new product or service. The auto parts merchant was talking to the bike merchant about a new swap meet opening up about 20 miles away. I walked over and asked him if he needed help.

He asked me for my card.

The management company was looking for people to help run the event.

I spoke to the vice president. He said the staff is so busy that they really aren't concerned with direct experience. They want a job done by trustworthy people, and they pay well to do it. Make mistakes and you're gone. That sounds fair enough because that means, "Do it right and you'll stay." Never a dull moment. What a place to learn!

There's also a need for office administrators, team supervisors, security personnel (uniformed in swap meet tee shirts and undercover), ticket booth cashiers, parking assistants, and other jobs.

The skateboard vendor bought the U.S. distributor's entire inventory of boards, and is selling them out of a truck. He says the exact same brand costs twice as much on the Internet. I believe it. People are buying them fast. He's looking for someone to help him find other deals, and pays a base salary plus a percentage of whatever they find.

All of these people (and many, many others at the meet) seem like very successful, savvy businesspeople. They smile and seem to greatly enjoy the swap meet spirit. Many have been at the meet for a long time. Nobody is particularly interested in experience. They're unpretentious entrepreneurs who want reliable, honest, helpers that reflect their values.

Some are weekly, some are monthly. At this swap meet, there are around a thousand merchants. Their backgrounds vary as much as what they sell.

In a separate area, there's a mini job fair. Around 10 private employers looking to hire. The sheriff's department, an electronics company, a supermarket chain.

Check the bulletin boards at your community center, look in your local newspaper, and watch for flyers about any swap meets, flea markets, road shows, or county fairs. The merchants are an entire subculture who often work from home and fly under the radar.

For weekend instant interviewing, there's *nothing* like greets at the meets!

Do 84: Supercharging Your Sphere of Influence

Now let's get your family and friends buzzin' like a bunch of bug-eyed bumblebees.

There are seven superchargers to awakening crazily committed people who love you or just depend on you for food and shelter.

You must do all seven superchargers because it's a system.

List Every Adult You Like

It's simple and surprising.

Go to your computer and list the name of:

1. Every adult relative living with you
2. Every local relative
3. Every local friend
4. Every local member of the clergy you know
5. Every professional you use (accountant, lawyer, doctor)
6. Every other provider of services to you (hairdresser, fitness coach, pet groomer)

7. Each representative of every retailer or other merchant who sells to you

8. Each representative of every vendor to your business

Do this in the order I've given. That will keep your list organized by type of contact.

The average I.I. has 27 names. That's 27X power magnification. V-e-r-r-r-y big.

Now number to the left with a 1 for those who'd stop a bullet for you, a 2 for who'd push you out of the way, a 3 for who'd yell "Duck!," and a 4 for who'd dial 911.

Then rewrite the list with the 1's first, followed by the 2's, 3's, and 4's. Leave some space (or use your computer) to insert phone numbers, fax numbers, and e-mail addresses.

You now have a prioritized list of all your many instant interview investigators.

This list is what recruiters call a *job intelligence network*—supercharged. Now you're ready to floor it!

Ask Instant Interview Investigators Right Away

Don't let your ego or your feel-low stop you. You must get busy before you overthink. You must not second-guess what every investigator will say or do. These are not like offerors (Do 41).

Call each person on the list. Here's the script.

You: Hi! This is Candi Candoo. Hope you're well.
Ron: Hi, Candi! I've been fine. How are you?
You: I'm doing great, but I didn't just call to say "Hi!" I need your help.
Ron: What's up?
You: I want to find another job, and I know you have many contacts.
    I need you to give me some suggestions about who to call.
Ron: So you want me to refer you to people I know?
You: Yes.
Ron: Well, I think I can do that. But I'd rather see if they're looking for anyone first.
You: I really appreciate that, but I don't want to impose on you.
Ron: I *am* busy, but I really don't mind making a few calls. What have you done? I really don't know that side of you. Do you have a resume?

You: I'll tell you what. Let's do both. For the ones you'd like to call, I'll e-mail and mail my background to you. I'll mail you some business cards too, so you can pass them around.

Ron: That's perfect. That way I'll sound halfway intelligent and can help you more.

You: Thanks. Now how about the ones I can contact myself?

Ron: Well there's Kermit, the newscaster I see at the club. Vidal, my hair-stylist. And Andre, whom I play tennis with. I'll give you their contact information.

You: Thank you!

Prepare Your Background Highlights

Just use your letterhead and title it "Background Highlights." Give an introduction and then start each item with an action verb. This is not a cover letter, broadcast letter, a resume, or any other direct communication to an offeror. It's just a helpful guide.

It reads like this:

Candi is the daughter of my college roommate. I've known her all of her life, and I recommend her highly for any opening you may have. Among Candi's many positive attributes is her ability to easily communicate with others.

In her last job as an associate vice president with Standard Finance, she inherited a small new business department of three trainees and only one senior loan agent.

Within eight months, Candi hired and trained a full staff of nine agents. She increased the loan business to almost three times the volume.

I am proud to recommend Candi. Her contact information is:

Candice D. Candoo
423 Marbury Rd.
Santa Barbara, CA 90723
555-555-5555 (H)
555-555-5555 (C)
555-555-5555 (O)
555-555-5555 (F)
cdcandoo@hola.com

Send Each Investigator a Gogetem Kit

The *gogetem kit* consists of your background highlights sheet, 25 of your business cards, and a handwritten, dated thank-you note in its envelope with the investigator's first name that reads:

It was great speaking with you!
My background highlights and business cards are enclosed.
I look forward to hearing from anyone you refer who can benefit from my contribution.
Please let me know by e-mail when I'm referred.
Thanks so much,
Candi

Follow Up in One Week

If you haven't received a call or e-mail confirming receipt of the gogetem kit, find out by a call.

Why a call? Because you called initially. Why *that* call? Because you probably didn't receive a reply.

You're an I.I. now. You know a phone call is strictly for setups and follow-ups. E-mail is for the convenience of an investigator who's helping you as a favor.

Then follow up every week by a call just to check in with the investigator. There is a cumulative effectiveness by the repetition.

He'll get to know you better and you'll be on his mind. Investigators are often offerors too!

Have a Conference among Intimate Investigators

Once you do these first five steps, your investigators will start becoming competitors after a few weeks. Parents, spouses, friends, business associates, schoolteachers, coaches, and others start talking up your fine self to others. They talk to each other too, and start doing what people *always* do when there's a challenge. They compete!

Is there competition in your family? Only if you have one! Would "insane jealousy" be an understatement? Among your friends? Your servers? I think so. I really do.

You can ignite investigators by mentioning how many interviews some other relative, friend, or business acquaintance popped for you. Would that be cruel and unusual punishment?

Setting up a contest—taking competitors to lunch and honoring the one who generates the most referrals? With a little inexpensive MVII (Most Valuable Interview Investigator) award?

Ouch!

Reprioritize and Update Your Investigator List Constantly

Pull up that screen and add the date of each referral and a short comment about it under the contact information of each investigator.

Add investigators and their contact information as they change.

Follow this procedure, and your sphere of influence will expand along with an avalanche of interview invitations.

Seven superchargers.

What's that buzzin' sound? Quick! Where do we get beekeepers' masks?

Do 85: Interviewing for an Instant Increase

A raise! For looking to leave?

Why not? Aren't you worth more today than yesterday? You're more experienced. Besides, we've got major buying decisions—business cards, thank-you notes, a decent pen.

Once you understand the dynamics of job e-x-p-a-n-s-i-o-n (Do 4), you can see the myopia of shortchanging yourself. Bosses want to get the most for the least. It's called *profit* and they want more of it. Keeping labor costs down means giving up nothing. So that's what bosses do.

You don't need a C.P.C. to know that employees are wired like this: Asking for a raise means hearing, "You're not worth what you're getting now and maybe nothing." It's injected into the veins at the time of the company physical. Mind games bosses play.

But it disappears in I.I.'s. Their self-confidence and freedom has them chuckling at this kind of foolery.

Here are the I.I.'s ways to get a raise.

Prepare a Raise List

It's all about objectifying your contribution. That's what raise discussions are all about. This immediately defuses the boss's bomb because *subjectivity* (whim) can't be credibly used as an argument. He'd look small and powerless.

So just make a *raise list* of everything you do *right*. We call these *raisers*, if you're thinking about what your boss thinks you do *wrong*, you need to keep reviewing that list. Do it 10 times, and you'll see the magic of positive programming. Objections are obfuscated by objectivity.

Around a dozen raisers are all you need. Twelve sentences that start with *I* (as in *instant interview influence*). Then an action word to make one concise, specific, positive sentence.

One might be, "I built an effective sales force in eight months." Another: "I exceeded my annual production goal by 30 percent."

Use that raise list as the foundation and you'll be unshakable.

Record Your Raise List

Use that little recorder we recommended (Do 25) to record your raise list.

Play it back once in the morning before work and once when you get home. A week of that few-minute exercise will have the list embedded in your subconscious ready to pop out naturally in context at just the right time.

Obsess on the Amount You Want

Convince yourself that you're worth it.

You do this by talking to others and convincing them. Also by writing the amount beneath a photo of you smiling, then taping the photo to your bathroom mirror.

Use the Magic Four Hello and Stay with the Eye Contact and Smile

The Magic Four Hello (Do 1) is all about what you *say* and *convey*. The physical part of your delivery is far more important than any words you use. What you *say* is *factual*, what you *convey* is *physical*. Big difference, little resistance.

You must rivet your eyes on your boss's. I always moved my head to follow his eyes. This is deadly. Continuous eye contact is s-o-o-o important. Looking down means you're weak. Looking away means you're not interested. Looking behind means you're trying to head for the door.

Sit Somewhere Besides the Front of Your Boss's Desk

We talked about the reasons for this (Do 38 and Do 56).

There's enough confrontation as it is. If he has (or you can gracefully move) a chair on the side of his desk, go for it. If there's a couch, sit on it with him. A coffee table and chairs? Okay.

Write Out a Script

It resembles:

You: Hi, Dean. Thanks for meeting with me! We've both got a lot to do today, so I'll get right to the point. I'd like a raise. (*Note the word ask appears nowhere in this conversation.*)

Dean: I just gave you one two years ago! Why do you think we should pay you more?

You: Well, for one thing, I have two more years of experience. For another, I've checked around and the going rate for my job is 20 percent higher than I'm earning here. And most important, I've accomplished a lot for the company.

Dean: I don't really see it that way. Weren't you excited to be MVP-of-the-month last year?

You: I appreciate all appreciation. (*Humor. It disarms and penetrates.*) Well, let me remind you what I've done. (*Write as many raisers from the raise list as you like.*)

Dean: I guess you're right. But the new safety program has increased our operating expenses.

You (*leaning forward—eyeballs riveted*): I'd like a 20 percent increase.

Dean: What do I get?

You: Well, you get what you got. And you got a lot. But you'll continue to have me becoming even more productive and I'll help with reducing the cost of our new safety program too.

Dean: Okay, let me sleep on it.

You: Sleep well. I'll call you tomorrow morning.

Shake Hands, Still Eyeballing and Smiling

You can stop leaning forward, get up, turn around, and get back to work.

Follow Up the Next Day

Don't lie in wait behind the water cooler.

Midafternoon, go in, smile, look at the eyes only, and say, "What are we doing about the raise?"

Note *we*, not *you*, and *the raise*, not *my raise*.

The *company* has a challenge.

We'll solve it.

You'll get that raise. And praise!

You'll never have to ask again.

Do 86: Magnetizing Muckety-mucks

Want to nose-to-nose with an industry mogul? Become a reporter on assignment! It's a sure way to get instants.

Roundup articles are surveys of business muckety-mucks about some subject that interests a trade magazine. They're a perfect opener to a standard I.I. (Do 1).

You google a subject, followed by *magazines*. That displays the mags that concentrate on that area.

Then you call (better than e-mail and *far* better than fax or regular mail) the publisher. Ask for the editor-in-chief. Tell her, "I'm writing a 'roundup article' on trends in the automotive additive industry. When would *Racing Maniac* be interested in running it?" The chief—directly, or indirectly through an editor—will say, "Sure! When do you plan to submit it?"

You now have an *assignment*. That allows you to honestly make up some questions like, "What do you think will be the next breakthrough in goosegrease gas goo?"

Then you call some huge company offeror (they call him their CEO) and ask away. It's occasionally hard to understand him because he foams at the mouth at the offer of free publicity.

This will require you to interview (read: interview *with*) him in person. Say you'd like to pick up a portrait of him to include in the article. (That will make it necessary to wipe off the foam oozing out of your phone.)

Expect an instant interview.

Bring that recorder you're using for your phone exercises (Do 25). It will save you a lot of time and you won't have to be taking notes. That means you can make eye contact with the offeror, smile, and carry on the basic no-more-than-15-minute interview.

As always, *buenos dias*, *pronto*, and *adios—hasta mañana* (Do 1)!

You can do this with as many offerors as you like. Try to pick a subject that is generic enough to snag a bunch of them. An example would be a wine survey if you live (or want to) in northern California.

When the article is published, mail it to the offeror with a thank-you note (in its envelope). Just:

Thanks for the great interview!

Best,

Mike

Or just walk down the hall to his office and give it to him personally! Yes, this *really* works!

You can also write an interesting article profiling successful people in a local industry. It's even faster than a survey because there's no preparation required. Just the publisher call. Choose a magazine the same way to read that runs pieces like that and google its name.

Magazines have an insatiable appetite for articles. You're not looking for fortune, only fame. Grant first rights and reprint rights but reserve all other rights so you can make your own reprints, display it online, or otherwise use it for publicity.

It's fast, costs nothing, and including it in your accomplishments increases the value of your resume (Do 5).

Distributing the article itself may be a great interviewgetter too.

You'll be magnetizing muckety-mucks in a moment *masterfully!*

Do 87: Getting Paid for Instant Interviewing

How'd you like to get paid right away for instantly interviewing? Too good to be true? Almost too good to *do*!

Pick an upscale area near you. Then google *party rentals* with the name of that area. Write down the names and addresses, call to find out the name of the owner (or general manager if it's a chain), go over, and poof, like a genie (Do 1), find out who they service and where.

There's a big difference here. Some are geared for small gatherings of seniors, family weddings, or baby showers. Others service major social and political gatherings where the beautiful people go. If you don't like carrying chairs and tables, google *caterers* again with the name of the area.

Caterers work from home, so you can't just show up. Call first, using the genie technique, then meet them.

If you don't like carrying or cooking, google *florists* with the name of the area.

If they have a shop, use the party rental routine. If not, use the caterer one.

Then work, but always attend the conflab. With your business cards and pen in your left front pocket. Instant interview the most promising guest offerors.

You've carried and sat. Cooked and eaten. Picked and arranged flowers. Instant interviewed too.

In a word, you're *qualified!*

Do 88: Getting Leads from Leasers

You won't know of office furniture leasers. They don't advertise in places you see. But they're the leaders of leads.

You can visit showrooms of the major chains (usually under "Office Furniture Rentals" in the *Yellow Pages* or googled for your area). You'll see these chains are *very* major—commercial furniture leasing is a huge business.

You simply walk in and make yourself a friend with a leasing consultant or whatever. An instant interviewer I've been helping went over to one of these places and took down the names and numbers of over 30 businesses. Over 30 local businesses that needed furniture! Chairs for employees to sit on. Desks for them to write on. File cabinets for them to stuff with orders. Busy businesses. New businesses expanding.

What? They gave her the names? Of course! You don't think she'd make a large leasing commitment without *references*, do you?

The independent leasers are even more forthcoming with names. I went in to one of them on my way to court about six months ago. I just stopped at an armoire to check my Windsor knot, and some salesman was glued to my jacket until I left. I just asked, "Who are some of your customers?"

He must have rattled off seven or eight before I took my jacket off (fortunately with his help). Then he took me over to the leasing office where I saw completed agreements from another dozen or so accounts.

I had to get to court, so I left after about 10 minutes. (The guy wanted to go, and I almost agreed. But one final tug and we unstuck him from my jacket.) I made it just in time for the calendar call.

It happened to be downtown. When my court appearance was over, rather than waste being dressed up, I drove a few blocks to the wholesale district. There were a few furniture places I remembered from my HR days. We bought furniture when we were moving our offices.

It wasn't laid out like the leasing place. There was a central counter area. I spoke with a very nice lady and asked who bought things recently. She told me. They had one of those displays with shelves so you can leave your cards. I took a dozen or so to share with I.I.'s.

If you're interested in a specific type of business, specialty leasers are dynamite lead sources. Among the most common are those who lease medical and dental equipment. They often have local showrooms and work exactly the same way (although much more in keeping with the elevator music set).

Getting leads from auto leasing companies is even easier (if that's possible).

You want fleet leasers because otherwise you get consumer leads. Many executives, but it takes too long to find them.

Auto leasers *really* want you to know their fleet customers. It's how they rate themselves in the car biz.

One I.I. reported that he saw a sign outside a lot that said "Fleet Sales." He drove in and just asked, "Who leases from you?" Pretty clear, right? The uniformed agent looked at him, turned an about-face and started walking back to the office. He followed her and she pulled out this big book with a computer-generated list of accounts.

New car dealers are also great leasing leaders. Cars, trucks, sometimes even heavy equipment.

How about uniform rental places? You can just call. They like to give out brochures with the logos of familiar corporate accounts. But you already know those, so ask for the names of *smaller* accounts. You can just google them and find out addresses and phone numbers for a genie visit (Do 1).

Who's increasing uniform orders? Who's giving new addresses for delivery? Who's changing sizes for new employees?

Once you know who leases commercially, you know who's actively employing. Then it's strictly appearing like a genie wherever and whenever.

This isn't exactly the Coke formula we're talking about. The information is there just for the hinting. Nobody hints, nobody gets.

How nice for us.

Do 89: Passing Instantly Through the Personal Screen

Employment applications are instant interviewgetters. But only for instant interviewers!

Finesse one properly and you'll instantly pass right through all screens. The reason is that the same questions are asked over and over again—usually in the same places. There are only so many questions that can be asked, and only so many ways to ask them.

Goof on apps, and you're screened out.

So print out a typical app from any employer and let's finesse it for once and for all.

In this Do, we'll cover the personal items you'll be asked even if you have a resume. (Do 90 is for when you're asked not to write, "See resume.")

Instructions

They may be only a two-word instruction in paper apps. If so, it's "Please print." Assuming you have access to a typewriter, use it for a paper app. Otherwise, print in handwriting as clearly as you can.

Just be sure to read the instructions on each app. There might be some minor differences (ways to abbreviate, most recent first, or spaces to leave blank).

Since offerors invariably use apps during the interview, it'll also help you to anticipate the order and types of questions you'll be asked.

If you don't follow directions, you won't get interviewed.

Name

Be sure the order is correct. Some apps require last name first.

If it asks for a middle name, don't use your initial (or vice versa).

Address

Customary post office abbreviations are acceptable. Include your extended ZIP+4 code (five digits, a hyphen, and the last four).

As I mentioned for resumes (Do 5) and all other printed matter, designate an apartment as "Unit." Doing so makes it appear that you own your home—a sign of stability. The "No." abbreviation should not be used because it's often the answer to yes-no questions and will attract attention. You're then likely to be asked whether you rent or own.

Phone Number

Hyphenate the area code to the seven-digit number.

Include cell, home, and office numbers, designating them separately.

If you're concerned about the calls to your office, after the word *Office* (not *Work*), in parentheses write:

"(Please leave message with name and phone number only)."

Date

Unless otherwise stated, this means the date you completed the app.

Don't write out the date unless it's clearly indicated by the space. And don't start with the year.

Use forward slashes with one or two digits like 12/3/XX.

Be consistent in designating dates throughout the form.

Referral Source

First name, middle initial (find out), last name.

If you've interviewed with the business before, don't include this person as a referral source. You can mention it and the details when you get the instant call.

Birth Date

Answer this question using slashes exactly as you do for all other dates.

Be honest (always).

Height

Use the proper ′ and ″ symbols for feet and inches. If you don't, *5′ 9″* will look like *59*.

Weight

Vanity or wishful thinking shouldn't change this answer.
The number should be followed by *lbs*.

Social Security Number

If you don't have one, contact the U.S. Social Security Administration and get one as soon as possible.

Length of Time at Your Address

This is asked primarily to determine your stability.
Address duration is easily verified by reference and credit checks, so be careful.

Previous Address

As with the present address, this can also be verified by reference and credit checks.
Be as careful here.

Salary Required

"Negotiable" or "Open" are the only two acceptable answers.
With any number (unless you know it and agree), the probability of you being too high or low is almost 100 percent.
That will screen you out.

Type of Work Desired

Write:

"Anything in the _____ field that will allow me to make a genuine contribution to _____ (name of business)."

Don't write "Unknown" or "Will consider anything" as unstants do.

Availability to Start Work

This should be answered:
"After I give notice to current employer."
If you're not working, write the date of the following Monday.
Don't write "Immediately," "ASAP," or "Now." It will make you appear anxious—even desperate.
You're instant—so they can wait!

Spouse or Partner's Name

If you're single, don't write "Separated," "Divorced," or "Deceased." Your reason for being single has nothing to do with the job.

If you're separated, write "Married" (you are, legally). Don't discuss a separation during the interview.

Spouse or Partner's Occupation

This shouldn't be asked, but it's permissible.

Incompetent interviewers inflate spouse job titles to impress the interviewer.

It has just the opposite effect—offerors want the moneymaker because she is more likely to be a long-term employee.

Number of Children and Ages

The number of children should be a word and their ages should be numbers.

So it looks like:
"Three—8, 7, and 4"

Be sure this is consistent with whether you're married. If not, be prepared to answer the question during the interview.

Bondability

If a direct question is asked about whether you've ever been "denied or refused a bond," answer "Yes" or "No" based upon your last job only.

Otherwise, questions about whether you are bondable are asking for opinion. Yours is always "Yes."

General Health

The only instant's answer is "Excellent."

Physical Limitations

Unless you have some disability that requires a special accommodation, "None" is the proper answer.

Mental Disorders or Treatment

Assuming there is no recognized mental handicap, the answer is "None."

Prior Work Injuries

Don't go back more than three years. Be prepared to show that you've fully recovered. The word *ever* on an app is just too broad. You can narrow it to a reasonable time. If the employer discovers the injury and you're well now, you're probably also fine.

Absenteeism

Fewer than 10 days per year over a two-year period isn't considered excessive. It gets an:
   "Occasionally absent for minor illnesses."
   More, and you'll be asked about it during the interview.

Military Status

Since dishonorable discharges are so rarely used, you should have no problem.

Conviction of Felonies

Answer "No" if you were under 18.

If you were convicted and the record isn't sealed, check your *Yellow Pages* under "Attorneys—Criminal." Call someone who offers a free consultation and ask about getting your record sealed.

You do not have to disclose misdemeanors or infractions.

Don't forget to sign the app.

See how easily unstants get screened out?

While you get instantly interviewed!

Do 90: Passing Instantly Through the Professional Screen

Now we get to the heart of the employment application—the crucial job-related information. Passing right through this screen is done differently.

It is only necessary if the employer doesn't permit "See resume" on the application.

Let's finesse this for once and for all too!

Languages Spoken

If the question doesn't say *foreign* languages, start with "English." Leaving it out will be a failure to follow instructions.

Special Skills or Talents

Unstants make the mistake of leaving this blank.

Offerors are impressed by people who have transferable abilities or skills. Be sure to include anything that will make you better at doing the job.

Don't generalize with conclusions like "Detail-oriented" or "I like people." Give specific accomplishments that demonstrate these attributes.

Outside Interests or Hobbies

As with special skills or talents, choose work-related activities that enhance your image as a superstar.

Memberships

Anything other than professional memberships should not be included.

Questions about social, fraternal, or religious groups get the response "None."

Other Job Interests

Unstants are often confused by the word *interests* and therefore leave the space blank. Big mistake.

Offerors interview people they think are flexible. The larger businesses also have computerized "skills inventories."

So include duties you'd like to have in the future.

Use keywords if you're applying online (Do 15). This is critical.

Computer Skills

Even if it's only on your personal computer, include any business software programs you use.

It makes you look professional.

Education

Some apps ask you to circle the highest grade completed, others ask you to write it down.

Do that, then note any degrees, certificates, honors, or awards received.

Dates of attendance should be written consistently (Do 59).

Be sure to include any other names used. Omitting this is a common mistake that screens out unstants without their knowledge. Their education can't be verified.

Present or Last Employer

Use the full name of the company, abbreviating the address where necessary. If asked, its kind of business should be stated in a few words.

Dates of Employment

Don't leave them blank. If you do, it looks like you're trying to hide an employment gap.

Call your last employer for accuracy if you're not sure.
This is routinely verified.

Past Compensation

Be sure to indicate the numbers with a dollar sign in front and /wk., /mo., or /yr. as appropriate for your type of job.

Past compensation is irrelevant to your worth to an offeror, but can be easily verified.

Just be sure to include every possible addition if it asks for compensation, not wages or salary.

Past Job Titles

Unstant written reference checks constantly pick up discrepancies in these. It's a bigger-than-realized reason for rejection.

So get your past titles right.

You can explain your duties and level of responsibilities on the form.

Immediate Supervisor

Give the first name, middle initial, last name, and title.

If you're worried about the reference, contact him (Do 43).

Regarding a present supervisor, write:

"Please do not contact without my consent."

Description of Job

Concisely summarize your most significant duties and highest responsibilities.

Use keywords if you're applying online (Do 7).

Job Duties Enjoyed Most or Least

Be careful here. Enjoy everything except poor work ethic, poor performance, or poor results.

Reasons for Leaving Prior Jobs

Use something like "Resigned for better position" instead of "Quit." Or "Reduction in force" instead of "Layoff."

Never "Fired." You just need to call your former boss to discuss an alternative (Do 64).

Gaps between Jobs

If they were more than five years ago, don't worry about being wrong. If within the past five years, be accurate on dates, and give some plausible reason other than "unemployed." Perhaps what you were doing (other than instanting).

Consent to Contact Present Employer

Always answer this, and always answer "No."

Otherwise your present employer could become your past employer instantly.

If there's space on the app, write:

"Please do not contact my present employer until mutual interest has been established."

Personal and Professional References

Be sure to complete the names, titles, addresses, phone numbers, and e-mail addresses (Do 63 and Do 64).

Consent to Verify Information

You can answer this way:

"Yes, except for present employer."

Don't forget to sign the app (if you didn't already).

That's how you instantly pass through the professional screen.

To an instant interview!

Do 91: Using Lead Cards for Instant Referrals

Let's start by taking your mental memos and writing them down on lined index cards. Each lead card should include this:

Name of lead

Title of lead

Name of business

Address of business

Office phone number of lead

Home phone number of lead (if known)

E-mail address of lead

Activity to get interview (date resume sent, dates of responses to follow-up calls, and so forth)

There are three basic ways to develop job leads. In order of priority, you should:

1. Look in the local Yellow Pages under whatever heading you like. Then call the target employer and speak with the receptionist or someone in the sales, marketing, public relations, or human resources department.

   You can even cold call into the department where you'd like to work.

   This is so easy, so much fun, and so effective that any other way is strictly for inactive interviewers.

2. Let your personal contacts (friends, relatives, acquaintances, former supervisors, and former coworkers) know.

3. Use an Instant Availability Announcement (Do 12 and Do 13).

This is a marketing campaign, and you're the product. You want *exposure*, so work up a deck of at least 50 cards. Delete cards as needed, but 50 hot leads is the absolute minimum at any time.

Contact every lead at least once. Discard and replace the less powerful, less influential, and less aggressive ones. Then select those you want to call on a regular basis and do so around every other week.

Many jobseekers divide the cards into:

Offerors

People who have direct control over who's hired (not merely intake interviewers who screen).

The routine calls to offerors are specific, since you're asking them for an opportunity to assist in any way you can.

Direct Referrals

People able to arrange interviews with offerors. This includes human resourcers.

Indirect Referrals

People who know many people but are not able to arrange interviews with offerors now. This includes people who are working at places that might be hiring soon.

Here are the kinds of questions to ask direct and indirect referrals when you call:

Who do you know who'd be interested in hiring me?

Does your company have an internal phonebook? If so, may I have one?

What other businesses do you know about that are hiring? Do you know anyone there I can call? If so, who?

You must follow through compulsively. That means if you say you'll let the referral know how things work out, do it. If you say you'll check back with her again at a certain time, do it.

Keep even the most casual commitment, be grateful for even the dumbest lead, and don't embarrass them about the people they suggest.

Do it right, and the people named on those lead cards will become your marketing department and sales force!

Do 92: Controlling the Offeror Like a Robot

It's like pushing one of only four buttons on a toy robot remote!
Beep, beep! Here's how.

Questioning Properly Controls Offerors

This is because strategic questions gain control of the offeror and direct the conversation toward loving you madly.

Let's say you've just appeared genie-style (Do 1), greeted with the Magic Four Hello, and are past the niceties. Usually this is a minute or two into the dance.

You push all four buttons by questioning with contracted words that end in *n't:*

aren't

can't

couldn't

doesn't

don't

hasn't

haven't

isn't

shouldn't

wasn't

weren't

won't

wouldn't

Pushing the Four Instant Buttons

Instant Button 1—Beginning a Sentence

Can't you get the project back on schedule with someone like me around?

Haven't you looked for anyone to help?

Wasn't the last person you interviewed qualified?
Now *you* push Button 1 by completing these sentences starting with:
Don't _____?
Isn't _____?
Wouldn't _____?

Instant Button 2—Connecting a Sentence

Since you suspect the staff is overworked, *doesn't* it make sense for you to hire me?

Now that the budget is approved, *shouldn't* we work together?
When the equipment arrives, won't you be glad I'm here?
Now *you* push Button 2 connecting these sentences with:
_____, can't _____?
_____, couldn't _____?
_____, doesn't _____?

Instant Button 3—Ending a Sentence

You really can retain your employees, *can't* you?

It looks like I can really do some good here, *don't* you agree?
We'd be able to get the job done right away, *wouldn't* we?
Now *you* push Button 3 to end these sentences:
_____, haven't I?
_____, shouldn't I?
_____, won't we?

Instant Button 4—Turning a Sentence from a Statement into a Question

You can verify my expertise with my supervisor, *can't* you?

My contribution will be significant, *won't* it?
Someone like me would definitely enhance the team, *wouldn't* he?
Now *you* push Button 4 to start these sentences:
_____, aren't _____?
_____, hasn't _____?
_____, wasn't _____?

Practice instant button-pushing for a day or two with people who wouldn't run away from home. By that time, pushing them will become as automatic as operating your TV (or a toy robot) remote.

Only *these* buttons control offerors to instantly interview. And only *you* know how to use them!

Do 93: Sending Icon Introduction Letters

Someone *big* introducing you?

Who else does that? Only instants!

An icon introduction letter uses the power of a third-party testimonial. Unlike a specific letter, it is not personal to the target. Someone with major credentials writes a letter about you aimed at senior executives.

When an icon writes the right words the right way and you mass mail it, the results are staggering. Often 100 percent interviews!

You're not looking for a job; you're marketing your abilities to a specific target—offerors that need you. Now you'll know what professional marketers know.

Understand the Reason It Works

This part of your marketing plan is a direct-mail campaign, with an important addition—phone follow-up. It's called *mailphone* and doubles—even triples—the results from direct mail alone.

You're in the interview industry. Its mission is to get you happiness, money, and prestige. Follow the methods that the pros use, and you can't lose.

The proof of direct mail effectiveness fills your mailbox every day. Focused direct mail is a multibillion-dollar industry.

Direct mail works because it's *targeted*. Unlike a commercial broadcast or advertising space, a direct-mail message doesn't compete with other advertisers for attention. If it gets to the interested party, and it gets opened, it gets the offeror's undivided attention. This is more than any media advertising provides. That translates into incessant interviews.

Direct mail is also the most scientific, controllable, and cost-effective method. A direct-mail jobseeker marketing campaign outperforms any you-against-the-world, one-step-at-a-time approach to the job market.

A phone or mail campaign leverages your time and gets your name in front of offerors faster. Then your body follows instantly.

Identifying an Instant Icon

Select or cold-call to find an icon—someone whose name or position will instantly impress an offeror. Perhaps a distant relative, or a friend of a friend. Someone who appears successful, trustworthy, and credible.

The Look of the Letter

The format for the letter is similar to the broadcast letter in Do 9. The process for identifying offerors is the same too. Managers, not human resourcers.

This letter should not look mass-produced. Do not use "To Whom It May Concern" or photocopies. Each letter should be on high-quality (at least 24-lb.) bond paper. The reference's letterhead, with raised type and watermark, is the best look for this one.

If you have access to a computer with a mail-merge program and a letter-quality printer, prepare originals on the reference's letterhead.

If the reference cannot supply you with 50 or more sheets of letterhead, you will have to resort to photocopies—but make sure they are on quality, 24-lb. white or ivory bond paper. It copies best. (The offeror may do a little internal mass mailing for you.)

All letters should be signed individually by the reference. Envelopes should be typed individually. Don't use a typed label.

This is personal correspondence. Offerors open envelopes that are personal.

The Content of the Letter

The letter should be sincere, measured, and factual, but it must be riveting and convincing. You have only a few seconds to capture the offeror's attention.

She'll look at the icon's letterhead first. If that interests her, she'll glance down at the signature and read any *P.S.* that appears below it. (Direct-mail pros pack their hardest sell into the P.S.) If an offeror is still interested, she'll read the opening paragraph.

Each element of the letter must captivate the offeror enough to go on. If she gets to the opening paragraph, it has to keep her reading. Study the example that follows.

Use language and tone to sell value, to create interest, and to stimulate response. When you call, the offeror will be ready to interview you!

SAFETY INSURANCE COMPANIES
Corporate Headquarters
One Founders Plaza
Davenport, Connecticut 06210
555-555-5555

Henry V. Tattersall, III
Chief Financial Officer

(date)

Edgar O. Winston
Chief Financial Officer
General Investors Group
1200 Park Avenue
New York, New York 70011

Re: Joel M. Adams

Dear Edgar:

As chief financial officers of multinational companies, you and I know the importance of an internal audit process. But talented, skilled, effective audit managers are almost impossible to find.

Joel Adams is one of them. As a manager of audit management with direct responsibility to the CFO, Joel uses his understanding of the audit process to solve complex financial problems.

Joel reported directly to me in my former position as CFO at Amalgamated Industries. Amalgamated's acquisition by Consolidated Brands has placed him on the job market. I'm letting you know he's available since you could undoubtedly benefit from the expertise of a highly qualified audit manager.

Please speak with Joel when he calls. I'm confident it will be mutually beneficial.

Best personal regards,

Henry V. Tattersall, III

P.S. Please let your secretary know that Joel will be phoning you for a meeting within the next few days.

HVT:mec

If you don't get through the first time, don't give up. I.I.'s don't—
ever!

Here's a typical offeror conversation:

You: Hi, this is Joel Adams. Henry Tattersall wrote to Mr. Winston about
    me. I'm calling to follow up on that letter. Is he available?
Secretary: One moment. I'll see if he can take your call, Mr. Adams.
    (*Pause*) Yes, Mr. Winston is available. I'll connect you now.
Edgar: Edgar Winston.
You: I'm Joel Adams, the audit manager our friend, Henry Tattersall,
    wrote to you about.
Edgar: Yes, Joel, I got the letter and would like to talk to you some time
    next week. I'll transfer you back to my secretary and she can arrange
    it. If we don't have an opening, I know who does.
You: Thanks. I look forward to meeting you!

That's the icon introduction letter. It gets interest—and instant
interviews!

Do 94: Slipping in the Back Door this Saturday

How'd you like to work this Saturday?

What's that? Pay? Who said anything about *pay?* We're talkin' instant
interviews!

Seriously, it's *the* way to do a backdoor hire. The front door's not just
locked on weekends—it's been locked for years (Do 57). That's why you
never make it past HR. They *screen* over there—screen *out.*

Stop and think about this. How can you expect some administrator
who's (1) never done the job, (2) doesn't understand the job, (3) is working from a committee-generated job description or a few-line job requisition, (4) isn't doing the hiring, (5) won't be supervising the employee,
and (6) isn't even in the department—to make a favorable decision based
upon (7) written background information from (8) someone who has no
idea about any of this.

Now you can see why calling managers directly is the only way to get
hired.

There are six steps to the Saturday slip.

Call a Hiring Manager Directly

Just pick up the phone and ask the operator for the head of the department where you have some experience (Do 1). This gives you some talking points.

Write a backdoor short opener for yourself.

You say something like, "Hi, Ron. This is Stuart Norcross. I have a background in finance with Competition Corporation, and wanted to discuss how it can benefit your department."

If he shows interest, say you have done or can do everything that's required (if you haven't, you can). Now you've gone from getting to giving—you are *meeting a need*.

It's all about *needs*.

The instant interview just happened. Now for your callback interview . . .

Offer to Do Something He Wants Done Free

Like the indemnification device (Do 44), this is simply offering to *do a task*.

All that's required is going to the facility, meeting the hiring manager, and doing whatever he'd like done.

Who gets offers like that? I.I.'s.

Handle Any Negative Drag

If he says, "Well, I have no open req," you say, "How could you? My experience is unique. And if you did, we'd have to go through all the red tape. I'd probably never even *meet* with you!"

Arrange It for This Saturday

Your challenge is not the *needager* (needy manager). Your challenge is all those people around him who can't *meet* his needs!

They'll sabotage your efforts entirely, since here you are coming in from outside and actually *accomplishing* something! That's why Saturday (and you) will work.

Saturdays are so *leisurely!* No pressure, no gatekeepers (except security), no eyes watching your every move. Happy talk about family, friends, food, fun, future.

This is primitive, basic *connecting*. The *only* thing that gets people hired. The *one* thing that going in through the front door *prevents*.

Saturday for *sure!*

Take the Paperwork Home

Usually a hiring manager will have certain items (an employment application, an employee handbook, whatever).

Take as much as you can get your hands on. It's either stuff you can fill out creatively at home or stuff that will fast-forward you into that department through the employment lobby.

Discuss How the Manager Will Lubricate the Hiring Process

This might be by opening a job requisition or generating a work order. It makes no difference what it's called.

Just learn all you can about the timing, who has to sign off (usually the needager's higher-up), and how you'll be notified.

. . . And *that's* how you do the Saturday slip!

If you get a chance during the week, here are five back-door openers for you to use when you call.

Use them to write your own short opener, just as you did with the Saturday slip.

> Hello Mr. Barton. My name is Stuart Norcross. Are you too busy to speak with me?
>
> I've been reading in the newspaper about International Industries' expansion. There are a number of ways I can assist with it, and I'd really appreciate the opportunity to speak with you.
>
> Do you have a few minutes you can spend with me next Monday morning?
>
> How about 9 a.m. or 11 a.m.? I'll be in your area on my way to an afternoon meeting.

Hello Mr. Barton. This is Stuart Norcross. Do you have a moment?

I wanted to let you know that I'm sending you a resume today.

As I mention in my cover letter, the research I've done on International Industries leads me to believe this is a perfect match for the project manager opening.

Before I send it to your HR department however, I wanted to speak with you a moment about what you're *really* looking for in someone you hire. I planned to send you a copy as well.

Hello Mr. Barton. We've never met, but I know of you by your great reputation in the electronics industry. I'm Stuart Norcross.

When the project manager position opened up at International Industries, I said, "Perfect." This is *exactly* the opportunity I've been seeking!

If you'll spend a few minutes with me on the phone now, I'd like to discuss how I can contribute to achieving your goals.

Do you have a few minutes to talk?

Hi Ron. You and I will likely become good friends! My name is Stuart Norcross, and I'm a project manager with Competition Corporation.

I noticed your display ad in the *Camptown Gazette* looking for senior project managers.

My qualifications and knowledge of our business fit exactly with the specifications.

Why don't we spend a few minutes to talk about it? Is this a good time for you? (If he says, "No," say:) "When would be a good time for me to call back?"

Hi Ron. I'm Stuart Norcross. Can you spare a few minutes to talk now?

From what I've read, International Industries is looking for project managers. I'm calling you directly because my qualifications are not only exactly what you're looking for, but I have worked for Competition Corporation. I have a demonstrated knowledge of the consumer electronics market. So I'm calling you now to arrange an interview for tomorrow. Are you available at 1:30? I'll be near International on business.

Now that you're hip . . .
Instantly *slip!*

Do 95: Making a Maven an Interview Mentor

Mentoring is one of those words like *networking*. Nobody quite knows what it means.

Except us. We know, because we just *decide!* A confused mind does nothing.

So here's our definition:

Somebody impressive who gets you more interviews faster than anyone else.

Here's how to make a maven a mentor.

Make a List of Maven Maybementors by Category

Just write down the name, phone number, fax number, and e-mail address of each. Prioritize the list with the most impressive, connected, and compulsive person (a major maybementor) first, then in decreasing order.

Break it down by category like this:

Former Supervisors

It doesn't matter whether the supervisor knew you that well or even liked you. Mentors act out of a desire to achieve a goal. In this case, getting you interviews.

Acquaintances

Friends are included here, but you can include someone you met just once—perhaps at a family gathering or on a plane during an instant (Do 38).

Friends of Friends

This is a huge population of maybementors that you don't even know exist. Your friends do, though. So ask around. Press hard for this. All the maybementors can do is say, "No."

Famous People

Perhaps someone who spoke at a convention you attended. Or a local politician. How about someone who writes a newspaper column? A community activist?

This is not about supercharging your sphere of influence (Do 84). It's about divining that *one person* whose mission in life is "You interviewing!"

Call the Maybementor

Write a little script.

This is a likely scenario:

You: Hello, Mr. Mentori. This is Pete Protege. You may not remember me, but I heard you speak at the Robot Roboat Roundtable last spring.

Merv: Yes, Pete. I'm very important, but you can call me Merv. To what do I owe the honor of your call?

You: Well, I wanted to meet with you to discuss my future. I want to become a mechanical engineer and thought you might be able to help me get interviewed for a drafter job.

Merv: But I'm a very important funeral director! How can I find you a drafter job?

You: I thought we could meet and talk about where the bodies are buried! *(laughing)*

Merv *(laughing too)*: Well, that's one I haven't heard! What about anything where you'd be around robots, like the bicycle factory in town?

You: I'd be honored to go anywhere you recommend, since you're so important!

Merv: That's right, I am. But enough about me . . . what's in it for me?

You: I'd like to be your protege. I know that sounds very forward since we haven't met, but all I need is a chance. I'd represent you very well.

Merv: Why don't we get together some time and talk about it?

You: How about this afternoon? (*If it ain't instant, it ain't important.*)

Merv: I'll be at the Hilldale Country Club getting my golf clubs polished. How'd you like to meet me at the snack bar? I'll be with my famous caddy, Hector.

You: That would be perfect. How does three o'clock sound?

Merv: I'm being interviewed by a local TV news reporter, but we should be done about three-fifteen. I'll meet you at the snack bar. Bring copies of your resume.

You: Oh, yes sir! I'll bring business cards too. (*A box of them!*)

Express Sincere Compliments

Mentors are volunteers. They're not being paid money to get you interviews.

So what *are* they being paid? Compliments. The following shows how Pete should compliment Merv when he meets him:

"I really appreciate your willingness to lend your prestige to getting me interviews." (Note it's not just a generalized "You're great." It's a specific link of *prestige* between the *act* of *willingness* and the result of *interviews*.)

"I'm so fortunate to have you taking me under your wing." (Note the roles of mentor and protege are being clearly defined.)

"Having you as my mentor is a great benefit to me. You won't regret it." (Note the elevation of the person to *mentor*, the acknowledgement of value benefit and the assurances that he's doing the right thing.)

Respect the Mentor and His Referrals

Mentors are *paid* compliments, but they're *motivated* by unwavering respect.

If you go out on a protege interview and have to wait, you wait.

If you're inadvertently mistreated by the mentor (say by an insulting remark), you don't insult him back.

If you're asked to do some reasonable favor by the mentor, you do it enthusiastically.

Say Nice Things about the Mentor to Offerors

You can be certain that whatever you say will get back to the mentor.

These are his business associates. He's putting himself on the line for you, and you pay by paying compliments.

Report Back to the Mentor after Each Interview

Let him know what happened and how much you liked the offeror and the biz. *Always*. It is an unwritten mentor mantra that you like everyone and everything—even if the *mentor* doesn't.

Then, order—er—*ask* the mentor to follow up. Suggest what he should say.

Mentors are well-intentioned volunteer guides who aren't usually adept at asking for favors on behalf of strangers. They need guidance themselves.

Make Sure the Mentor Understands His Mission

You're not looking for career planning, constructive criticism, or psychotherapy. You're looking for *instant interviews*.

This is a very *specific* relationship. Its effectiveness is measured by the speed, quality, and quantity of interviews.

Give the Mentor as Much to Work With as Possible

- Your rest-you-may (Do 5)
- Your background highlights (Do 84)
- Your business cards (Do 1)
- An icon letter for him to sign (Do 93). Send it for him whenever and wherever you can.

Go Out of Your Way to Do Nice Things for the Mentor

This isn't always easy.

Some mentors refuse to take anything in return. Others resent being asked.

But you can bring him a surprise lunch and eat with him informally. You can wash his car. You can buy him a thoughtful little gift with a card expressing your appreciation.

Recognize How Fortunate You Are to Be a Protege

Somewhere along the line, *every* successful person figures this out. Many more would be mentors themselves, but nobody asks.

So they join mentoring groups (google *mentors* and 5,740,000 links appear). Or they find some unworthy underling in their family or office.

It's just as much about *their* needs as it is about the protege's.

I really hope you take charge of this mentoring project. Follow these guidelines.

. . . And make the maven you select an interview *mentor!*

Do 96: Doing Informational Interviews Instantly

How'd you like to go from a cold call to one that's instantly incendiary?

Can it be? Enter instant informational interviewing.

Let's S-S-S-I-Z-Z-L-E!

Understand Why Informational Interviews Are So Effective

The informational interview doesn't meet with rejection because you're not looking for a job.

You're just gathering information. So no decision has to be made.

That means no initial doorslam.

The power to increase instant interviews is found in the role reversal with an offeror.

Powerful power—'cause *you're* doing the viewing!

No need to try switching seats with the offeror—just . . .

Question Your Way to Success

You ask from your first hello. In fact, right after the Magic Four Hello (Do 1).

Here are some ways:

> I saw you speak at the Electronic Paperclip Association last month and learned a lot. I just had to ask you a few questions. Do you have a minute?

You've identified yourself as a fan, complimented him, and are being time conscious. It's easier to say, "Yes" than "No," since "No" means another interruption.

> I was in the area wanting to get some brief information from local success stories for a book I'm working on. How about us talking now?

Here, time consciousness, a compliment, and a reason. Now he's thinking about free publicity and self-promotion.

> I'm fascinated with your business and just wanted to ask you about how you got started. It should only take a short time. Are you available for a moment now?

Now a compliment, a reason, and time consciousness.

No question about it—
You're instantly *in!*

Memorize These Questions

Just glance at them before you go under as you're relaxing (Do 42).

After a week or so, they'll be stored and ready for instant recall as needed.

There are three separate areas of inquiry:

Business Profile

How long have you been in business?
What are your products?

Who buys from you?

What is your share of the market?

What are your annual sales?

How many employees do you have?

What are your future plans?

What is your management philosophy? (This answer gives you more instant insight than the first seven combined!)

Hiring Profile

How are your hiring decisions made?

Who makes them?

Is a position open now? (Here we go!)

How long has it been open?

Why hasn't it been filled?

What kind of person are you looking for?

If someone is qualified, how long does the hiring process take?

Who interviews the candidates?

How many people have you already considered?

Have you extended any offers?

Why were they rejected?

What was wrong with the other candidates?

Why haven't you hired from within?

Instant Interview Intelligence

In order of magnitude, what are the three most important functions of the job?

What was the background of the last person who held the job? (If it's not a new position.)

What can someone who's done the job do better than someone who hasn't?

What personality traits are important to do the job well?

Would you hire someone instantly (*I couldn't resist*) who had those traits?

Glance at these exclamations before relaxing too (Do 42):

I'm a walking job description for you!

You're talking to the person who can do this job immediately!

I can't understand why you haven't filled the position. I could do that for you!

I'm made for that job!

This sounds like a terrific opportunity. I'd love working with someone like you!

Conducting an informational interview still keeps you well within your 15-minute time limit (Do 1).

Psychologically it's the best way to move an offeror from cold to hot. . . . And when you're hot, you're *hot*. Instantly *incendiary!*

Do 97: Consulting for Instant Resulting

Your easiest entry to a job interview is to market yourself as an consultant.

Someone who gets *results*!

All you need is:

- A judicious look on your face (when not smiling, of course)
- A suit or dress
- An ability to pronounce at least 20 of the latest buzzwords and buzz-phrases in your field (Trade publications are the best place to find them)
- A brochure about your expertise and services (a resume)
- A business card
- A local business license (if required)

The reason consulting is so easy to discuss is that there is almost no expense or risk to the client. According to the U.S. Chamber of Commerce, up to 30 percent of a typical business payroll is spent on administration alone. This isn't surprising considering the recordkeeping, bookkeeping, cash flow management, payroll taxes, paid holidays, paid vacations, paid sick leave, paid insurance, and paid everything else involved.

As an independent contractor rather than employee, there's no concern about you running to the EEOC or state compliance agency with a discrimination complaint. No concern with group medical workers' compensation or disability claims either.

You complete a W-9 form and receive a 1099 after the end of the year to compute your self-employment taxes (Do 44).

This arrangement isn't available for hourly (nonexempt) jobs, unless you're doing the activity on a freelance basis. Call your state's labor department to find out whether you're eligible.

Phone solicitation is the best way to obtain an appointment. Simply look in the Yellow Pages in any field you like with an appointment calendar open, and start in the A's.

The beauty of the consultant routine is that it positions you immediately to talk to an offeror without alienating the human resourcer. It's an accepted practice for consultants to discuss projects directly with those responsible for them.

Even HR has management development, training, human factors, wage and salary, recruiting, outplacement, insurance, pension, employee benefits, safety, communications, labor relations, information technology, and other consultants.

It's easy to sound knowledgeable when you don't understand the situation.

Listen well, probe, ask questions, use the same vocabulary as the client, and avoid shooting from the lip.

The appointment is an *end in itself*. The call is the means! It's usually about five minutes in length. Any longer will reduce the chances of an instant interview. This is how it sounds:

Receptionist: Good morning, Unreal Company.
You: Hi. What's the name of your director of finance?
Receptionist: We don't have a director of finance. Would you like to speak to our chief accountant?
You: Yes, please. Who is it?
Receptionist: Moe Money is his name.
You: Thank you.
Receptionist: One moment, please. I'll ring . . .
Secretary: Accounting. May I help you?
You: Hi. Moe Money, please.
Secretary: May I tell him who's calling?

You: Helen Helper.

Secretary: May I tell him what it's regarding?

You: Sure. I wanted to speak to him about your cost control system.

Secretary: Is there something I can help you with?

You: No, I'm sorry. I really must speak with Moe.

Secretary: Just a moment . . . I'll see if he's available.

Moe: Moe Money.

You: Hi, Moe. My name is Helen Helper. I'm a consultant in the finance area, and would like to discuss how I might assist with improving your cost control system.

Moe: Our system works fine. Well . . . there are a few things that could use improvement.

You: I'm really familiar with this, and have been very successful in reducing costs with clients. What areas do you see as needing improvement?

Moe: Inventory control has really become a problem. We're just unable to keep track of our costs!

You: Your costs? Why?

Moe: Well, our production control group hasn't been following up on status reports.

You: An objective appraisal can often help to straighten this problem out.

Moe: Really? I never thought of that.

You: I'll be in your area on a consulting assignment later this week. Why don't I stop by to see you at nine on Thursday morning?

Moe: I'm on a very limited budget. What do you charge?

You: Why don't we see whether I can be of assistance first. There won't be any charge at all. If I can do you some good, we can discuss it further. However, it appears we'll be able to reduce the costs substantially at Unreal without a major change.

Moe: Okay, you're on.

You: Thanks. I estimate we'll be about an hour.

Moe: Fine.

You: I'm looking forward to meeting you! See you then.

Moe: Sounds good. Bye.

You: Goodbye.

While the call can start differently and take an infinite number of turns, you're controlling the dialogue. It should be a *dialogue*, not two *monologues*. Listen actively, but don't give away information when clients are willing to pay for it.

How much is too much? Anything beyond just enough. You're giving away the sample, not selling the product.

Fee or free—which will it be?

You may have to leave a few messages before you swing into action. If the offeror calls back, be courteous but too busy to talk.

Ask if you can return the call in a few minutes. This makes you appear in demand. It also enables you to organize your thoughts, review your notes, and relax. Then by initiating the call, your control position is increased.

You'll note that the emphasis is on helping someone else. We are using one of the most basic success principles:

You will get what you want if you give others what they want.

The call also considers the natural insecurity of any offeror who depends upon someone else for emotional and financial support. That's why you don't mention an interview.

The last thing you want to say to an offeror who is in trouble, whether real or imagined, is that you intend to replace her. You're a genie (Do 1). You do and disappear.

As you go down the alphabet, making notes on the Yellow Pages and calendar, you'll notice that you become adept at finessing around front-liners.

You want to be honest, not only for moral reasons. Misrepresenting destroys your self-respect. This is conveyed in your delivery. Start out believing in yourself, forgetting about time of day, the day of the week, the last call, an errand to run, or any other excuse to procrastinate. Offerors await!

An appointment around one hour after the start of business is best for this caper. Overworked offerors are often behind schedule.

Let those optimum morning hours work their magic. Schedule a meeting an hour after business starts. This gives the offeror time to get down to business. It also gives you time to arrive and scope out the situation in advance.

You'll have your instant *consulting assignment!*

Situation Wanted Advertising

Before we leave the subject of consulting, one other technique deserves honorable mention. The situation wanted classified advertisement in a metropolitan newspaper. It's the opposite of a help-wanted ad, and might read like this:

Engineering Executive

Proven ability. Presently consulting with a diversified manufacturing company. Seeking assignment in:

- Feasibility
- Planning
- Acquisitions
- Mergers
- Patent Review
- Licensing

Box 3780, *Daily Sun*

Or this:

Marketing Consultant

Seeking assignment in hi-tech electronics. Experienced in component marketing, sales, merchandising, distributing, planning, and advertising. Assisted in corporate reorganization. Phone 555-555-5555 or Box 8773, *The Register*.

Or even this:

Buying Problems?

Experienced purchasing consultant looking to assist growing manufacturing company. Highly qualified in cost reduction and vendor selection procedures. Immediately available and willing to travel. Please reply to:

P.O. Box 2306

Denver, CO 88521

Since your identity isn't disclosed, it makes no difference whether you're currently employed. Display ads are also a possibility. They're more expensive but enable you to be more creative and perhaps elicit more responses.

As you read the situation wanted ads, you'll begin to see a pattern in the layout. If you want to enter a new field, try to pick something in your background that's related.

Trade journals, newsletters, and related periodicals are also possibilities, but check lead times. They're usually too long, so these should be considered secondary sources.

Use of print media advertising is a painless way to let hiding offerors know your capabilities.

Consulting for instant resulting.

Apply now. No experience required!

Do 98: Infiltrating the Secretarial Secret Service Instantly

In every business of two or more, the *real* organization chart is a grapevine!

The secretaries, assistants, and other support people are the inmates in charge of the asylum. Collectively, they form the *secretarial secret service*.

Yet average jobseekers think these folks get in the way of communication with an offeror.

We don't.

Consider an Offeror's Secretary to Be the Offeror

She frequently *is!*

The influence of their opinions can't be overstated. I consulted with my secretary and assistant before I made a decision to interview someone. In fact, I don't remember hiring *anyone* without having them interview the person and approve.

Their perspective made me better at evaluating, because they frequently interacted with a jobseeker when the spotlight was off.

Was she courteous? How did she react when she was asked to fill out an application? When she was asked to wait? How did she act while she was waiting? When she was interacting with other candidates? What did she talk about in the reception area?

Even without getting a sneak peek, they often had far more insight than I had. I'd say, "I don't think he's got enough employee benefits background." My assistant would say, "That's just a matter of reading our insurance, pension, and other information." Of course!

Assume the Secretary Knows Everything about the Offeror

Everything you'd like to know.

Is there any secretary who doesn't know the most intimate details about her boss? What he likes or dislikes? His every whim? His every mood? Who he'll accept calls from about what, when and why?

When you call and when you appear (Do 1), always ask things like:

I hear Leon really takes care of his people! How do you like working for him?

I'm really looking forward to meeting Leon. What can you tell me about him?

Does Leon usually like to see examples of someone's work, or does he prefer to just talk about it?

Think of the importance of asking the right people the right questions. You're getting marketing intelligence, showing you value their judgment, and (most important) getting them to buy into your success!

Assume the Secretary Has Access to Secret Records and Scuttlebutt

Secretaries continuously prepare and see business records. So they know everything from new products still under wraps to unannounced hires and fires.

Since the juiciness of the gossip is directly related to the status of the secretary, disclosure is the way to succeed.

So even a file clerk knows things you can learn to get interviewed.

How valuable is it to know that someone's about to be let go? Or that some new manager is being hired? Or that a department is being reorganized?

You can find this out by discreetly asking a secretary something like, "What's been happening at Rapidrate over the last week? I've been out of town."

Then listen carefully.

Name the Secretary in Your Thank-You Note

It costs you nothing to say, "Many thanks for the courtesy extended by you and Denise during my recent visit."

But it shows sincere appreciation and much class.

Respect deputizes a secret agent to work for you.

Infiltrating is one of those little but large things that make interviews *instant* and offers *often!*

Do 99: Jolting Overworked Offerors

There are 20 jobjungle jolts we've developed to get you offers from the most likely offerors—those too overworked to even talk!

Use one or more of them whenever you want to shock offerors into action.

Dressing Up

Looking powerful is a huge jolt after you arrange an interview with a professional offeror. Perhaps one missed in your genie appearance (Do 1).

Let's say it's a law office. A dark blue suit, white shirt, and striped tie is the uniform. Even if you're applying for a nonlawyer job, lawyers will *identify* with you. That's the way interviews happen.

In all interview situations, you can always dress down. But if you walk in with no tie or jacket, it's over.

I use suits for high impact by removing my jacket, rolling up my starched white shirtsleeves, and sometimes even removing my tie.

The animation and the control are incredibly powerful. What traditional jobseekers would even dare?

Women can remove a suit jacket with just as much effect.

As any successful actor will tell you, "Look the part, and the part plays itself!"

Announcing No Phones

When you finish the Magic Four Hello (Do 1), ask the offeror, "Would you mind holding your calls and turning off your cell phone? I'd like to speak with you a few minutes without interruption" (Do 43).

Who says that? People with *power*.

You're saying, "It's important!" "Listen up!" "Pay attention!" "Interview me!" "Now!"

Then, shut the door and sit down.

Of course, you don't carry your own cell phone on any instant interview (Do 1).

Mentioning Another Interview

You're in her office instanting, and after 10 minutes, you sense the offeror is hesitating to offer you a job. You instinctively feel that you want to turn up the heat (Do 96).

So you say, "I've got to get going. Someone has been calling me to discuss working for him. I have an appointment in an hour, and I'm always on time. This sounds like a great opportunity. I know I can contribute a lot. Are you going to make me an offer?"

Imposing a Deadline

Getting to the close with a deadline can work wonders to dislodge a stuck offeror.

Drop, "I must make a decision. I've become a very popular guy. Please let me know whether you'll be making an offer by the close of business Friday. I'd really like to pursue this position, and we'd be terrific together!"

Setting a High Expectation

You think you'll get an offer, but it's not what you're worth. You know they're anxious to have you join them.

Tell the offeror, "I'd love to be here and know I can turn your business around. I must receive at least 15 percent more than I was earning to leave, however, and I want a company car. Since I'm up for a promotion, this only makes good sense."

Giving a Fairness Ultimatum

You like what you see. But the offer must be more than the employee in the position earns, since you have more education and experience.

You state, "I know you recognize that I'll be able to do far more than Joel, since I have a bachelor's degree in business and have done much larger financial plans than he did. So I expect you'll be fair, otherwise I won't accept the offer or won't stay."

Stating What Is Needed

Instant interviews get offerors interested on the spot. Many times they just haven't had time to figure out their needs. You want to strike while the iron is hot.

Tell him what he needs in a way like, "I know you aren't thinking about hiring someone. I'm here now—ready, willing, and able. The best way for me to help is to update your training program with new manuals and a series of classes. Let's start Monday morning."

Using Your Pen as a Magic Wand

You see that the offeror is just in over her head and won't make an offer in that state.

So you reach in your left front pocket for your pen, pull it out, and say "Pretend this pen is my magic wand. I'll wave it if you tell me what you wish for most in the person you hire."

Moving the Next Interview Away from the Business

Whether it's a lack of privacy, jealous employees, or an offeror who allows interruptions, get her out of the office. This will also diminish her power over the interview and you.

Get her away with, "Why don't we meet at the Metro Cafe next Wednesday at 3 P.M.? I'll be in the area, and we can speak privately."

Using a Survey

Whether it's the introduction of a new manufacturing idea or supporting a salary demand, surveys are super third-party corroboration. You can get a source by searching for a trade association or government agency on the Internet. You may even find the actual survey—or do your own (Do 18)!

The approach is, "Here's the *City Gazette* salary survey on technical support management positions. As you can see, I should be paid commensurately with 'Midrange Technical Support Managers.'"

Mentioning Your References

References are instant enhancement to a candidate and will generally cause offerors to go from uncertain to certain.

You mention them with, "You might want to talk to my references before making a decision. I didn't plan on that, but they've become my greatest fans. I don't like to talk about myself, but they'll give you the perspective of those who've seen me in action" (Do 63 and Do 64).

Taking Away Your Expertise

Offerors don't always buy what they think they can always get. When you instantly interview, they perceive you'll always be available.

Use a classic takeaway close by saying, "I'm just not interested in doing your books. My unique specialty is in segmented financial analysis that results in higher operating revenue every quarter. I need to leave and will be making a decision tomorrow. Please let me know tonight if you recognize I can turn this situation around."

Confronting without Condescending

You may think giving your opinion will result in an offer. If you're going to express it, avoid anything that puts down the offeror like, "Your idea for new monitors won't work."

That's not likely to generate an offer, only resentment. *Your* and *won't work* are mistakes.

Just toss, "My experience with monitors is that you're better off upgrading the computers at the same time. I know where we can find a system that will cost almost the same amount as the monitors alone."

That's "you and me against the problem," not "your silly self against me" (Do 85). It's also a *solution* that gives the offeror an instant incentive to hire you.

Getting into Instant Gratification

Frequently, a delay in getting an offer is simply a sign that you haven't fully aligned with the offeror.

This can be simply adjusted with a few strategically spoken statements:

I'm from the Midwest too.
I agree with your idea about the miniblinds.
You see things the same way I do.

Admiring Something in the Offeror's Office

Traditional jobseekers are so uptight that they never get past a phone screen. You're in the office, so go for something like:

Gee, that's a beautiful bookcase.
I've never seen such a clever paperweight.
Your desk layout fits your personality—so organized and efficient.

Asking, then Listening

Sometimes that's all it takes. When offerors talk, they agree with themselves.

Traditional jobseekers don't know what to say. That rarely stops them.

You can listen to almost anything for a few minutes. So use the candidate can openers to get the offeror talking and you listening attentively.

Just ask what, how, where, when, or why:

What projects are you looking to do?
How are you going to staff the new marketing department?
Where will you be moving?
When are you ordering a new phone system?
Why is the manufacturing outsourced?

Questioning an Objection

Questioning an objection doesn't work in traditional interviewing because objections are *conclusions*. The decision has already been made.

Not so with instant interviewing. *You* control the outcome (Do 92).

The offeror says, "I like you, but you just don't have experience selling hair products."

You ask, "That couldn't prevent you from making me an offer, could it?"

The offeror thinks, "Could it? Would it? *Should* it?"

Your question caused him to reflect in a much more critical way.

That gets you the offer.

Making Feel-Felt-Found Statements

This is an instant steering mechanism. The offeror says, "I'm just not ready to hire this month because of our cash flow."

You counter, "I understand how you *feel*. I *felt* that way when I was meeting a payroll. But I *found* that hiring the right accounts receivable person can change 'cash no' into 'cash flow' very quickly."

Placing Yourself in Alternative Jobs

Another jolt is to place yourself in an alternative job, then let the offeror decide.

Suppose the offeror wants the product catalog and product brochures redone.

Say, "I can either redo the product catalog or redesign the product brochure. What would you like me to do first?"

Asking the Offeror Why No Offer

Don't just take procrastination as a reason. If the offeror has not yet extended an offer, it's a symptom—not a cause.

Lob, "I know we have a great match here, and I could already be making far more money for the company than I'd be paid. Why haven't you made me an offer?"

These are the 20 jubjungle jolts. Still don't take more than 15 minutes (Do 1). *Jolt then bolt!* Successful, high-voltage supershocks!

Do 100: Pursuing Your Passion

"It doesn't matter how you start, where you come from. The ability to triumph begins with you. Always."

I'll tell you who said this shortly. But you should already know.

Do what you love, and you'll never work another day in your life. Someone who loves what she *does* is the *best* at it. The reverse is also true: Someone who's the *best* at what she *does* loves it.

Don't you agree? You can't not!

Are you so passionate about your j-o-b that you can't wait to start? Does time stand still? Do you forget to eat? Develop your bladder control? Are you the one who locks up every night?

Would you pay the one paying you so you could do it? Would you literally give up everything you own and sleep under a bridge if you could just do that one precious, all-consuming, reason-for-being job? With every one of your 2,000 parts?

I remember being on tour in the mid-'80s when I got a call from my publicist. She was jumping up and down because she'd just booked me on *AM Chicago*, and wanted me to write it into my itinerary.

I didn't think much about it. Actually, I didn't think much about anything except my next interview with a newspaper reporter.

Major book touring is like walking through a blizzard in the middle of a marathon. You can barely see, and you rely on the escort to pick you up at the airport, take you to the morning wakeup TV and radio shows, feed you, help you get dressed, run to the one-hour cleaner for you, take you to the noon talkers, check in with the publisher, get you to the newspaper offices in the afternoon, plop you on the evening news set, get you on the phone for some radio talk show in another time zone, then pour you into the last plane out to the next city, where (if you're lucky) you're picked up by the escort there.

This was another booking, and I wrote it down. "Okay, got it. AM Chicago. WLS-TV. Be there at 8 A.M. Fine." Chicago was just another whistle stop.

I eventually wound my way to O'Hare International Airport, checked in at the hotel and flopped down to sleep. My escort picked me up the next morning. A few phoners and she whisked me off to WLS.

Drove in, signed in, checked in. The sign on an easel said, "AM Chicago."

Whoa! Did you feel that? The house is a-rockin'! What's this? I-I-I'm from Los Angeles. I know that feeling. Is this the great Chicago earthquake?

Everyone, everything was buzzin' about the new host. She was making a movie. Someone mentioned "purple." So we had a guest host. My escort said, "You'd have loved her! You guys would have become best friends. She's going to change the world."

I said, "Oh!"

Even in my altered state, I got it right.

Oprah is quite simply passion personified. Her success couldn't be due to anything else, for she had nothing else. (Nothing you'd see outside of herself, anyway.)

Raised by a strict father from age 13. Me too. What's that all about? Age 13, strict father—little more than a smile—unimagined success.

She just "went for it." (Rhymes with "Winfrey.") These days she "goes for it" with that same passion.

Pratfalls? Sure. Regrets? That she didn't do more.

Those words at the beginning of this Do are hers. They say it all.

Wherever you look, there are people who make a living telling others what jobs they should do. It starts with child guidance counselors and ends with adult career counselors.

Well-intentioned folks with their tests and texts. They should be accountable like criminal lawyers—goof and your client's sentenced to lifetime imprisonment. Solitary confinement, without the possibility of parole. (Until this little book finds its way into the prison library.)

They'd do more good on a busy street corner dressed like Harpo holding up a sign that reads, "Do what you love—success will follow."

Need the DOT (Dictionary of Occupational Titles)? Hardly. Gimme a break. Embarrassed to sound lazy? Dumb? All that money wasted on a master's in fine arts?

Stop. Here. Now.

What would you like to do? Your hobby raising parakeets? You'd rather clean cages than eat? Fine.

Find a bird vet (maybe yours) and tell her you're ready to rock. Instant on her.

Go over to that bird sanctuary and find someone who'll appreciate you. Drop your fine self on a pet store owner. It's not my thing, but what do I know?

I've got mine. Go get your own! Say, "Outta my way—I'm comin' through!"

What time have you got? AM Chicago? Don't look at your watch—the answer's not there. The answer's not for you to know.

Is it tomorrow? Tomorrow is promised to no one.

Do 101 and DONE! Deciding Which Offer to Accept

You'll be instantly inundated with offers once you start using the first 100 techniques.

Don't panic!

Now I'll show you how to buy some time to decide, then show you how to do it.

Recognize that You're Not the Same at Do 101 as You Were at Do 1

When you began following *Instant Interviews*, you had to beg for a job and take whatever was offered.

Now you know what a *job* really is, and how to make your own.

So if you're considering an offer, the only question is, "What am I giving up by not having more instant interviews?"

The answer is, "More opportunities."

It's a tough decision, and really comes down to whether you love the gig or need the money.

We'll get to the Offer Comparison Checklist in a few.

But first . . .

Take at Least One Day to Accept

Asking for a day to sleep on it can be a challenge. But you owe it to yourself to really think all offers through.

It also makes you look just a little more in demand—an important way to position yourself if you start working there.

The day can be used to call any offerors with possible, probable, or pending offers.

I'm going to take you through a dialogue of the most agonizing fact pattern. It's the phone call with an offer, but not from the company with your dream job. That offeror hasn't called.

You need to work now. It's a good offer. But that dream job may be offered within a week. So you probably need more than one day.

You just received the call and the offer's been made . . .

Oliver: I know you were waiting to hear from us. We'd like you to start on Monday.

You: The offer sounds good. I'd like until this Thursday to get back to you.

Oliver: What? I thought we'd get this wrapped up today! We've got the Constellation program coming in here within the next week, and we need to staff your department.

You: I understand, and I'm almost certain I'll accept. But I have another offer in the works, and I owe it to that company to let them complete it. (*Good! You didn't say, "I'll have to talk it over with my wife." You used a professional reason.*)

Oliver: Who is it? Are they offering more?

You: I'd rather keep its identity private. (*Perfect! Classy, in control, mysterious.*) I really don't know what they'll offer, and would like to accept yours now. But as a matter of professional courtesy, I'd like to give them the opportunity to extend an offer too.

Oliver: Let's see . . . this is Monday. Are you sure you'll know by Thursday?

You: Whether I hear from them or not, I'll let you know by the close of business this Thursday. Does that sound fair? (*Good again! You're still in control. Nobody revokes an offer because someone wants a few days to reply. When you ask whether it sounds fair, it forces the offeror to admit that it does.*)

Oliver: Sure. Considering it took us almost a week to sign off on your offer, how can I really object?

You: I'm looking forward to a long and productive relationship at Offset Office Outlet, Oliver. Thanks for your patience. I'll call you by 4 P.M. this Thursday. Sooner if I've made my decision.

Oliver: Sounds good. If I'm in a meeting, just leave me a voice mail and I'll call you back.

You: Fine. Have a good week.

Oliver: You too.

Call the Other Offeror(s) Immediately

You need to move instantly—just like you did when you interviewed.

In our fact pattern, the dream job offer was nowhere in sight.

You simply call the dream job offeror and say, "I haven't heard from you and I have another offer. The company wants an answer immediately and I asked the hiring manager for time to consider it. When will you make a decision?"

You can give the offeror until Wednesday, so you can stall one day for a reply.

This call will accelerate a pending offer or let you know the offeror wasn't ready.

You can still pursue the gig—but you'll be working.

Ask for an Offer Letter

I didn't use this device in our fact pattern because it was too easy.

If an offer letter hasn't been discussed, it usually takes at least a few days to crank one out, obtain the approvals, get a signature, and mail it to you.

So you automatically buy enough time to call the other offerors, decide, and accept or reject.

Aside from the negotiating benefit, asking for offer letters is a good practice to clarify and document the deal. It's no longer considered a sign of mistrust.

Evaluate Each Offer Objectively and Thoroughly

We've experimented with all kinds of ways to evaluate offers—grades, point systems, percentages.

This simple but comprehensive checklist has consistently been the fastest and most objective way to make the decision. It forces you to ask the right questions before accepting too, since you wouldn't have thought about (or remembered) them at the interview stage. For salary, vacation, or any other item that's a comparison, write in the amount.

Many I.I.'s use the checklist as a guide while the offeror is extending the offer too. Some use it to negotiate further as well.

Here it is:

Offer Comparison Checklist

	Offer 1 Name of Business	Offer 2 Name of Business	Offer 3 Name of Business
Challenge			
Company car			
Company culture			
Convenience			
Coworkers			
Expense account			
Facility			
Health insurance			
Job satisfaction			
Life insurance			
Long-term disability insurance			
Memberships			
Office			
Opportunity to advance			
Opportunity to learn			
Paid time off			
Professional growth			
Retirement plan			
Salary (gross annual)			
Stability			
Status			
Title			
Tuition reimbursement			
Unpaid time off			
Vacation (weeks per year)			
Other			
Other			
Other			

Decisions, decisions! Always between better and best.

As one I.I. remarked, "I feel sorry for anyone who isn't me!"

Congratulations on your new livelihood, your new life, and your new future.

Best wishes for success—*Instantly and always!*

Acknowledgments

Special thanks to my editor, Shannon Vargo, for recognizing the importance of *Instant Interviews*, and to my assistant, Gerald Jones, for working with me day and night to complete the manuscript.

Truly, you are the awesome genies who made the wish come true. Now it's time for the miraculous results.

Index